Penguin Books
Tibet

Thubten Jigme Norbu was born in Tibet on the sixteenth day
of the eighth month of the Water Dog Year (16 August, 1922).
As a child he was recognized as the twenty-fourth incarnation of
the fifteenth-century Tibetan monk Tagtser. He was himself
educated as a monk, and became the abbot of one of Tibet's
greatest monasteries, Kumbum, on the Chinese border. His
younger brother was recognized as the reincarnation of the Dalai
Lama, thus officially assuming at the age of seven the position
of the head of the Tibetan church and state.

Norbu stayed on in Tibet after 1949, when the Chinese
arrived, and remained abbot of Kumbum monastery for as long
as he was able to fulfil his functions. He then joined his brother
in Lhasa, and eventually fled to India in 1959. He now lives in
the U.S.A. and has initiated programmes of Tibetan study at
the American Museum of Natural History and at the University
of Indiana.

He is married and has three sons.

Colin Turnbull was born in London and now lives in New
York, where he is Curator of African Ethnology at the
American Museum of Natural History. He was educated at
Westminster School, Magdalen College, Oxford, and the School
of Oriental and African Studies, London University. For two
years he held a research fellowship in the Department of
Religion and Philosophy at Banaras Hindu University, India.
During that time (1949–51) he made several visits to Outer Tibet
and followed a number of pilgrim routes in the Himalayas,
spending some time in various Tibetan monasteries.

He is the author of *The Forest People*, *The Lonely African*,
The Wayward Servants and *The Peoples of Africa*.

ཆོས་པའི་སྒྲུང་།

བོད་ཀྱི་ཚེས་དང་མི།

རྟ་ལའི་བླ་མའི་གཏེན་ཁྲབ་བསྐུན་འདྲེགས་མེད་ནོར་བུ་དག

ནགས་མེའི་ཁྲིས་སྐབས་ཁ་ལེན་ ཅམ་ ཁྲི་དན་འབོལ་ནས།

Tibet

Its History, Religion and People

THUBTEN JIGME NORBU
COLIN M. TURNBULL

PENGUIN BOOKS

Penguin Books Ltd, Harmondsworth, Middlesex, England
Penguin Books, 625 Madison Avenue, New York, New York 10022, U.S.A.
Penguin Books Australia Ltd, Ringwood, Victoria, Australia
Penguin Books Canada Ltd, 2801 John Street, Markham, Ontario, Canada L3R 1B4
Penguin Books (N.Z.) Ltd, 182–190 Wairau Road, Auckland 10, New Zealand

First published by Chatto & Windus 1969
Published in Pelican Books 1972
Reprinted in Penguin Books 1976, 1983

Copyright © Thubten Jigme Norbu and·Colin M. Turnbull, 1968
All rights reserved

Made and printed in Singapore by
Richard Clay (S.E.Asia) Pte Ltd
Set in Monotype Ehrhardt

CONTENTS

Chapter headings of ritual objects and sacred symbols by kind permission of Antoinette K. Gordon, from *The Inconography of Tibetan Lamaison*

INTRODUCTION

The Human Body, at peace with itself,
Is more precious than the rarest gem.
Cherish your body, it is yours this one time
   only.
The human form is won with difficulty,
It is easy to lose.
All worldly things are brief, like lightning in
   the sky;
This Life you must know as the tiny splash of
   a raindrop;
A thing of beauty that disappears even as it
   comes into being.
Therefore set your goal,
Make use of every day and night to achieve it.

– TSONG KHAPA

This book is not an autobiography of Thubten Norbu, for that has already been written (*Tibet Is My Country*, Dutton, 1961). It is effectively a history of Tibet, though its objective is not the presentation and interpretation of facts as historians think of them. We call it a *history* because it attempts to give an understanding of the Tibet of today, its people and their way of life and thought, by connecting them with their past *as they see it*. On the one hand the book is factual in that it deals not with fictions of a romantic Western imagination, but with the reality of the thoughts and beliefs of the Tibetan people themselves (and far from being in a perpetual state of levitation Tibetans have their feet very much on the ground). Yet, as told by Thubten Norbu, this history is stranger in some ways than most of the glowing

7

accounts that have constantly harped on Tibet's other-worldliness, making of its religion something inaccessible, of its people something mute and unreal, and of the country itself something cruel and harsh. Here we deal with the reality that is Tibet in the eyes, mind and spirit of one man, Thubten Jigme Norbu, twenty-fourth incarnation of the fifteenth-century Tibetan monk and teacher Tagtser. Here we see the country and people as he sees them, as he has known them, and as he believes them to be.

Many think of fact as something empirical and demonstrable, and hold fancy to be undemonstrable; but here fact blends with fancy, and together they form a single powerful reality. There is, for Norbu, no discrimination between the two ways of looking at the world, and indeed the difference is not even relevant, for each has its own contribution to make, and each finds its ultimate and highest reality only in the mind of the beholder, be he thinker or dreamer or, as is Norbu, both. The most empirical and demonstrable of facts are seldom welcome, and are even rejected if they shatter our fond dreams; falsehood finds a more ready acceptance than unwelcome truth if it only supports our wistful world of make-believe. Despite man's growing materialism this is still so, for man still hopes and yearns and dreams.

Fact and fancy, then, have each their own reality, and Norbu, in looking at the past of his country explores both realms insofar as he sees them as being of significance for the present purpose. The book starts and ends with what the West would call fancy, pure and simple. We call it legend, for legends often have a basis in fact; these legends of the beginning and the end of the world, and others that Norbu recounts during the course of the book, may or may not be related to fact in the Western sense, but they are related to truths of an equally high order. Yet even to consider them as parables or legends is to miss much of the point, if the reader wishes to begin to see the world as the Tibetans see it.

Norbu first gives a brief picture of the country and people of Tibet, as he knew it before the Chinese occupation, to give the reader a general familiarity with what would otherwise be a strange and confusing scene. The rest of the book then follows a chronological sequence, though throughout, to emphasize the personal nature of the story (or history), Norbu draws on his own experiences and beliefs for illustration, so this is very much Norbu's Tibet, not the Tibet of the historian or the philosopher. It is Tibet as he sees it from its remotest beginnings to the present day. It is not an account for academics who are concerned only with lesser, petty forms of truth; it is for dreamers, for people with souls, who are concerned with a larger truth. To them the truth that is Norbu's will speak, and the real Tibet will be revealed, for better or worse. History becomes something more, it becomes part of man's religious experience.

The reason for the book lies in Norbu's religious training and belief. The teachings of the Lord Buddha may bring an inner peace and beauty to the lives of many Tibetans, but they also bring a dynamic urge and drive that almost smack of impatience. There is a sense of near frustration in the simultaneous acceptance of the beauty of life and of its fragility. The Buddhist doctrine of rebirth is not one to be comprehended in the facile interpretations of condensed and abbreviated handbooks on the religions of the world, crowded and cramped into small type on small pages. It is something to be *lived*, through space and time. Previous and future births are not to be looked back upon nor anticipated, not to be considered with eagerness or anxiety; they have been lived and they will be lived, and that is enough to know. What concerns the Tibetan is the life he is living now, for it is his master, absolute and irrevocable, demanding that he live it well.

There are many forms of existence, and we may be born to any of them. To be born in human form is indeed precious, but it is also precarious – because with the beauty of freedom it bestows upon us it also gives us the means for self-destruction. All around us are those who would lead us along the path of ignorance, holding to false values. That is why Tibetans say that you should know your friends before you call them friend. The man who steals your property is more truly your friend than he who steals your vision. Properly cherished, however, the human form enables us to soar to the heights of ecstasy, to tear the veil of ignorance that surrounds us and to come face to face with the supreme truth of existence. That should be our goal, our single purpose. The rest will follow of its own accord.

This is no selfishness, leading to a sterile mountain-top asceticism. Each human form is different and each imposes certain limitations upon us. The basic obligation of developing the body to its fullest potential will lead us all in many different directions. Thus some come to the truth of existence by seeking seclusion from the world, though not many would envy them their lot. Others become teachers of wisdom, leaders of men, farmers or herders, manual labourers, beggars, or thieves. Each, in contributing to his own development, contributes to the development of mankind. The thief teaches us by his example just as surely as the sage.

Norbu's lot is not an easy one. As a young monk he devoted himself to his studies and became abbot of one of Tibet's greatest monasteries, that of Kumbum, in his home province of Amdo, on the borders of China. As abbot his obligations were to his monastery, to its thousands of inmates, and to the many Tibetan people who lived all around, their whole existence tied up with that of the monastery and dependent upon it. When the Chinese came, in July 1949, Norbu stayed on. He stayed for as long as it was physically possible for him to fulfil his obligations, but a time came when he was not even allowed to pray alone, and he was faced with the greater duty of alerting his brother, the Dalai Lama.

Once in Lhasa, return to Kumbum was unthinkable. Once out of Tibet, Norbu's whole being as a monk became pointless. He had left his monastery in the belief that he could help save his country. He was beset with news of tragedies that had fallen upon those he had been unable to take with him; unable to pursue his life as it had been shaped for him, Norbu renounced Holy Orders. There was something else he could not renounce, however, namely his existence as a reincarnation of Tagtser. As such he had been reborn with a very special purpose. It is believed that some of those who manage to achieve enlightenment, or *mying di*, elect to return to the world of suffering for the alleviation of those still struggling upward, to help, guide and teach.

The Tibetans believe that the monk Tagtser has returned in Norbu's body to continue his work, begun hundreds of years ago, as a teacher. As Tagtser, then, Norbu has very particular obligations to the people living around the monasteries founded by the monk and to the monasteries themselves. These obligations he can no longer fulfil, being physically divorced from his homeland. But from his being as Tagtser there was, and is, no escape. This is something Norbu has to reconcile with his new life.

Now, as a layman, Norbu must live as a layman, with other obligations and responsibilities. There is no dishonour in renouncing Holy Orders, but as an incarnation *and* as a layman Norbu faces a great conflict. The conflict is in part resolved by his untiring efforts at creating a deeper and wider understanding of Tibet. This book is part of that effort. To some extent then, it is not only the work of Norbu, it is also the work of Tagtser, the ancient teacher who gave himself to be reborn through all time for the enlightenment of his fellow beings. It is hoped that these pages will evoke at least some of the feelings of respect for life, of compassion and love, of the truth that is goodness, which are the qualities of the Tibetan Buddhist.

The work of collaboration has been a privilege, a joy, and a heavy responsibility. It has been arduous and difficult for we have been working in three languages: Tibetan, Sanskrit and English. The dangers have been many, for our imperfect knowledge of each other's language has led to constant checking and cross-checking, and it was agreed at the outset that this was to be the book, in the sense of the thought, of Thubten Norbu. The co-author's task has been to perceive that thought, to grasp it, and to present it in his words but without intruding any of his own thoughts.

We believe we have achieved this, at least to a large extent, because we are both, with all our human weaknesses, dedicated to the pursuit of the one great truth we believe to underlie the existence of mankind. It matters not to one of us if the other sees or thinks or dreams differently, for the truth is the same. The aim of all translation, direct or indirect, has been to present that truth, and words have been used and constructed to that end, not to satisfy the narrow limitation of dictionary usage.

Our claim is a small one. This is not intended as a definitive history of Tibet and its peoples but merely as an image of Tibet as seen by one man. This image, with minor variations, is probably shared by many other Tibetans, but our hope is that by avoiding the almost insuperable difficulties of attempting to be definitive, consistent and complete, as well as truthful, we have been able to present an account that represents, for better or worse, right or wrong, Tibet as seen and understood by a Tibetan. If the reader can but share that vision he will have more understanding than he would ever gain from a more formal, academic presentation divorced, as it would have to be, from the religious belief that alone makes life significant to the Tibetan. That, at least, is our belief and our hope.

THUBTEN JIGME NORBU
COLIN M. TURNBULL

The problems of accurately representing the sound of Tibetan words in Roman type in a book such as this are many and difficult. For one thing there are many different pronunciations that are all equally Tibetan, though some are local to particular areas and others are confined to specific contexts, such as usage in official circles. Norbu, while born in eastern Tibet, became increasingly familiar with the tongue of central Tibet and with the official 'court language' following his younger brother's accession as *Gyalwa Rinpoche* (Dalai Lama). We have tried to render as simply as possible the pronunciation used by Norbu. A glance at the standard transliteration will suffice to show the general reader how futile it would have been to attempt to convey, let us say, the truth that the name of a certain famous monastery is pronounced (near enough) *Drepung*, by adherence to the academically correct form of *hBras-spüngs*, or that the words *sGra-mi-snyan* conceal the name for the worldly land of the north, pronounced as *Dra Minyen*. Our own efforts may not be perfect, but at least they will get the reader closer.

Where we have used *Gy* as in *Gyalwa*, the G is to be pronounced somewhat between a hard G and a J. So with *Ky*, which should almost sound like *Chy*. Where we break words up into two or more parts it is for ease of pronunciation and does not necessarily correspond to the more formal usage. Some terms used have counterparts in other languages, particularly Sanskrit, better known to Occidental readers. We give some of these in parenthesis on their first appearance; but the terms being better known, the misconceptions that for so long have accompanied them are also more firmly entrenched, and we have decided to retain, thereafter, the Tibetan term. It is better that the reader should come to Sanggye Sa as an entirely new concept, for example, rather than for us to use the term *Nirvana* and raise up a whole host of associated ideas that will only confuse and mislead.

Tibet

ཅོད།

PROLOGUE

The Legend of the Beginning

The Four Worlds lie beyond
 a great mountain, Rirab Lhunpo.
Rirab climbs to the heavens,
Rising eight times ten thousand pagtsad*
 above the mighty ocean,
Sinking as deep below its surface.
Its nature is to have four sides, each a precious
 stone.
East is crystal, and beyond, in the outer ocean,
Is Lö Phag, Land of Giants.
The South, of malachite, gazes from afar upon
 our own fair world of Dzambu Lying.
Silver is the western face;
There lies Balang Chö, rich in cattle.
The North is made of solid gold;
Northward lies Dra Minyen, blessed but
 worldly land
Where all beings are born with wealth,
Destined to lead their lives in peaceful leisure.
But that seeming happy land is land of the
 unpleasant voice,
That speaks of Death.
Land without religion.

– from GRUB-MTHA CHENMO

*A Tibetan unit of measure, given sometimes as 500
arm spans.

A void, a dark emptiness, was before all time. From within this nothingness came a wind, gentle and quiet. From east and south, west and north, it filled the void, growing in power with the passing of years. After many, many years, the wind became thick and heavy, forming *Dorje Gyatram*, a great double thunderbolt in the form of a cross. From the thunderbolt came clouds, one upon the other, growing thick and heavy like the thunderbolt and the wind. Then, from the clouds, came the great rain, each drop as big across as a wagon wheel, each drop enough to cause a flood. For countless years the great rain fell, and when it stopped falling it had created *Gyatso*, the primeval ocean.

When gyatso was still, its surface smooth and quiet, there came once again a wind, gentle and smooth like gyatso, moving the face of the waters softly back and forth. As the churning of milk brings cream to the surface, so the moving of the waters caused a light foam, *Wangchen Serkyi Sashi*, to cover them, becoming heavier as the wind grew in strength, until the foam was heavy and yellow, like *Tri*, the milk given by a cow when her child is born. And as cream becomes butter, so earth was created from the ocean.

The earth rose like a mountain, around the top of which blew the tireless winds, covering the peaks with clouds. When the rain fell once more, the water it dropped was salty – and so, ocean upon ocean, our universe was made.

In the centre was the great mountain, Rirab Lhunpo, a four-sided column of precious stones, the abode of gods. Around it lay a lake (*tso*), and around the lake a circle of golden mountains. Beyond the golden mountains was another lake, encircled again in turn. In all there were seven lakes and seven rings of golden mountains, the innermost being the mightiest. Seven times earth, seven times water. Beyond the outer mountains lay the outer ocean, *Chi Gyatso*. It is in chi gyatso that the four worlds are found, like islands, each with its own shape and different nature. The world of the south is pointed downward, like a cone; the western world is circular; the wealthy land of the north is square in shape; and the eastern world is a crescent. On each side of each world is a smaller island, of similar shape: four worlds and eight islands. This was the universe, and it was dark.

To Rirab Lhunpo came the gods and demigods. They divided the mountain between them, into different levels, the highest being the most blessed. The centre of the universe was like our own world, with hills and valleys, rivers and streams, with trees and flowers and all beautiful things; but everything was more beautiful than we can know, being most beautiful at the top. There live the *Lha*, the embodied gods. Even they, like us, must suffer and die, but they cannot be compared to us for they do not know the suffering that is ours.

Far above the universe of the desired and the formed worlds of Rirab Lhunpo exist other heavenly worlds, the formless universe of Sugme Kham. The mountain itself is, in its lower regions, the six worlds of Do Kham, the universe of desires. Above this lie the seventeen formed worlds as Sug Kham, peopled with gods embodied, who can be called on when in need. At the very summit is the single world of Ogmin, the world of enlightenment, a realm of peace and tranquillity, where suffering is unknown, the abode of the Perfect Ones. About these worlds we know little, and in any case they do not much concern this world of suffering.

Of Rirab Lhunpo we know more. This great mountain has a tree, whose name is Yongdö Dölba, rising up through its very centre, bursting into flower and fruit at the top. The mountain is populated by gods and demigods, living at four different levels of the mountainside. Those at the top are the most power-ful. The gods of this level do not have bodies like ours, but those of the other three levels do; they have bodies you can see and touch, bodies that suffer and die (though they suffer much less than ours). You can pray to these gods, to be born amongst them on Rirab Lhunpo. But each level is more powerful than the level below it, and constant fighting is the suffering of these gods, for the demigods of the lowest level say that Yongdö Dölba does not merely grow on the top of Rirab Lhunpo, it has its roots way down at their level and nourishes itself from the base of the mountain, and therefore they are entitled to a share of its wonderful fruits. So with the gods of the other lower two levels, they all fight to force their way to the top of the mountain to claim their share of the fruit. Even on Rirab there is suffering.

Rirab Lhunpo is the centre of our universe, and each of its four sides looks out across the seven lakes and the seven rings of golden mountains, to the four worlds. The gods on the side of Rirab Lhunpo facing south concern themselves with the southern world; those facing northward look after the northern world, and so with the worlds of the east and the west. It is said that the chief of the northern gods, and guardian of the northern quarter, is Nam Thöse; the guardians of the east and west are Yulkor Kyong and Chen Misang. The guardian of the southern quarter, in which our own world of Dzambu Lying lies, is Phagkyepo.

After Dzambu Lying was created, a *prakcha* tree grew up in the middle of a river. When its fruit was ripe it would fall into the water, making a noise that sounded like 'dzambu'. Many *klu* (water creatures) lived in that river, and they ate the fruit of the prakcha tree. Their excrement turned to gold, so wonderful was the fruit. The best gold in our world comes from the waters of the prakcha tree, and our world takes its name from the sound of the falling fruit. We do not know now where the river with the tree is, but it is here, somewhere.

At first Dzambu Lying was empty. There were no people, no animals, and no trees. But some of the gods of Rirab Lhunpo, because of all past deeds, came from the upper part of that mountain to our world. Because of their power and their greatness they did not need to work. Food was there for the taking; there was no famine, no hunger even. There was no sickness, and the gods lived a long time, far longer than any of us can live. Their power lay in *samten se*, a deep meditation in which creation issues from the mind. Their power was such that there was no need for light; each god was his own light, and by his own power his body glowed like a heavenly body.

After many years of contentment in Dzambu Lying, one of the gods noticed a kind of fat, like cream, called *sashag*. This fat came from the earth itself. Touching it and tasting it, the god found it good and told others to taste. The gods from Rirab Lhunpo began to eat the sashag rather than other foods. The more they ate, the more their powers diminished, the more feeble the light they created. Finally, when all the sashag was gone, they had lost their long life, they had lost their light, for they had lost the power of samten se. They lived in darkness. It was then that the sun and the moon and the stars were created for Dzambu Lying, for the light of our world that had been the light of the gods, and their power, had gone. It is only because of the gods' previous good deeds that we have the sun and the moon; if it were not for them we would be living in darkness.

In this way the gods became people. They depended on the sun and the moon and the stars for light. They ate a corn-like plant called *myugu*. It bore large fruits. Each day each person took one fruit, and the next day there was another ready for him. Thus there was no hunger or famine; it was still a world of plenty. Each person had his own myugu plant. One day a greedy person, finding that his myugu had provided two fruits, plucked and ate them both. The following day there was no fruit at all and he became hungry – so hungry that he took someone else's fruit. The latter having no food, in turn became hungry and took the fruit from yet another person's myugu plant. Soon everyone was forced to take what was not his, and in this way theft came into our world. So also came work, for everyone had to start planting so that he would have enough food even if some were stolen from him.

All this time these people, who had been gods, were in the shape of men. But once they started stealing, and then planting, they began to feel and think strange things. One man felt that his genitals were troubling him; he found them uncomfortable, so he tore them from his body. In this way he became a woman.

Having contact with men she gave birth to children, and from them came more children, and soon the world was filled with men and women, all having more children.

With so many people there was always more and more difficulty in finding enough food and in finding places to live. Instead of living together peacefully, each family began to look after its own needs, no longer bothering about the others – and they soon began fighting each other. After much fighting the people came together in a huge assembly determined to end the fighting and chose a leader. They called him Mang Kur, meaning 'many people made him king'.

Once made king, Mang Kur taught the people. He taught them how to build houses, telling them that each family should have its own house and its own fields, each family planting, growing and reaping its own food. In this way we became human beings, having been gods. In this way we became subject to the round of life and death, for while living we must work, fight, steal and get sick. Thus this world was created. That is what we believe.

Beyond our world is Chi Gyatso, the outer ocean, and beyond that we know nothing. It is to Chi Gyatso that bad people go, or so children believe: their bodies are taken alive to Chi Gyatso to die there.

The sun and moon and stars, the sky and the clouds, are not seen by the other worlds. Nor can we see those worlds or travel to them, unless we have supernatural powers. Some of us may go to these other worlds when we are reborn; some of us may have come from them. They have people living on them, but they are very different from us.

Lö Phag is the eastern world, shaped like a half moon. The people living there are giants, with moon-like faces. They live for five hundred years. They have many kinds of food and eat mainly rice and vegetables. They are not like us because they do not fight. They are quiet and peaceful. But they have no real religion.

The western world is Balang Chö, shaped like the sun. The people there are like those on Lö Phag, though their faces are round. They are large and live for five hundred years. Balang Chö is a land of cattle; many, many cattle, and the people eat mostly butter and cheese. They are a strong people.

North of Rirab Lhunpo, and furthest away from our own world of Dzambu Lying, is Dra Minyen. Unlike Lö Phag and Balang Chö, Dra Minyen is square in shape. People there have square faces, like horses, and they live for a thousand years before they have to die. There is no fighting and no work. Dra Minyen is the land of plenty, where food grows in abundance and needs no tending. When you are born on Dra Minyen you are born with everything you need. Never in your lifetime need you look for clothes, shelter or food. When you die on Dra Minyen, your wealth dies with you. It is a land of utter peace and bliss for all of your thousand years – except for the last seven days.

For Dra Minyen is also the land of the unpleasant voice. Seven days before you die you receive a sign. The clothes that have always been kept fine and clean for you become dusty and torn. Decay sets in. And you hear the chilling voice of death whispering in your ear – a sound that brings the first pain in a thousand years – telling you that now the time has come to die. The voice whispers to you and tells you how you are going to meet your death, where you will be sent afterwards, what hells and sufferings are in store for you. For nearly a thousand years the people who live on Dra Minyen do not know suffering, want, pain or fear. For the last seven days of that thousand years they know more suffering than we know in a lifetime.

We know more about Dra Minyen than the other two worlds, apart from our own, because each world has its own chief god, and the god of Dra Minyen is the god of wealth, of prosperity and contentment, of all riches. We pray to him a great deal. He can grant us wealth without the seven days of suffering. We pray to him not only for ourselves, but that his wealth may fill our whole world. If my monastery is in need of food, or in need of money for food and clothing for the monks, it is to the god of Dra Minyen that we pray.

But for all its thousand years of happiness and wealth I would not want to be born on Dra Minyen even though, with good deeds to help me, I could escape after the seven days to a heaven, and not suffer in hell. For on Dra Minyen there is too much luxury, too much comfort, too much wealth. There is no want and no religion. Not knowing any religion, he who is born in the northern world goes through life without preparing for his end. When the end comes and the unpleasant voice is heard, when at last he realizes that he is to die and suffer, he has no time to strengthen himself to meet death. Far more fortunate is he who is prepared through religion, even if his life on this world seems less full of riches.

I would always choose to be reborn in this world, for here we have religion. We are not so big, nor so long-lived, nor so well-fed and comfortable as people in the other worlds, but we are more fortunate. If I *had* to choose one of the other three I would choose Lö Phag because there they have some kind of belief, though it is not like our religion. One of Buddha's disciples, Mongal Gyibu I think, went to Lö Phag. He had supernatural powers. There, very huge, were three priests. They were so huge that they saw him as an insect, formed like a human and wearing a yellow robe. They picked him up and said, 'What a strange insect, shaped like a human being, with arms and legs, hands and feet, and wearing the yellow robe of a monk. How strange.' When Mongal Gyibu came back to Dzambu Lying he told us of all this, and that is how we know the people on Lö Phag are big people and have some form of religion. But I would always pray to be reborn on this world.

All this is found in the *Chöjung*, the Tibetan history books written by scholars going back to the thirteenth century, perhaps even earlier. History and legend, they are the same, telling of the past. All are found in scriptures like the Chöjung. This story of creation we call the *Jigten Chagtsul*, or 'narrative concerning the creation of all worlds'. Not all the accounts are the same. The old *Dzö* scriptures say that Rirab Lhunpo is square, but the later *Tökhor* writings teach us that it is round, at the heart of a round universe. Personally I think it may be round, but it does not matter very much. What matters is that we believe there *is* such a place. Perhaps there are some Tibetans who do not believe that Rirab Lhunpo exists at all; if so they believe in something else. When I believe in Rirab Lhunpo it does not matter whether it is round or square, or looks like anything else. What matters is what my belief means to me. Perhaps it is square, but if I believe it round, for me it *is* round. Even if it does not exist at all, for me it is still round. So long as we have *some* belief, we find much to learn from all these legends; they help us lead good lives. That is all we need to know about them – that is their truth. The real truth will come to us later.

Thus some people think that Rirab Lhunpo may actually be in this world, somewhere in the high mountains between India and Tibet. Some think it may be near Bodh Gaya, for that is where the Buddha received enlightenment. Perhaps from somewhere there we should look to the north and east and west for the other worlds. To the south, for instance, is the world that was the real world to the people of the Buddha's day, India, which is just the shape of the southern world, Dzambu Lying.

We Tibetan Buddhists always say that the Buddha preached many things, and that we do not necessarily have to believe that what he said has actual form. He himself said we must examine all his words as we examine gold; we must cut his speech and put it to the test of fire. So we find the truth by testing the Buddha's words, rather than in the words themselves. What each of us finds may be different, but whatever it is, that is reality and truth for us. What we *think* to be the truth, having tested it for ourselves, *is* truth; that is what we have to believe, that is what we have to follow. The Buddha taught one thing, and his disciples took that one thing in many different ways, for they each heard what they thought. To each of them that was the truth, and in following that truth each was following the path of the Buddha. Hence many of us seem to be following different paths when, in fact, we are really following one.

It was not long after the Buddha died that his disciples split into two schools, *Theg Chen* in the north, and *Theg Man* in the south. Each understood the Buddha's teachings in different ways.

If you look at a piece of gold from one place, and I look at it from another, we each see different shapes – yet the gold is the same. The truth is one, no matter how we look at it, and most of us can see no more than a small part of that truth. Ignorance lies in thinking that we see it all.

There is a story of a very powerful and fierce Indian lady who set out to kill a hundred people. One day when she had killed ninety-nine, and hunted everywhere for one more to kill to make up the hundred, there was nobody to be found except her mother, so she chased after her mother to kill her. The mother ran to the Lord Buddha who hid her in his begging bowl. The would-be murderess then tried to kill the Buddha, but he too disappeared. When he finally showed himself to her he demanded why she had wanted to kill him. She said it was because she believed that she could not achieve liberation until she had killed a hundred people and she needed one more victim. Rather than dissuade her from her goal, or make her think her goal unattainable, the Buddha did not forbid her to kill, or say it was a crime. He delayed her, saying that he would help her find her goal, so getting her to accompany him. By his teachings he gradually showed her that the killing of the hundredth victim was not necessary. But at the time she believed it necessary to kill a hundred people, *that* was the truth for her, and that was the path she had to follow. At least she believed in a path – her only crime was ignorance. The Buddha's task was merely to show her a higher truth. We should all be seeking for a higher truth while still following the one we hold.

That is why we do not mind people of other religions in Tibet. Outside Tibet everyone thinks that we have kept our doors closed to foreigners. That is not so. People have come to our country from all over the world, for many centuries, and found welcome there. Eight hundred years ago we received a Muslim delegation in Lhasa, and there has been one ever since. They have their mosque and worship as they choose, following their faith in peace. So we have had Hindus and Christians for hundreds of years. The ways all look different, but we believe the goal to be the same. If a man lives by his belief we think him a good and honest man. We do not judge him by his outer clothing.

We think Tibet the most fortunate of lands, however, for the Buddha sent his teachers to us, and our country has been blessed with many *Changchub Sempa* (bodhisattvas), teachers who have willingly re-entered the round of rebirth and suffering for our sake, to teach us and help us. We have always lived where we are today, in the mountain land north of India. It is said that we come from a union between two incarnations, one of which had taken the form of a monkey, the other having become an ogress, evil and given to the eating of human flesh.

After the creation of the universe, and of Dzambu Lying, we believe that our country was under water. Through the blessings of Chenresig, Lord of Mercy, the water slowly dried up leaving our country surrounded by great mountains. It was a lovely country of valleys and hills, peopled with *Mimayin*, invisible and intangible spirits. Sometimes they can still be seen, like ghosts, and they can do both good and harm. There were no human beings to begin with. But into this country both Chenresig, Lord of Mercy, and Dolma, his consort, sent their incarnations. Chenresig's incarnation took the form of a monkey, Trehu Changchub Sempa. The monkey incarnation was under vows of celibacy, and lived alone in quiet meditation. Dolma's incarnation, however, was an ogress and a cannibal, called Tag-senmo. Senmo, the ogress, became very lonely, having nobody to live with her. She cried and sang and cried. Trehu, the monkey incarnation, heard the crying and singing and hurried to where Senmo was and asked her what was wrong, being filled with pity. She told him of her loneliness and begged him to stay with her and her husband. At first Trehu refused, saying that this was not why he had come into the world, that he came to fulfil his vows. But Senmo was so distraught that the monkey incarnation was overcome with compassion and using his supernatural powers went straight to the great Potala, abode of Chenresig, to ask for advice. Chenresig told Trehu that the time had come for Tibet to have children of its own, and that he was to return and take Senmo as his wife.

The monkey and the ogress married, and they had six children which some people say were drawn from the six kinds of creatures that fill the world: gods, demigods, human beings, ghosts, animals and fiends. Others say the six children represent the six kinds of people found in different regions of Tibet today. In any event, the monkey father left the six children to fend for themselves. On returning a number of years later to see how they were faring, he found that they had multiplied, with children and grandchildren. All these offspring were real people, human beings, the first Tibetans, but there were so many that there was not enough fruit on the trees to feed them all. Trehu set off once again for the Potala, and Chenresig gave him different kinds of grain, from Mount Rirab, to take back and plant. So the first seeds of life were planted in Tibet.

We believe this all took place in the south of Tibet, at a place known now as Tse-Tang. Tse-Tang means playground, and this was the playground for the six children of the monkey and the ogress. Near by is the mountain Konpori, where Trehu and Senmo first met. But the human children quickly became too many, so they spread and went six different ways, to different parts of Tibet, living separately until Nyatri Tsanpo came to be Tibet's first king, so called because he was carried into Tibet on the backs of those who found him . . .

Tibetan children love to listen to these stories of the beginnings of the world, and of the beginning of Tibet. They tell them amongst themselves again and again. To them the stories are very real. Chi Gyatso is a frightening place to which they will be carried off if they are bad. But it is not used by parents to frighten their children into being good; it is something that the children themselves believe in. They often talk about it, far more than their parents. So also the countryside is full of very real things that are quite invisible. Early on, through these stories, children learn both that things are not what they seem to be and that there are many things that do not seem to be anything. The invisible Mimayin are real, to the children, as spirits that have powers quite different from those of human beings. Some of them can

31

help in times of need. They may be known to live in a certain lake or on a certain mountain, and even adults will go there and pray when in need. These good Mimayin send us harvests and look after us but if angered, they can harm us. That is why, all over Tibet, you find prayer flags on hills, mountains, by lakes, and always on the crest of passes. Again, it does not really matter whether these Mimayin exist, as the children, and many others, believe they do; what matters is that through these stories we have come to believe that everywhere, all around us, at all times, there is some power that is greater than ourselves.

Mimayin may be spirits of those who have died with an un-fulfilled wish in their minds. We may live all our lives well but we may die in a moment of anger. In such a case we may be reborn as a bad spirit, to work out that anger, for whatever we wish for, we get.

There are many kinds of bad Mimayin. One is *Yidag*; he has a huge stomach and head but very thin arms and legs. Even worse, he has a very small mouth and throat. His big stomach makes him always hungry, for his mouth and throat are so small he can never swallow enough food. Some have human bodies and animal heads. All are frightening, and live in one or another of the eighteen hells to which our bad deeds may bring us when we die. Every bad thing we do has to be answered for, just as every good deed will have its reward.

The hells are truly terrible places, each with its own kind of torture. In some people are boiled, in others they are frozen on an icy mountain. In one the victims are torn to pieces, then rejoined, only to be torn to pieces again – this is particularly for people who have killed themselves. Eight of the hells are hot, and eight are cold. Other hells, less severe, exist right here on this world. Even the guardians of each hell must themselves suffer the torments they inflict on others.

Again, one person cannot say for another that these hells do or do not exist. Like the sun and the moon and the stars, they exist if we believe in them. Our children learn that the world they live in is what they make it, good or bad. There is one truth, however, that none can deny, and that is the truth of suffering. The

Buddha taught the truth of suffering and the way to escape from suffering. It is this way that we follow in Tibet.

The Buddha also taught that suffering arises from desire, for however often our desires are fulfilled, still more remain un-fulfilled. This is the first cause of suffering. Until we can escape from desire we must continue to suffer, to be reborn again and again until by continuous good deeds we are able to escape from desire, escape from suffering, and achieve enlightenment. Each life offers an opportunity to acquire by good deeds a better birth in the next round of existence. But while life as a human offers the most opportunities to advance, it offers as many opportunities to lose ground by bad deeds. If our deeds are bad then we may be reborn in one of three lower stages of existence, as animals, ghosts, or fiends.

To be reborn as a human is not easy. The Buddha said it was as rare as for a solitary one-eyed turtle, swimming beneath the surface of the eastern oceans, to come up once every hundred years with its head through the hole of a solitary ox-yoke floating in that same vast ocean.

For this reason we are very careful about death. When a man is dying, we whisper good things in his ear so that his mind may be occupied with goodness when death comes. This will help his rebirth. If a man dies alone he may die in anger, or with bad wishes, and so secure for himself a bad rebirth. Often people like to have worldly goods taken away from them when they are dying, so that they will not die feeling attached to them, desiring them. At the moment of death a man seeing some meat near by might wish it, and so be reborn a wolf with a craving for flesh.

But the Buddha does not want us to live well, with good deeds, just because we hope for a good rebirth . . . indeed to wish for a good rebirth in itself leads us back into the round of suffering. Instead he asks us to cast our eyes about us, to think of the world around us, to recognize the truth of suffering. Suffering is every-where. Birth is suffering, so is sickness, and so are old age and death. Suffering is also experienced throughout life in the mis-fortunes that daily cross our paths, or the punishments meted out to us for wrongdoing; in the many things that offend our senses; in the non-fulfilment of our desires; and in the separation from our loved ones and from our cherished possessions.

This is the truth that the Buddha taught, the truth of suffering. The answer is release, and the Buddha also taught the Path, the way to release from suffering. It is a path demanding right belief and right aims; the aspirant must seek neither spiritual nor material well-being, only release from the round of rebirth, which is suffering. He must practise right speech and right behaviour, earn his living lawfully, be right in all he does and in all he thinks; and he must practise meditation. This is the good life, the life of the true Buddhist, and the Path teaches us to follow this good life, at peace with ourselves, at peace with our neighbours, not in fear of hell nor in hope of heaven, but secure in the knowledge that at the end of the path lies *Sanggye Sa* (Nirvana), the end to suffering.

CHAPTER ONE

Khabachen: The Land of Snow

Before the Perfect Buddha left this world
He called to him the best among the Changchub
Sempa.
He called Chenresig and told him to go to the
north,
To Khabachen, Land of Snow, there to teach
the perfect religion.
In Khabachen, the Buddha told Chenresig:
Your work is for the welfare of all living
creatures;
For all moving things, for all born into life,
You are to work.
The people who dwell in the Land of Snow are
brutal,
Touched by the three-poisoned evil.
They are selfish, jealous, and lazy;
They kill and steal.
To convert them to the Way of Truth will be
hard,
Find your disciples by many paths.
As long as there is a living creature in
Khabachen,
So long will there be a Changchub Sempa there,
for his welfare.

– from MANI BKAHBUM

We believe that there is an eternal source of Changchub Sempa, or enlightened ones, whose sole reason for existence is the salvation of all living things. They are those who have achieved enlightenment, and who could have escaped from the wheel of life, the round of suffering, but who out of compassion chose to stay. Some of them are always with us in bodily form; others are waiting for their time. Chenresig was sent to Tibet to help the Tibetan people, but Changchub Sempa may be reborn anywhere, wherever there is a living creature subject to suffering.

Tibet was chosen not because we were a good people but because in those days we were given to much fighting and killing and stealing. We were fighting with each other, fighting with our neighbours. Even the Chinese feared us because we were so warlike and so powerful. Then, some 2500 years ago, the Buddha prophesied that Chenresig would come to Tibet, and all that changed. We became so peaceful, so unwilling to take even animal life, that our enemies thought they could make us captive and take our country. Several times they nearly succeeded, but Chenresig gave us strength, and we had the even greater power of religion. We were never conquered.

I believe that Chenresig will once again save his country. What has happened must be because of our own failings, our own past bad deeds. All humans are subject to the 'three poisons' – we in Tibet as much as people anywhere. These are: *döchag* – carnal desire; *shedang* – anger; *timug* – blind passion.

It is not easy for a human being to escape being touched by the three poisons, yet in many ways we are better off than some Gods. In Tibet, while we are in some ways most blessed by Chenresig, we are also open to the greatest sin. A man who does not believe, but who has not been shown the truth, is not to be blamed – he is merely unfortunate. But if those to whom the truth has been shown spurn it, theirs is a great sin indeed. In Tibet, even the poorest farmer or cattle herder is taught the truth, through the words of the Buddha, from the moment of his birth. For him there is no turning back – he is born bound to the eightfold path.

We say that there are eight blessed states of being and eight states of restless being. Blessed are they who follow their religion, who have developed both physically and mentally, who are, if not religious, at least not heretic, and those who are not savage or wild. Blessed also are the gods and demigods who dwell on Rirab Lhunpo. It is even blessed simply to be born human and blessed not to be born in space.

Restless beings are those who are born as demons, ghosts or animals; humans who have a different form, lacking parts of the normal physical body; the wild tribes living in border countries not believing in any religion; those who actively disbelieve; the *Lha Lö* or beings of indistinct speech, whose belief is confused; and restless are those gods who because of the pleasures of their being have desired to live too long, and so were born into a heaven from where there is no escape to Sanggye Sa. They are like beings who sink into meditation and then go to sleep for aeons.

We in Tibet recognize that we are blessed indeed, because we are born with religion, we are guarded over by our protector, Chenresig, sent by the Buddha himself, and we are nearly all blessed with healthy bodies and minds. We possess all the blessings except those of being gods – and it is better to suffer as a human and eventually reach enlightenment than to live as a god and enter Sanggye Sa only after countless ages.

To understand this is to understand the Tibetan people. Tibet is not a land of saints or miracles. It is a land of people committed to the path of religion, who follow that path not as a mournful duty but with enthusiasm and great happiness. It is also a land where we can always expect the help of our protector, Chenresig, so long as we deserve it. If that is a miracle, then Tibet *is* a land of miracles, for Chenresig is always revealing himself, guiding and helping.

The countryside itself helps, perhaps. I know that those of us who have had to leave Tibet feel a real loss not being able to see our mountains and feel our winds and breathe the cold clear air. It is a countryside that takes our thoughts directly to a state of existence far above our own. Its very size and splendour make a man's thoughts turn inward. In Tibet we live with the world around us, not just in it. In itself it seems part of our blessedness.

We are surrounded by huge mountain ranges, always covered with snow, high and perilous. On the narrow trails that hang from the side of great cliffs the winds can sweep a whole caravan to its death. The wind can kill by its very coldness. It may take days or even months of travel to get from one safe resting place to another. But even in these most desolate and barren heights, far above the level where trees and shrubs can grow, there is a constant beauty and a kind of rough gentleness. We who live in Tibet know how to deal with the heights and the cold and the wind, but in any case all the discomfort in the world is worthwhile just to stand for a minute, alone with one's thoughts, in those mountains.

In the midst of the frozen heights, however, lies another country. That is the real Tibet, where people live and die, dance and sing, raise families and take them off for month-long summer picnics. It is a land of soft meadows filled with fruit trees (peaches and pears) and strawberries in the woods. Neither much rain nor snow fall down there, though the land is well watered by the melting snows all around us. Even in winter we sometimes let our young children go naked, and in the summer it is warm enough for swimming. It is so warm in some places like the Lhasa valley that people from the mountains have to leave since they suffer so much from the heat.

Some authorities say that this central region used to be a great ocean at one time – the Sea of Thetys – but however that may be, it is now a gentle and kindly land, full of beauty. Antelopes abound, and a day without bird song would be unthinkable. Even the mountains and the lakes seem to have a life of their own, and it is no wonder that some claim that they speak to us. They can tell us many things about the weather for instance, and many a life has been lost through ignoring their warnings. But they seem to speak to one in a different way too, putting strange thoughts into the head, setting strange visions before the eyes, and filling the ears with sounds that were not there. Some lakes, in particular, are so famous for this that they are consulted as oracles. I have myself been to such a lake, and seen a vision that I still cannot explain or understand.

Some explain such things by saying that these places are the dwelling places of certain spirits or gods. This belief is sometimes so strong that shrines are built and offerings made. Even those who do not believe in these disembodied spirits believe that Chenresig, in his mercy, is all around us, at all times, and may choose to reveal himself in any of these ways. To the Tibetan, then, there is nothing particularly miraculous about happenings of this kind. We live too close to our belief to doubt that help will be given when it is sought.

Even in the cities and towns, where one might expect religious belief to give way to the five poisons, one cannot escape. We do not even want to escape, for the meanest peasant finds the way of religion the way of happiness. That, for us, is the proof of its truth. But should we be tempted, even in towns there are reminders all around us, not only in the temples and monasteries, but in the people. Towns are peopled mostly with traders and merchants passing through, or with pilgrims. But trader and pilgrim alike can be seen wandering through the streets, looking at goods for sale, swinging a little silver-encrusted prayer wheel. Inside may be fragments of scriptures written on paper or cotton, and an invocation is carved into the metal wheel itself. As it twirls around, these prayers and invocations are carried to heaven for the salvation of all beings. It is the same with the monastery walls, which are surrounded by scores or even hundreds of prayer wheels – huge wooden cylinders, elaborately carved –

balanced carefully on spindles so that as the pilgrim makes the holy walk around the monastery, his hand outstretched, he sends a thousand prayers heavenward. There is hardly a rooftop or a horizon that is not broken by prayer banners fluttering in the wind. Even the most sophisticated women carry elaborately carved and jewelled reliquaries that contain sacred prayers and are worn like necklaces. But then even the sophisticates, the aristocratic town dwellers, do not scorn religion in any form. They may recognize prayer wheels and banners as mechanical devices, without any power of their own, but they also recognize that they generate a spiritual power by constantly directing people's minds to the goal of life, the cessation of suffering.

Our belief in this goal leads us to be strangely considerate, some think, towards our fellows. It is the reason that in a city like Lhasa you will find no hotels or restaurants. The pilgrim or trader has only to knock on a door and ask for food and shelter and it will be freely given. Some town dwellers feel that if such a guest stays too long, say for a year, they are entitled to ask for some recompense; it depends on their means. But even the poorest home will open its doors to any who ask.

In the country homesteads may be few and far between, but wherever he finds one the traveller may be sure of a welcome, whether he is a wealthy merchant or a beggar. Usually merchants travel with large caravans and carry tents to sleep in with all the supplies they need. Even a small caravan must have thirty or forty mules with eight or nine men and two or three dogs. When they make camp the dogs keep guard. They are very fierce, and we feed them meat and milk to make them strong. Then we make collars of yak hair and soak the hair in boiling water with a special grass. The hair comes out bright red, and it makes the dogs look bigger and fiercer than ever. During the day the dogs have to be kept chained because they will attack any stranger coming near. At night they are left free to roam around. They are the best guards to have. Fierce as they are, they are gentle with their owners.

As small children we used to play with our dogs, wrestling

41

with them and teasing them. Whatever we did, they would never bite. But if a caravan came and made camp near by, we would not think of going near *their* dogs.

Sometimes these caravans are on the move for a whole year, from one part of the country to another. Wool is one of the most important trade goods, and we even send it out to neighbouring countries. There was for a long time an important trading route into India, and the Indian towns of Kalimpong and Darjeeling were always filled with Tibetan traders unloading their bales of wool and stocking up with goods for the return journey. Inside Tibet, Gyangtse was the main wool-trading centre, and caravans came there with the soft wool of the valley sheep or the coarser wool of mountain sheep from many hundreds of miles away. In Gyangtse itself some of the finest woollen cloth in Tibet is made.

Goat and yak hair are also used, but mainly for blankets. We import dyes from China and India, but many people still prefer the old dyes made from roots and grass, special kinds of wood and stone and earth.

Individuals who want to travel from one part of the country to another, or groups of pilgrims, often attach themselves to caravans for protection. Up in the wilder and more barren regions, the hills are full of bandits, and they are likely to attack any caravan or group of travellers, large or small, However, poor travellers in company with a large and wealthy caravan will get off more lightly even if they are attacked, for these brigands are a deeply religious people and are dangerous when they can afford to be. We do not even think of them as thieves. A thief we call *Kunma*. He comes in the dark, and silently steals what he can and creeps away. You may never know who he is. A brigand is not like that. We call them *Chagba*.

Near Lhasa these brigands live with their families mainly in caves. When they go out to rob there may only be eleven or twelve men. But further north, up in the mountains, a band of brigands may number one or two hundred, and they wander about the countryside like nomads, living in tents. If a particularly large and wealthy caravan is seen, several groups will join together to attack it. Sometimes they will attack each other. But they never come down to the valleys to attack villages or the homes of poor farmers. They just wait for wealthy travellers. Even then, they always announce beforehand that they intend to attack on a certain day and at a certain time. If you can defend yourself, well and good, they consider themselves beaten. If you cannot defend your caravan they will take nearly everything you have. They do not take all, however, for sometimes you may still be days or weeks from the nearest shelter and to leave you without anything would be to let you die and the brigands never like to kill. After they have robbed, they always leave enough food and mules to get you to safety. They will even show you the quickest and safest way.

When I was a monk I used to go and visit these bands, and I was always very well received and well treated. They are among the most religious people in Tibet. They pray before they go to rob a caravan, and they always give a part of what they win to the monasteries.

Some of them are Buddhist, some are Bön, followers of the old religion that was in Tibet before the Buddha sent Chenresig to us. Others believe only in the gods and spirits of the mountains. But they all believe in something, and they are good people. If you trust them they will do anything for you. There are others, mostly thieves who have been driven from cities like Lhasa, who live by attacking caravans on the India road. They kill. They have no gods, and they are bad people. They are Kunma. Yet even they are not without religion.

The real brigands build shrines to their gods near mountains or hills where the spirits are thought to live. I have seen some of these, made of wood like small houses without roofs. Inside they put spears and guns and lots of prayer flags. Each person puts in a prayer flag, coloured according to the year in which he was born. Each year is named after one of the six elements, and each element has its own colour. Travelling through the mountains you see these shrines with bright-coloured prayer flags flying, and if you want, you too can make an offering of a prayer flag and some weapon to it. But if you put in a real gun you must first break it or damage it in some way, so that it can never be used. The spears are usually just wood, or else broken so they cannot be used. Once a year the brigands have a special festival at their shrines if they are not too far from their homes. Eventually they visit even the remotest shrines, one by one, to pray.

A brother of my teacher, who came from a family of nomads, once got to know some brigands. Then he joined their band and accidentally killed someone in a fight. Being honest he told everyone what he had done, and had all his wealth taken away from him. He came to our monastery, entered as a layman and gave his services to help atone for his crime. There was no need for him to do it, but he wanted to.

At the monastery we often had brigands come to us and confess to such accidental killings. Others came to confess that they had been hunting and living off the meat of wild animals. They usually gave us their weapons and vowed never to take life again and promised to try and make up for what they had done by prayer. None of these were really bad people for they all believed.

Sometimes they are so religious that they make the pilgrimage all the way from Kumbum, where my monastery was, to Lhasa, measuring their length on the ground for the thousand or more miles it is. They prostrate themselves full length, with arms outstretched. Then they stand up again, but on the spot touched by their hands. Some do not even stretch their arms out, but measure their length by touching the ground with their foreheads. Pilgrims come to Lhasa this way even from Outer Mongolia and Siberia. It is called *Kyangchag* and considered a very holy thing to do, but it is also considered very healthy. It is very popular in the fourth month, for that is the month of the Buddha's birth, and any actions in that month, good or bad, will bring rewards a thousandfold. When I was at Kumbum I used to like to measure my length all the way around the monastery during the fourth month. It was not very far, about four or five miles, and I would do it early in the morning, and again in the evening. At first it is terribly painful to the knees and arms, but the exercise gives you a good appetite, and you sleep better than at any other time. It is good for the body and good for the mind.

While we are doing this, or while on any pilgrimage, we think. In a monastery service it is easy just to chant and to get into the habit of chanting without thinking. But slowly measuring your length over a long distance, lying down and standing up, gives you a chance to do nothing else but think about your beliefs, and that is good. To chant or say prayers without thinking is not bad – at least it keeps harmful thoughts away – but it is best to use one's mind to think of good things.

Many people outside Tibet think we are strange because we are religious. They think it strange that a farmer or a wandering cattle herder should be religious, and wrong that a brigand should be. Yet these people have as much right to religion as anyone else. Few people are all good or all bad, but the more bad deeds a person has behind him, the more he needs religious belief. For us religion is nothing strange or fanciful: it gives us a very real pleasure, as well as helping us to live in peace with each other. Without it we would be unhappy, and we would fall into quarrelling and fighting, lying and stealing. Our lives would be poisoned.

If we believe, as many do, in spirits and gods around us, it is because it helps to explain things. We do not fall into the belief that they will do everything for us, that they are our servants. On the contrary, such beliefs help us to live our lives well. Many people tell stories of magical happenings in Tibet as though they were everyday happenings. We too hear such stories – of people who can raise themselves into the air, or make themselves invisible, or move themselves instantly from one part of the country to another. There are stories of men who fly in man-made kites high above the peaks, of others who can leave their bodies at will yet still appear to others far away and talk to them. There are stories of men who live for hundreds of years, of others who can see into the most distant future.

These things are common talk in Tibet, and we wonder at them as much as any. I myself, even though I was chosen by the oracles as an Incarnation, have never seen any of these things; I cannot see into the future or even into the past. But I do not disbelieve them. I have seen enough to make me understand that

45

there are many things about ourselves that we do not know and many powers that lie hidden through ignorance or lack of proper teaching and training. Those of us who have gone through the long and difficult training for the priesthood all know of hidden powers, powers that may someday come to us. We are constantly warned not to seek them, nor to expect to find them in others. If they come, it is merely part of the growth of the whole being – physical, mental and spiritual. They are only to be used for furthering that growth towards ultimate enlightenment when ours shall be the greatest power of all, the power to release ourselves from the chain of rebirth. Until then we have no right to use such powers as we acquire for any other purpose.

They are most certainly not to be used as mere displays, nor for selfish ends, nor even to help others. Until we achieve perfect enlightenment we lack perfect wisdom, and lacking perfect wisdom we might, in seeking to help others through our power, interfere with their *Lei* (normal course of life) and do them harm. There are some sects that deliberately cultivate these powers, but only for religious purposes. They are not revealed to the un-initiated, and anyone who breaks the vows of secrecy is subject to terrible retribution and possibly to punishment.

I suppose that we would all like to see a miracle, and hearing so much about them many of us – particularly the simple country folk – are drawn to anyone claiming such powers. In all the towns and at all the festivals and in all the markets you will find magicians performing their tricks and soothsayers selling their services to any willing to pay. But even they, with all their trickery, do no conscious harm. The fortunes they tell are so vague that they are not likely to make anyone act in a way he would not have acted otherwise. People who have had their fortunes told merely go away with less money in their pocket but somehow feeling more confident about the future. Perhaps these people, whom some call charlatans, are really doing good, despite all their trickery.

There are some, however, who sell their services to do harm. They claim to have supernatural powers that can reach out and strike people with sickness, even death. These sorcerers are truly evil people, for their thought is evil.

There are stories about strange tribes living in Tibet. Some are said to be giants and ruffians who kill and steal and take women. Others are said to be a people in the east who dig gold from the ground and become wonderfully rich. In the south are said to be the Loba, who live on human flesh. These are all travellers' stories. Mountain people are big and fierce looking, and brigands are a real threat to wealthy caravans, but they never harm people unless they are forced to fight – in fact some of them prefer not to fight at all, and will take tribute, given voluntarily, in return for safe passage through their country. And they certainly never take women. Even Kunma, the thieves, will not do that. We live an open life in Tibet, in the countryside, and there is no need for such things.

In the east there *is* a place where there is gold, and the people there scratch a little of it from the surface. But they do not dig and burrow for it, because they believe this would anger the gods. They prefer to remain poor.

The southern tribes, particularly along the Assam and Burma borders, are very different. They are not really Tibetans, and they are not Buddhists. They go naked and hunt animals in their forests with bows and arrows. Stories were told by travellers very long ago that these southern tribes would kill any young person who was fat, healthy and had a nice complexion and then eat him. In Tibet we know nothing of such stories, but we do think of some southern people, particularly the Loba, as wild. Every Monkey Year (that is, every twelfth year) many Tibetans go on pilgrimage there and bring presents and money so that the Loba will not harm them. But I have never heard, except in our old legends of the days before Buddhism, of their being people who ate human flesh.

We have many different kinds of people in Tibet: mountain people and valley people, people who farm the land and others who wander through the mountains with their herds of cattle. The customs are different, too, from one part of the

47

country to the other. In the north the Mongolian customs are practised. In the east, where I was born, there are many things that are Chinese. Our religion is also influenced, containing many gods in common with the gods of the Hindus, and it is divided into many sects. There are even those who still practise the ancient religion of the Bön. But we think of ourselves as one people, a people who love our country, and who believe that no matter what disaster strikes we will be saved in the end by our protector, Chenresig. All we have to do is to try and follow the way of life taught by the Buddha.

CHAPTER TWO

A Peasant Childhood

One treasure, and one alone,
Can no robbers steal.
One treasure, and one alone,
Can one take through the doors of death.
The wise man's wealth lies in good deeds
That follow ever after him . . .

All perfections, even that of Buddhahood,
Are by this treasure won.
So great their power, so rich their fruit,
Good deeds are done by all with reasoning
   mind.

— from KUDDAKA PATHA

The people of Tibet, even today, can be best understood through an understanding of their past but, before we look back into the remote past, something should be said of the material side of life in modern Tibet because that too has been the subject of much misunderstanding.

Briefly, there are four main ways of life in Tibet: there are the valley farmers and the mountain nomads; there are the traders whose caravans endlessly ply back and forth, supplying such needs as the people cannot supply for themselves; and there is the monkhood, the vast body of those who have taken holy vows, a body to which almost every family contributes at least one member. The monkhood is organized into a hierarchy from which springs the government of the country. The government is not confined to the religious order, however; it is divided equally between priests and laymen. The lay members of the government form a fifth division of the population, the nobility. It is a small group and its members are often, but by no means always, wealthy. It must not be confused with the kind of hereditary nobility known in Europe, for although a Tibetan noble is accorded respect it is not because of his birth but rather because of his responsibilities. Anyone can become a noble by entering government service and acquiring an official position. Frequently it is the sons of those already in office who enter service, but not necessarily. The nobility, then, is not strictly a hereditary class. Children who do *not* enter government service may eventually return to the land as farmers, losing their noble status. Many stay on in Lhasa, either in the hope of appointment or simply because they enjoy the life there. It has an elegance and an air of leisure and ease that might seem attractive to some, but it is not a way of life that the majority of Tibetans would envy. The nobles who are conscientious in their duty are hard worked, have heavy responsibilities and little freedom. They are always at the beck and call of the central government, whether it is in session or not. Authority in itself is nothing the rest of us would desire; even the job of being a village headman is not coveted, for it brings worry, distress and little reward. The only real privilege a noble or a village headman has, by virtue of his position, is the satisfaction of doing a particularly difficult job.

There are always, of course, those who abuse their position, using it to accumulate material wealth or to wield personal power. These are some of the temptations that come with nobility, and they are among the reasons why the rest of us have so little envy for this class of people. It is not that we have no use for wealth; on the contrary, it would be a strange Tibetan who did not enjoy haggling in a market place and getting a good bargain. But we haggle and bargain for the necessities of life, not for the luxuries, so our lives are that much more secure. We do not live in poverty, our homes contain the comforts we need, and we find it no hardship to do without those things we do not need. It is important to realize how little we care for the life of the nobility, for it is often alleged that we are abused by them. The only people they can abuse are themselves. The rest of us are content to leave the problems of politics and economics to those whose jobs they are, being thankful they are not ours. And it is often said that the most contented nobles are those who have given most of their wealth away and retired from the affairs of state.

Coming from a peasant family, I should start by saying something about those who live by working the fields. My family comes from Amdo, an eastern district that fell, in the old days, under the jurisdiction of the Chinese government. But geographical boundaries mean little, and we never thought of ourselves as anything but Tibetan, owing all allegiance to the *Gyalwa Rinpoche* (Dalai Lama), our political and religious ruler. Our houses were a little different – mainly in that we sometimes had one room in which there was a heated platform on which people could sleep. Elsewhere in Tibet, despite the cold, the houses are heated by small copper braziers that can be carried about, filled with glowing charcoal. My family was poor and Tengtser, the small village in which we lived, was equally poor, with a dozen or so houses like ours. The only time our home saw any wealth was after I had been recognized as the incarnation of the ancient and highly revered monk Tagtser and was about to be sent to Kumbum Monastery for entry into the monkhood to occupy the seat of Tagtser there. The Tagtser *Labrang*, as the living was called, had accumulated great riches over the ages, given by pilgrims and wealthy patrons. It used these riches to support four monasteries, including its own monastic seat within the huge monastic city of Kumbum. Those monasteries in turn worked for the good of their neighbourhoods – teaching, lending out land and money to farmers, supplying grain in times when the harvest was poor, and, of course, fulfilling all manner of religious duties. I spent some months as a young child at one of these monasteries, and it was from there that I had to make my way to Kumbum for my enthronement as Tagtser *Trülku*, the reincarnation of Tagtser. The way led through the little village where my parents still lived, and although I was only some eight years old, the whole village turned out to greet me and the escort that was bringing me to my new home. I was to spend three days in Tengtser with my parents before continuing the journey, so the Tagtser Labrang sent them as a gift a number of beautiful carpets and hangings, as well as food and money, so that they could provide hospitality not only for me and the score of monks who accompanied me but also for the whole village.

Some years later, when my youngest brother was recognized as the incarnation of the Gyalwa Rinpoche, my entire family had to leave their humble home and move to Lhasa, where they were provided with wealth far beyond their dreams to enable them to live fittingly in their new station. But I have in many ways regretted having had to leave that simple life of ours in Tengtser. It was poor, but never without warmth and comfort. There was always enough food, and on festival days my mother never failed to find ways of cooking up special delicacies for us and for any visitors who might come. Nor did we ever refuse hospitality to travellers. Poor as we were, we all had our fine clothes, carefully kept in the huge wooden cupboards in our best room, for special occasions. Above all we had very real wealth in the companionship that extended beyond our own family, uniting all the families of Tengtser and giving us the assurance of a warm welcome in other villages where we had relatives. We had no more than three or four cows to send out daily to join the village herd, and our little strips of land were smaller than most and required long and hard work since we could not afford to pay for much help – but it never struck us for a moment that we were living in poverty. We were only conscious of our happiness as a family and as a village.

My earliest recollections and fondest memories show how close our religion was to us, even as tiny children. One of the favourite spots to play used to be around the household shrine that stood in the main courtyard. It was a clay tower containing various sacred images, and it was the centre of certain rites concerning the protection of the home. It was equally the centre of attraction for my friends and me, and there was no place to play that we liked better. We were not particularly conscious of its religious significance – we were simply aware that somehow this was a warm, safe and friendly place. In fact many of my childhood associations with religion were far from religious. Even the family shrine inside our house was not safe from my prying eyes, and I once tried to roast a potato over the sacred butter lamp.

Like many children I used to dream of running away. But my idea of excitement, shared with many of my fellows, was to pretend that I was running away to a monastery to become a monk. Once I actually did run away. I rolled up a few of my old belongings in my rope, and with this bundle over my shoulder I escaped through a hole in the wall. I was about six years old, and I ran as hard as I could to a little path that led to the near-by monastery. I followed it, but then it divided; not only did I not know which path to take, but also I didn't know how to get back. My mother knew where to find me, and she soon came to bring me home. Later I was told I was the reincarnation of Tagtser. My parents had known for some years, but it had been kept a secret from me. Then the monks came to tell me, bringing all sorts of gifts, and there was no more need for me to run away.

My mother is in nearly all my childhood memories, I suppose because she and my sister were the ones who always had to look after me. My father was busy working and I saw much less of him. In a Tibetan household the women are all important. I remember that it was my mother who tended the family shrines. At first light she went up onto the flat roof of our house taking some charcoal or yak-dung fire with her, and when I was old enough I would go too. There she lit a little fire and made offerings of cedar or juniper wood, and of a little food such as *tsampa* flour, dried fruits and butter. Every house in the village did the same thing, and it is done all over Tibet each morning as the sun strikes the snowy peaks of the mountains. From every roof a wavering wisp of smoke rises up to the sky, and the air is filled with sweet smells and the sound of prayers.

When that was done we went down into the house, and my mother lit the butter lamp and put it on the altar, where it burned all day. The whole family came together there to say prayers, morning and evening.

I was too young to be able to help my father in the fields – a boy must be ten years old anyway before he can be of real use, and in any case parents like to see their children playing. I had many friends in the village, but most of all I liked playing with my sister. My very earliest memories are like dreams, and I can see myself being bundled up in woollen blankets by my mother and put in a corner of the house where I could not get into trouble while she worked. The first real memory I have is of a day in the autumn when all the colours in the fields and on the sides of the mountains were changing. My sister and I went into the fields to play almost every day because the straw that had been cut was piled up and we had made a little house by burrowing into the pile and making little rooms. Into one room we had brought some flat stones, making a table. Other smaller stones we used as dishes. This particular day, as usual, we brought a few grains of barley and some peas, and we pretended we were having our meal. But as winter was approaching it was cold even inside our straw house so we lit a fire to keep us warm. Of course the whole pile of straw was soon alight, and our parents came running to beat it out with sticks and blankets. We were more frightened at the beating we would get than at the danger, but everyone was too busy putting the fire out to do more than shout at us. We were never allowed to play in the straw again and it was the last house we made together.

We used to go for walks together too, up into the foothills that lay around Tengtser. In the summer the hills were full of berries, and we filled baskets with these and brought them home for our family; it made our parents happy to see that we wanted to help, and the wild fruits were a welcome addition to our meals. We were often joined by other children, and we played as we gathered. I was about three or four years old when on such an expedition I produced a candy I had brought with me. Another boy, about the same age, wanted to eat it too, but I would not give it to him. We played together, and in the middle of playing he suddenly bit me in the face. I did not give him the candy, even then, but I cried loudly and my mother's sister who was with us had to pick me up and carry me. That is one of the unhappy things I remember.

Our family had a number of relatives also living in Tengtser, and like many Tibetan villages people thought of themselves as related even if they were not. The Tibetan village is spread out among the fields and meadows. Each house has a stone wall around it, with a gate leading into an inner courtyard. Inside these courtyards the great black mastiffs are allowed to roam at night. Some houses are all by themselves, but mostly they cluster together, perhaps three or four of them separated from the next cluster by open country. In Tengtser our own family cluster was the largest, having seven or eight houses in it. A number of the men were called 'brother' by my father, but they really were not. Their mothers I called 'Grandmother'. One was blind, and whenever I went to see her she let her hands feel all over my face as she talked to me. Another 'grandmother', who lived next door, sometimes used to fight with her son's wife, and that used to give me bad dreams. But one in particular I liked to visit. She was very old, and she sometimes looked after my sister and myself when my mother was busy. She always carried her beads in her hand and when she was doing nothing else she would murmur invocations to the gods. Many Tibetans do this. I liked to play with her and try to take her beads away from her. Then she would put them in a bag and I would try to take the bag. She was old, and very kind to us.

We were quite free to go and play with other children, and we came and went as we liked. But mostly we played in the courtyards and not inside the houses themselves. The New Year season was the time for making more formal visits, and then every day we visited three or four houses. Sometimes we went with our parents, sometimes my sister and I went alone, on some excuse, knowing that we would be given candy and perhaps a few pennies. Sometimes we were given rare treats like dried fruit, and we were never expected to be polite and stay. As soon as we were given our candy we usually ran off to the next house.

Visits to other villages we never made on our own; for one thing there were a lot of wolves about in the country and they would be quite likely to attack children. But sometimes my parents would be invited to visit friends or relatives in other villages, and then the whole family would go. While the grown-ups were eating or drinking home-made wine, the children would play. But I did not particularly like these visits; other villages did not seem as friendly as ours – everything was strange and even the children we did not know.

There was a little monastery about ten or eleven miles from Tengtser, and we children always looked forward to a visit there. On festival days the whole village went, in groups of two or three families, bringing butter lamps to light and offerings to make. We liked it because it seemed such a friendly place, and it was so full of interesting things.

Sometimes a priest came to our house to say prayers for us. Then he would wash my sister and me with holy water, to remove all the bad things in us. My father used to like to invite him to stay for several days so that he could read from the religious books to us and do honour to our ancestors. But we were not expected to sit and listen to it all, and nobody minded if we ran out to play.

Small as we were, we liked to help, and our mother gave us a number of jobs of our own. One was to take any food that was left over and mix it in a small bucket with some meat and bread, then take it out to our watchdog. We also used to feed the pigs, and when a sow gave birth we had to look after all the piglets to make sure they did not wander away too far. They were always kept in the courtyard, just near the gate, where there was a shelter for the animals.

My sister used to help with the cooking and made sure the stove was always fed with fuel. Sometimes we used yak dung, horse and sheep dung being used mainly in the fields, but we also had plenty of wood. It was not large wood, for we used to get it from the bushes that covered the hills near by, but it was good fuel and we were never without warmth.

Since I left home when I was eight to become a monk, I was never able to go and work with my father in the fields. My parents contributed to the hire of the village shepherd so there was not even that work for me to do. As a matter of fact I was strictly forbidden to go up into the hills where the sheep and cattle were grazing, but it was one of the things I liked doing best as I grew older. If my father was away I would run off and join the shepherd and go with him way up the mountainside. Other children did the same thing and we spent wonderful days playing with each other, or by ourselves, and best of all listening to the shepherd tell stories. We all used to steal some food from our homes, some potatoes, dry bread and some cheese, put it in string bags and tie the bags to our waists. This way our hands were free. We stayed out all day, returning only when the shepherd brought the flocks back at dusk. Then we generally had to face a beating, but it seemed worth it.

I had no younger brother to play with at that time. One was born a year or two after my own birth, but he did not live long. My mother cried a little, but we try not to cry on such occasions, and if we do, then we try to hide it. I remember being very worried and giving my mother what comfort I could, telling her that we should take my young brother to a nice place and bury him properly.

My father would have been badly off for help had he remained a farmer. At eight I joined my monastery, the next son had already died, the third was, like myself, chosen for the priesthood, and the fourth was to become the Gyalwa Rinpoche. Our family could not afford much in the way of outside help. My mother and sister did all the work in the house, and for most of the year my father worked the fields alone. In springtime he might hire a man to help him with the ploughing and sowing, and when it was time for weeding everyone had to hire help or help each other. That was a busy time. And again he hired help when it was time to get the harvest in. We children were really too small to be of much help for the work was hard, but even so we did what we could, and neighbours always came to help each other. Our fields were all mixed up, because no one person had all his fields in the same place. It had always been the custom to divide the land, grading it from good to poor, each family taking a share of the poor land as well as the good. Our nearest field was only three minutes away from our house, but we had three other fields to look after, north and east of the river, and travelling back and forth looking after all these fields made the work even harder.

In a case like ours the land is usually all left to the eldest son, in the hope that brothers will stay together and keep what little land there is intact. But parents always watch their sons and daughters-in-law carefully to see how they get on with each other, and if they foresee trouble they divide the land before their death. When land is divided it is a sad occasion because it means that a family is divided; even brothers no longer have the same obligations towards each other. If in this way anyone finds that he has not enough land to support his needs, he can always get a grant of land from a near-by monastery, and many people live by farming monastery land. Monasteries also provide seed when it is needed. In return they take a small percentage of the

59

crops; even on cash loans the rate of interest is only about two per cent.

When all the work of the harvest was done, my father used to set off on journeys to near-by markets or trading centres, taking donkeys laden with goods for exchange. Others from the village often joined him, and they made up quite a caravan in this way. They brought grain and wool and cloth woven by themselves and their wives. At the markets they bartered their grain and wool for trade goods, returning home after two or three days. It was always good to hear my father's voice calling out as he rode back through the gate into the courtyard.

Sometimes traders came to our village bringing their goods with them, and then it was like having a market of our own. Different traders made friends with different families, and each year when they came they would stay with that family, usually for several days, while they traded their goods. When they came to our house all their goods were laid out in a room, and the door was locked. I used to try all sorts of ways to get in, but it was impossible. The best I could do was to make a little tear in the cloth that covered the small window panels, and stare inside at all the treasures laid out there.

When the fruit traders came my sister and I were more lucky. These people used to take all the fruit from their bags and baskets and lay it out on the floor for inspection, and we usually managed to sneak a few small apples away without being noticed. But whether there was anything we could steal or not, we always enjoyed visits from outside. Not all were traders; many were craftsmen – tailors and shoemakers, who travelled around on a regular circuit, year after year, from village to village. Even from them we children could expect little gifts. From one end of the year to the next our lives were full of variety and interest. Although I only spent the first eight years of my childhood in that little farming village, it is plain from everything I remember, apart from all that I have seen since, that for the adults too life was good.

Some of our customs seem strange to other people. Many families are made up of a number of brothers all of whom have the same wife. Some say that this is because in such regions there are more men than women, but whatever the reason it seems to work out extremely well, and it has the great advantage of keeping all the land together. To some people it also seems strange that parents often arrange marriages for their children. But it is seldom that children are married against their wishes, and the wise guidance of older people often results in a happier marriage than when the youthful heart follows its desires. There could scarcely have been a happier family than ours, yet the marriage between my mother and father was arranged by their parents.

Most strange of all, I suppose, are our funeral customs. Poor people are often just put into rivers. Others have their bodies carried to mountain tops, to be cut up there, the flesh laid out in strips on a rocky ledge, and the bones pulverized, for the birds to eat. Others are cremated. Only the bodies of lamas, great teachers, are kept intact, or their ashes are sealed in urns and set into funerary monuments. The general idea behind all these practices is that even in death the body can be of use to our fellow creatures – animals, birds or fish. It only seems an unpleasant idea to those who think that somehow the body can continue to have an existence of its own after life has departed. Great teachers are exempted from these practices because it is believed that their relics can serve a better purpose by becoming enshrined as a reminder to future pilgrims of their teachings.

For us the human body is a wonderful gift, so long as it is inhabited by life. But once that life departs, the body has no further use, except by making of itself a final gift to other forms of life.

CHAPTER THREE

Mountain Nomads

He who feels shame where there is no cause,
He who is shameless in the face of shame:
Both are condemned by their falsity.

He who is afraid where there is no danger,
He who, in the midst of peril, ignores it:
Both are cast from The Way by falsity.

He who considers a good thing perverse,
He who considers a perverse thing good:
Both are lost through the falseness of their
    vision.

– from DHAMMAPADA

Even a large monastery like Kumbum depends for much of its support on the mountain nomads. Every year there is a festival, for instance, during which large towers are made from butter fashioned into all manner of shapes and gaily decorated. As a young monk at Kumbum, when I was around fifteen or sixteen, I used to be sent out to the mountains to collect contributions from the nomads to help pay for this festival. By that time I had been studying hard for seven or eight years and I knew many of the scriptures by heart. I was always made welcome by the nomads because I would be able to say prayers, make sacrifices for them and recite the scriptures. I went from group to group, often answering calls when there was any sickness.

Later on I visited the nomads during winter, but these visits from Kumbum were made during the summer, and I used to stay away for about six months. Their country is a high plateau, about ten thousand feet, with mountains rising still higher. It is an open country, with few trees, swept by powerful winds. In winter though, the winds have their use, for they blow the snow away and leave patches on the hillsides where the herds can get a little grazing. Only nomads live up in these mountains, and there is no farming until you get down into the lower country, such as my own Amdo province, which is about seven thousand feet high. To the west there are a few scattered groups of Mongolian farmers.

I used to go from Kumbum by horse, a small caravan of donkeys or mules carrying my tent and provisions. If I was only going to stay a short time with any one group, I would not bother to unpack my tent but would stay with them. There was always a genuine and friendly welcome and some groups I came to know so well that they treated me as though I were one of their own family. They used to send out to meet me and help bring me to their camp. Some groups consisted of only two or three families, and the largest was never larger than twenty families. Each family, which might be made up of several brothers and their wives and children, had one main tent made of yak hair, which they weave into a heavy coarse material. If children marry, they sometimes put up an extra tent. The tent is used for living, not merely for sleeping, and all camp life revolves around it. In any one group the individual family camps were never much closer than a mile apart, just close enough so that a really loud shout could be heard from one camp to the next. In this way the herds did not get mixed up, and there was enough grazing for all in the hills around. The grass was never plentiful so most nomadic groups had only about ten families.

The tents are four-sided, with sloping roofs, and there is usually only one entrance. For a large family a tent might be thirty feet long and about fifteen feet wide, and the property of the entire camp will be kept inside. During the summer a wealthy family might put up a cotton tent, really just a four-sided screen without a roof, for entertaining visitors; but the yak-hair tent is the real centre of family life.

At the entrance a fire pit is dug, and over this a stove is built to hold two or three large cooking pots. Close by is a box containing the barley flour we call tsampa on one side, with cheese and butter on the other so that when tea is made, the butter and tsampa are ready to serve with it. Four or five feet away is a low table, twelve inches high, and around this the family sit on sheepskins for their meals. Between the stove and the table is an open space where people just sit and talk. All around the walls are wooden chests and yak-skin bags containing personal belongings and food stores. Wealthy nomads like to keep grain stored in bags so many generations old that they become quite black. This is just for show, a way of proving they have so much food that they never need touch these reserves.

Saddles and swords are hung from the roof poles on one side of the tent, while on the other is kept all the kitchen equipment, including the tall wooden cylinders used for churning up the tea and butter. Sometimes a curtain is hung here to screen this part off. At the far end is the family altar with the images of Buddha and the family butter lamps, and just beside it a chest made of wood and decorated with wrought silver in which jewellery and other valuables are kept. Even poorer families have some fine pieces like this to show off, and every woman has gold and silver jewellery to wear on special occasions. The tent is kept warm by the stove, and there is sometimes a charcoal brazier. There is always a special little brazier on which herbs are burned to make the air sweet and clean.

At night the only light is the dim and flickering light given by the butter lamps. The altar lamps are kept burning day and night; the cotton or cloth wicks hanging from their rims are trimmed by the women. If guests come an extra butter lamp might be set on the table in their honour. In the winter people sometimes sleep inside the tent, particularly if they are old, but in the summer, when I used to visit the nomads, we all slept outside, on sheepskins, with a rough yak-hair blanket to cover each of us. If it was cold we pulled the blankets right over our heads, and lying so that our feet were all together helped keep us warm. If the feet are cold the rest of the body will be cold.

In the morning, before dawn, the young men get up and milk the yaks. Then the women stoke up the fires and prepare a brew of boiling hot butter tea. By then everyone is awake and up – except the children, who are usually the last to awaken. When everyone is up, fire is taken from the tent and placed on a kind of altar, a pile of stones about four feet high, just outside. Tsampa and butter and perhaps a few dried fruits are put into the flames, with rhododendron leaves and juniper wood. As this is done everyone chants invocations to the *Könchog Sum*, the 'Three Precious Ones': *Sanggyela Kyabsu Chio* – I seek refuge in the Buddha; *Chöla Kyabsu Chio* – I seek refuge in the Teachings; *Gedunla Kyabsu Chio* – I seek refuge in the Monkhood.

We always start, however, with an additional invocation:

Lamala Kyabsu Chio   I seek refuge in the Teacher of Religion –

because no aspirant can reach the Könchog Sum without the guidance of a teacher.

We Buddhists believe this is the basic law for all laymen. If they honour the Buddha, believe his word, and heed the monkhood, they will find release. Release must be found in all three; it cannot be found in the one without the other.

One of the old people takes a ladle of butter tea and sprinkles it into the air, calling on the Buddha and Changchub Sempa, naming their protective deities, and finally the mountain gods and goddesses. Then the last of the tea is thrown to the sky and everyone gives a loud shout that can be heard many camps away. In this way they offer the first food of the day to their beliefs and to their gods. Even when this is over many of them go on chanting prayers, sometimes all day long, simply because it makes them feel good, not because they have to.

When the morning sacrifices are over everyone gathers in the main tent for breakfast. The whole camp comes together at meal times, children, parents and grandparents. All think of themselves as one family. Those who are going to take the herds up into the mountain pastures usually fill their bowls with tea, put some tsampa or cheese in it, and walk around outside getting ready, drinking their tea as they work, letting the yaks loose and coiling up the ropes. Tsampa is often scarce, but there is always dried cheese or yogurt, and perhaps some meat, to take with the tea at breakfast. From every camp you hear the great shout as the sacrifice is made, and soon after you can see the yaks and sheep slowly wandering off to graze. Each camp grazes its flocks and herds separately, though if one family is very small it may join up with another to share common pasture and for protection.

Women and small children stay behind in the camp, with newborn calves and lambs, and dogs to help guard them. The men take turns staying behind to keep watch over the camp during the day. There is always plenty to keep everyone busy, particularly spinning, weaving and making felt. Feltmaking is hard work. An old piece of felt is taken and on top of it wool is laid, the amount depending on how thick you want to make the new blanket. Some blankets are a good twelve feet square and over half an inch thick. Water is sprinkled over the wool, and then the whole bundle is rolled up, tied loosely and beaten. Men and women join each other at the work, beating with sticks, stones, even with their hands. After each beating the bundle is folded and tied up a little tighter. After about three hours it is unrolled and pulled and stretched into whatever shape is needed. All the time they are doing this, instead of talking to each other the workers chant prayers and verses from the scriptures.

Small babies are always carried by their mothers wrapped in a small piece of felt. But when they grow up a little they are put in yak-hide bags on a little bed of yak-dung ashes. The babies are kept clean and comfortable by changing the ashes. As soon as they can crawl they begin to play with the other children, who help look after them and keep them out of trouble. All children up to four or five years old go completely naked in the summer, no matter how cold it is. They have no toys of any kind, but they play with stones and different kinds of grass and pretend they are adults. They also collect sheep dung and play with that, throwing some into the air and trying to pick up more from the ground in time to catch the first lot. They have the animals to play with, the calves and lambs that stay behind in the camp, and the large mastiffs. Those dogs will let anyone from their family play with them, but nobody else can even come near without being attacked. Like all children these nomad children love to listen to stories – usually stories about the wild men who live in the mountains and eat berries and fruits but are always on the look-out for children to catch and eat if they can. There are lots of stories like this, all over Tibet, but I have never met anyone who believed that such people existed, and I never heard the word 'yeti' (the Abominable Snowman) until I left Tibet; it is a Nepalese word. For us these are just children's stories.

There are real dangers in the mountains, though, and it is good that stories of this kind frighten the children enough to make them careful. There are wolves and bears, and every nomad, man or woman, always has with him a special sling hung from the sash tied at the waist. The sling is made of yak hair and has a felt pocket in the middle. At one end there is a hole for a finger or thumb, and at the other end there are a number of loose yak hairs. You put a stone in the felt pocket, hold the loose end between your thumb and fingers, and swing it around your head. When you let go, the stone flies out, and the loose yak hairs crack like a whip, making a sound almost like gunshot. A good marksman can hit an animal at two hundred yards on the level, and even more if he is higher up. At night everyone has his sling beside him in case of attack by animals or thieves, and a little pile of stones is kept in the middle of the sleeping area. The dogs give plenty of warning of any such attack.

When the herders are out during the day they have to keep a sharp eye open for either animal or human tracks that might warn them of danger. Hands are always busy with some kind of work. Over his shoulder a herdsman carries a hair bag, and in it some wool that has been spun by children back in the camp. As he follows the herd he twirls this into yarn, rolling it into balls and twisting the thread on a stick. He may also bring skins with him to tan, which have already been softened with buttermilk and cream. By constantly rubbing, twisting and wringing a good man can tan a small sheep's hide in three or four hours. On the way home, of course, herdsmen pick up all the yak dung they can find and bring it back to the camp for fuel.

It is a long day, from dawn to dusk, and sometimes the milking cattle have to be brought back to the camp for a midday milking. Then the herdsmen have to take all their herds to water, after which they must be kept quiet for an hour or two. During this time the men are able to eat a little dried cheese or meat that they bring with them, or they may even cook themselves a meal if they have brought a small vessel. Fire is easily made with a flint – even the older children know how to do it. A kind of cottonlike substance can be made by rubbing special leaves, found all over the mountains, and this is held on top of the stone, in one hand, while it is struck with the flint. One strike is enough, then the cotton is alight without any fanning or blowing, and can be set on top of some yak dung to make a fire. All men and women and older children carry flint bags and a supply of this cotton with them, but younger children are never allowed to play with flints.

There is always the danger of starting a grass fire, and as there is only just enough grass for the cattle, a fire could be a disaster. But young children are gradually taught how to handle fire by letting them work the bellows used to build up hot fires under the stove in the camp. These bellows are hard to work, since they are no more than hide bags that have to be opened and closed by hand as they are pumped up and down. So everyone is glad to let the children have this work.

When people get back from the mountains they all gather together again in the tent, where they can rest and get warm. The women cook the evening meal, which is usually a soup with boiled meat in it, perhaps with some rice or barley added to thicken it. This meal is taken sitting around the table, and it is the main meal of the day. Evening time is the time for talking, but when the meal is over it is already several hours past dusk, and everyone is ready to go to sleep. Some go straight outside and cover themselves in their blankets, others stay in the tent for a while, in front of the altar with its flickering butter lamps, saying their prayers and chanting. Then they too go outside to sleep, leaving a few old people to sleep in the warmth in front of the altar.

During the summer months the nomads move about in groups, from one pasture to another, changing location perhaps every month. Every tribe has a fixed territory that belongs to it, and members of the tribe can move freely within that area, usually in groups of several family units that camp separately, but near one another. Each camp within a group has a headman of sorts, a *gowa*, but the gowa's job is mainly to see that taxes are collected, and he cannot decide such matters as when to move. No one family can decide – all the families that make up a group get together and make the decision among themselves. If one camp has a particular reason for moving, someone from that camp will get on his horse and go to talk to the people in other camps. Some may decide to stay, and others to move on, but generally a group always moves together. All the belongings are packed up and tied onto the pack animals and the whole caravan moves off together. Before they leave, a last fire is kindled in the fire pit above which all the family meals were cooked. The nomads believe a fire god comes to live near such hearths, and they make a final offering by putting a little of their precious tsampa into the fire. As they ride away they look back to see if the tsampa has caused the fire to smoke. If a fine column of smoke is seen rising up into the sky, then they know that their sacrifice has been accepted and that the next camp will be a happy one. If there is no smoke they expect trouble and take extra care in their new camp.

When the winter winds begin to blow all the nomads move down from the heights to the foothills, where they can find shelter. The camps they set up there last for the whole winter, six or seven months. Winter lasts from the ninth to the second month, and it is very cold indeed, and dangerous. Once I was travelling from my home to Lhasa, in winter, and one night a boy was too lazy to take off his felt boots when he went to sleep. The next morning his feet were frozen and he could not walk. He felt no pain, but he could not stand. We took his boots off and wrapped his feet in warm cloths; they were swollen and red and became worse. We were still eleven days from Lhasa, so we carried the boy, sometimes on yak, sometimes on horse. Sores spread all over his legs, and they were continually dripping water and blood. There was nothing we could do. First his toes came off, and then the feet. In Lhasa they tried all sorts of herbs, all the medicines they knew, but it was too late. Both his legs rotted away up to the knees. Then the doctors bound his knee joints up in yak-hide covers, and after a time he was able to walk on the stumps.

He should have known better. Everyone knows of this danger, and the wise ones not only take their boots off when they go to sleep, they leave them off in the mornings when they are milking the cattle, and they even walk short distances barefoot, though the temperature may be thirty or forty degrees below zero. While they are working, either milking or loading the yaks, they are not only barefoot but they also bare their shoulders. They never get frostbitten. They continue to sleep outside, and I found that I preferred to do so. The winter camp is a permanent one, so they are able to protect it in various ways. One is to build a wall of yak dung. This keeps the wind away from the tent, and at the same time dries the dung out so that it makes better fuel – and it is a convenient way for storing it. We used to sleep between this wall and the tent. The older people sleep inside during the winter.

In addition to the yak-dung wall, we used to make windbreaks by piling up our saddles. Then the dogs used to come and sleep on top of us, and that kept us warm. There are the sheep too, and some of us used to sleep with them, using our boots for a pillow. The yaks were warm, but they were not good to sleep with, for they always kicked. Sometimes it snowed and we got wet, but still I preferred to sleep out. Once I went from Koko Nor, the great lake not far from Kumbum, to Lhasa. It was in midwinter, and the journey took one hundred and eleven days. I had a tent with me, but every night I slept out, even when it snowed. There must have been about a thousand of us in that caravan, with some ten or twelve thousand yaks, horses and mules. It was the only safe way to travel in winter.

After the winter camp is set up, in the ninth month, everyone gets ready for the expeditions to the markets that will follow, from the tenth month on. It is a good time of year. The farmers have got their harvest in, and all the great nomad herds are strong and healthy after a summer's grazing. Markets are plentiful, and this is also a time for religious festivals. It may be a twenty-day journey to the nearest market, so it is quite an expedition. The farmers bring their grains, and the nomads bring their livestock, as well as other products like butter, cheese and meat. In exchange the nomads want mainly barley to make their tsampa, and tea. But they also buy other foods like dried fruit and rice, and with whatever money they have left they buy cotton materials, sewing needles and thread, and extra cooking utensils.

At this time of year livestock is killed and the meat is dried for use during the summer. In summer the animals are not so healthy, and it is considered bad to kill animals for food then. Autumn and spring are the best times, though in the spring it will only be old animals or those that are beyond giving birth. Some meat is cut into strips and hung on the tent ropes to dry. Some is brought into the tents and frozen and kept there to be

73

used when wanted. The really choice fat meat is wrapped up in hide and put into special boxes made of squares of yak dung. These boxes are then covered with fresh yak dung, and left to freeze. When they thaw out in the spring there is plenty of fresh meat to eat.

Many nomads revisit the same villages and trade with the same farmers. They become very good friends. Some farmers go up into the mountains and try to steal some of the nomad sheep. Then there is fighting, and the nomads come down to raid the farms and get their sheep back. The nomads, however, prefer not to fight and are really a very gentle people, and completely honest. If someone cannot get down to his trading partner one year, he will send a friend in his place, and the farmer will honour and trust him in just the same way. Sometimes a farmer who has managed to get an extra stock of goods such as sewing needles and thread, may send his son, together with supplies of food, grain and tea, up to the winter camp of the nomads. It even happens that he may meet a girl among the nomads and make her his wife. This does not happen often, but when it does everyone is perfectly happy, and the couple are free to live where they wish, as nomads or farmers.

The nomads love to sing, particularly when travelling on horseback and when in the mountains. Sometimes they sing about horses. 'When a grey horse travels with two white horses, he must travel fast. If he travels slow, he will bring shame to the two white horses.' They also like to sing about the moon, and such songs are often love songs. 'When the full moon rises on the fifteenth day, high over the eastern mountains, if my lover is not beside me, the moon shows me her face.' Then in the evenings sometimes they dance. The girls may sing and dance by themselves, watched by everyone, or else men and girls may dance together in a circle, holding hands. They may, on the other hand, just spend their winter evenings sitting and talking.

Two favourite games of the young men are wrestling and riding. They wrestle with each other often, trying to throw their opponent on to the ground. They have horse races. Some nomads have a special game played from horseback, while riding at speed.

A target is set up, and as the horseman rides by he hurls a spear at the target. Around the shaft of the spear is a rope, and as this uncoils the horseman is able to jerk the spear back into his hand.

There is no drinking, though the men like to smoke a little. They say that to smoke too much makes you cough and makes your chest bad when you leave the mountains. But old people who do less moving about smoke a great deal. They like a special pipe made of the bone of a sheep's leg, with a hole bored in it to hold the tobacco. They have never picked up the habit of drinking and prefer to avoid it. Often when they go to towns where the farmers and others like to drink lots of *chang*, a beer made of barley, the nomads will set up a tent outside, rather than stay in town. They make good friends, but on the whole they prefer to stay by themselves.

There is little law and little need for it. The people lead such an open life that any disputes become immediately known to everyone and are quickly settled within the camp. Even arguments are rare, and crimes such as theft simply do not exist among the nomads. The headman, who is called *Gowa* in some areas and *Garpön* in others, is always respected, chosen for his wisdom and his religious nature. He has no real authority, but people often go to him for advice. When the time comes to collect taxes, he sees that everyone contributes his fair share. He has to know exactly how many people are in his group and how many cattle they have, but above all he has to be absolutely honest. This is the quality the nomads value above everything else. It is the very centre of their life.

It is their honesty, perhaps, that makes them so religious. Being Buddhists, they know that it is wrong to take any form of life, yet being nomads it is the only way they can survive. They accept their lot, believing that previous bad deeds must have caused them to be born as a people destined to live by killing animals. So for all their lives they are trying their best to outweigh this great sin by good deeds. They are not morose or bitter about their lot, and they do not perform their sacrifices and chant their prayers as some kind of painful penance for past sins. The past is past, and rather than being sad they are full of joy at the fact that they have

75

at least been born in knowledge of the Way, the way to release. When they make their sacrifices or say their prayers, it is in happiness and out of faith. Nomads make the most ardent pilgrims. The longest pilgrimages they make on foot, or even by measuring their length on the ground. They give a great deal of such wealth as they may accumulate to monasteries, and they are friendly and hospitable to all travellers. When they get older, most of them like to give up their lives as nomads, take holy vows and enter a monastery. There they pray continuously for forgiveness for all the lives they have taken, and so they end their own lives in peace, striving towards the goal.

Those who can afford it always pay a monastery for a monk to come and live in their camp. The monk will not only read the scriptures and say prayers for the family, he will also teach the children. All other children near by come then and are made welcome. It is good to have such monks, especially when there is a marriage or a death. If there is no monk when a death occurs then someone who has been taught by one will say the prayers that send the spirit of the dead man on his way. The body is kept for twenty-four hours, placed in a sitting position, and all the time people sit around and chant and say prayers. The main prayer is to make sure that the soul does not stay behind but departs from the old body and goes to seek its teacher. Prayers are also offered to all the gods, then the corpse is simply taken up into the mountains and left there for the birds and animals.

When the boys and girls are around eighteen or nineteen they start looking towards marriage. The parents of a boy will look around for a suitable girl, and the father will tell his friends and relatives. The boy too will be searching. When a likely girl is found, if the parents of the two young people know each other they will meet without formality. If they do not know each other, then the boy's parents have to send a friend with the traditional scarf given in all formal greetings, and a gift of butter, cheese and meat. The friend will say why he has come, and if the girl's parents are agreeable then the young couple start visiting each other and exchanging gifts. Gifts are also exchanged between the parents. Friends join in to help make the wedding a splendid one, by giving cloth or food. First of all the boy's parents visit the girl's parents with gifts, then the girl's parents make a return visit with gifts that must be slightly less valuable. These exchanges must go back and forth seven times, and often it takes two years.

Once that is done, the parents from both families consult an astrologer to fix an auspicious day for the wedding. They will almost certainly have consulted him in the first place to make sure that the young couple are suited to each other, but it is most important that the wedding be on the right day. This is so with all Tibetans. They believe that there are good and bad times to do anything, and whenever possible they consult a soothsayer or astrologer.

On the wedding day – or before if the girl's camp is a long way off – the groom's family sends out seven or eight people on horseback, with a special horse for the bride. The saddles are newly decorated, or even newly made for the occasion. When the party arrives, the bride's family and friends come out and shout at them, insulting them, asking who invited them, and pretending to get ready to fight. The girl is hiding in her tent. The men from the groom's camp reply in the same way. 'Who are all these ugly people? Where is the stool to help me dismount from my horse? What an unclean lot of people, and what poor clothes they are wearing. Where are the people who are meant to be here to receive us?'

Actually nomads never use stools for mounting horses, this is only done by nobles and perhaps a few farmers. A nomad would consider you as good as dead if you could not mount a horse without a stool. Often they don't even bother with saddles, but simply leap onto the horse bareback.

After this is over the groom's party enters the tent. Then they start again, complaining about the poor quality of the food. This may go on for two nights, if the distance between the camps is far. All the time people are joking and insulting each other. But in the end the groom's party leaves with the bride on her new horse. Her parents do not go with her, just her brothers and sisters and friends. If the camps are near each other, instead of sending a horse the groom's family may send a splendid white yak, all saddled and decorated in rich finery. But when the bride finally arrives, and is met by her mother-in-law with a gift of a bucket of milk, even though she may have been longing for this day to be with her lover as husband and wife, she has to start crying and pretending that she wants to go back to her own home. Some girls make such a fuss that it seems as if they really mean it. She refuses to take the bucket of milk, but finally one of her sisters takes it, and the bride dips her finger in the milk and flicks a drop into the sky.

At that everyone goes inside, where a great feast has been prepared, and that is the end of the wedding. Usually a separate tent is set up for the privacy of the young couple, and for a while they will live in this separate tent.

If the girl's parents have no sons, then it might well happen that the boy goes to live with his wife, and takes membership in her family, so that her family line will not die out. This may also happen if the boy's parents cannot afford the expense of a large wedding. More often the girl will be taken into the boy's family, but there is no fixed rule. The important thing is that the new-comer, be it the boy or the girl, is not treated as an outsider, as a relative only in law. He, or she, is taken as a full member of the family, and welcomed as such. Before long the couple will be sleeping outside like everyone else. The nomads have no time for false modesty, and they see no cause for shame in things that they know to be right and necessary. That, too, is part of their honesty; being honest with themselves, they are able to see things as they are, and give them their true value. As devoted and religious as the farming peoples are in Tibet, the nomads are even more devoted and religious.

Illustration Section

DRAWINGS BY LOBSAN TENDZIN

Dress in Tibet, as elsewhere, varies for men and women not only according to rank and status but also according to region and season. Sometimes the differences are subtle, sometimes extreme. The most elaborate dress may be worn on everyday occasions, and the simplest on occasions that are most solemn and special. Even monks, who always wear the simplest robes, indulge in varied and elaborate headgear. They have special hats that they wear on special occasions or at particular times of the year. And we also know the kinds of hats worn by the great religious teachers in past periods from paintings of them that were preserved and hung in our monasteries.

A lady of Lhasa City wearing a typically elaborate head-dress, jewellery of precious stones, a gold or silver charm box around her neck, and a wide band of pearls over her left shoulder. Over her long skirt is a multi-coloured apron, the upper corners of which are embroidered with gold thread.

A lady from the countryside near Lhasa, dressed in a style quite like that of the city, with a similar reliquary or charm box, but with much less jewellery.

A lady of Tsang with the distinctive head-dress of that area. She is wearing a richly embroidered dress, and her jewellery marks her as a person of rank.

Ladies of the nomadic people of eastern Tibet wear less elaborate head-dresses than the ladies of the cities, but their clothing, often made of silks imported from neighbouring China, may be equally rich. Their jewellery is mainly of amber, turquoise and coral.

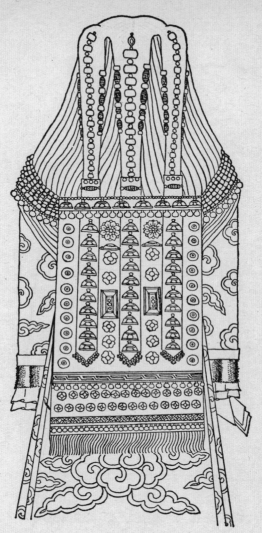

Back view

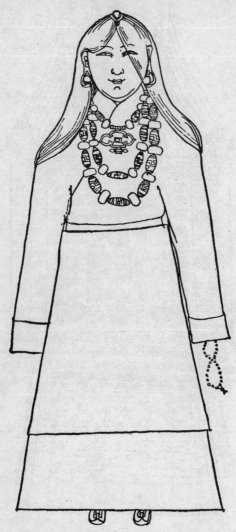

Another costume worn by the eastern nomads

Back view

Naring: *Tsong Khapa's hat*

Changchub Semsha:
*the kind of hat worn
by any Changchub
Sempa*

Gomsha: *the hat of one
who is an adept in meditation*

Ritö Bensha:
*the hat of a
recluse*

Kunga Gyaltsen's hat

Phagmo Durpa:
*hat of the leader of
the Karjurpa sect*

Lopon Rinpoche's hat

*Another of
Lopon Rinpoche's
hats*

*Hat worn by all
leaders of the
Sakya sect*

Hat worn by Srontsan Gampo and Ralpalchen

Trison Detsan's hat

King Ripong Chögyal's hat

Gushri Khan's hat

*The hat of Chamchenchögyi,
founder of the Sera Monastery*

Tonmi Sambhota's hat

89

Drochama: *the kind of hat that can be worn by any monk*

Tagdroma: *the hat worn only by monks of the Gelukpa sect*

Tsogsha: *a hat worn by ordinary monks for Assembly or other special gatherings*

Tasha: *the winter hat of a monastic or government official*

Setheb: *the summer hat of a monastic or government official*

Shanag: *the hat worn by dancers of the Black Hat sect*

Atisha's hat

Life among the nomads is by no means as hard as may be supposed, and what it lacks in material comfort it makes up in conviviality. The term 'tent' gives the impression that comforts are far more scarce than in fact they are. When the nomads move they carry not only their tents but yak-hide bags and wooden chests filled with foods of different kinds and with all the normal household items that would be found in any permanent dwelling. Above all, they carry the great churns in which the daily tea is prepared, mixed with butter to fortify the people against the cold. And, of course among the most treasured possessions of any nomad family is the altar, which is to be found set up in every tent and which is attended with great devotion and care.

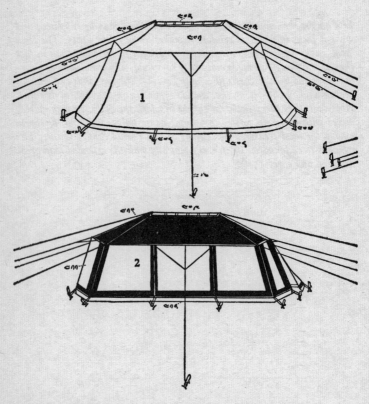

1. *A simple family tent of yak hair*
2. *A more elaborate living tent decorated with strips of black cloth*
3. *Scarecrows for protecting livestock from wolves*
4. *Watchdog (khyi), an essential part of every household*
5. *Animal compound for special animals, such as milk cows*

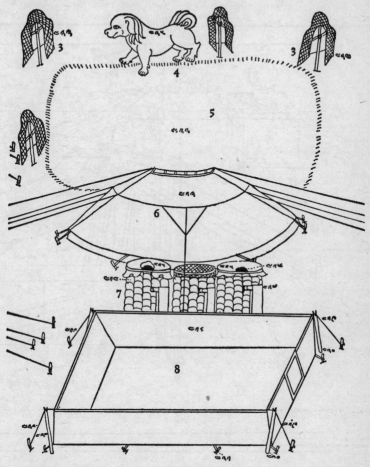

6. Tent (ba) *made of yak hair, used for storing goods. Note the vent on top*
7. *Stored yak-dung cakes, used as fuel, sometimes arranged to form a wall for protection against the wind and also to assist the drying of the cakes*
8. *Compound for ewes and their lambs*

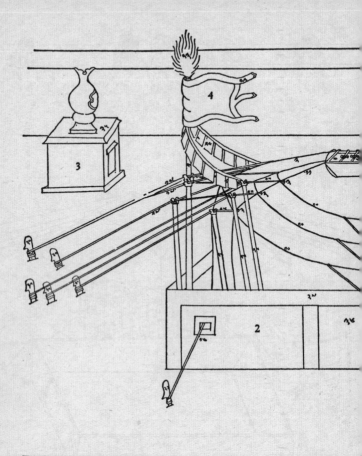

1. *Showing how a tent is erected. Note open vent at the top with a flap that can be closed against rain. The tent poles are of wood, the ropes of yak hair*
2. *Walls made of yak dung*
3. *A small altar for burnt offerings (sang) of juniper, dried fruits and tsampa*

94

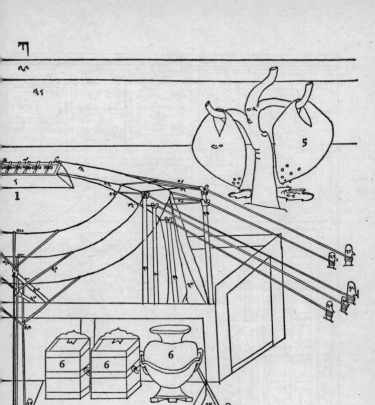

4. *Prayer flat* (tarjog)
5. *Cheese being strained in bags*
6. *Water buckets* (som): *two of wood, one of clay*

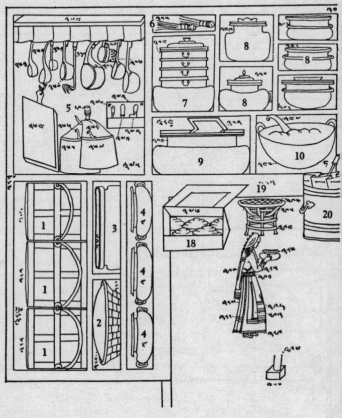

INTERIOR OF A TENT SHOWING TWO SIDES

1. Milk buckets
2. Basket of cheese
3. Container for cooked meat
4. Cooking pots (dig)
5. Kitchen utensils, including cutting board, dishmop, knife, pots, spoons, etc.

6. Pot scourer (jog thur)
7. Multiple steamer and pot
8. Pots
9. Food container
10. Pot for yogurt
11. Box for butter (margam)
12. Tea churns (ndonmo)

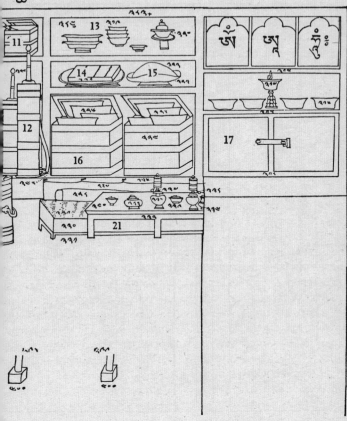

13. *Dishes* (kader)
14. *A kind of cheesecake* (thud)
15. *Dried cream* (pumar)
16. *Storage boxes* (nyindrog)
17. *Family altar* (chösham), *with bowl for holy water, butter lamps and treasure chest*

18. *Container for yak-dung cakes*
19. *Brazier for roasting barley*
20. *Tsampa bag* (tsamkhug)
21. *A sitting cushion behind a table set with two drinking bowls, two tsampa bowls, and two prayer wheels in stands*

97

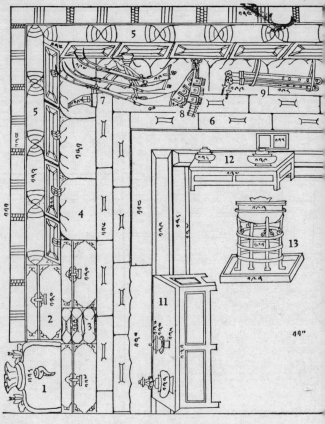

INTERIOR OF A TENT SHOWING TWO SIDES

1. *Bag for storing the family wealth. This wealth is added to yearly. The contents of the bag should never be used or given away*
2. *Storage chests (tobo)*
3. *Grain bags*
4. *Yak-hide bags for barley*

5. *Yak-hide bags*
6. *Storage boxes*
7. *Guns (menda)*
8. *Cartridge belt (ndeshub)*
9. *Swords (tri)*
10. *Butter churns (marsom)*
11. *Table (jogtse) set with tsampa bowl and teacup*

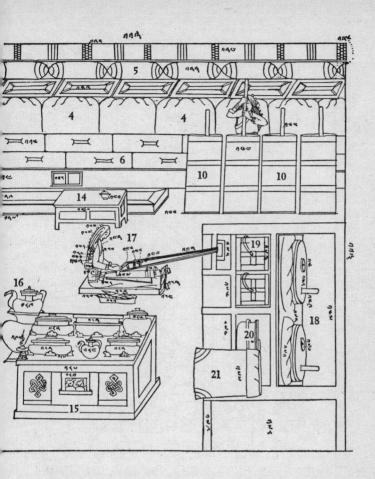

12. Table set with two tsampa bowls
13. Brazier holding pot for making cheese
14. Table set with single teacup
15. Stove with teapot and five cooking vessels

16. Teapot on brazier
17. Woman weaving at loom (thag)
18. Mills for grinding tsampa
19. Tsampa boxes
20. Pot for boiling milk
21. Bag for roasted barley to be used as tsampa

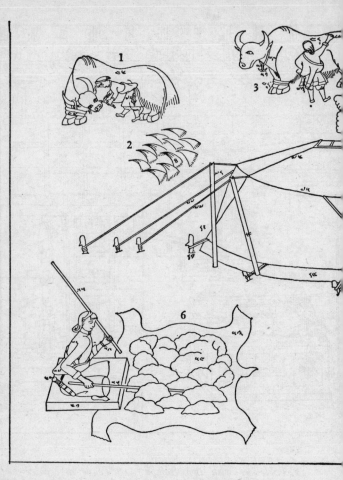

1. *Cutting the long hair of the yak, taking care to leave one to two inches.*
Yaks are not shorn
2. *Bundles of long hair that require no beating and can be made into ropes*
3. *Combing out the short hairs. Short and long hair each have separate*
uses
4. *Bundles of short hair*

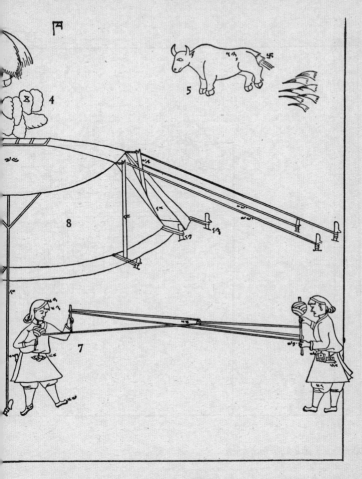

5. *The yak after the hair has been trimmed. Some tail hair is left to protect his rear from the cold winds. The long hairs are set aside for making ropes*
6. *Beating the short hair prior to spinning and weaving*
7. *Making ropes from the long hair*
8. *Tent with woven yak-hair sides and yak-hair ropes*

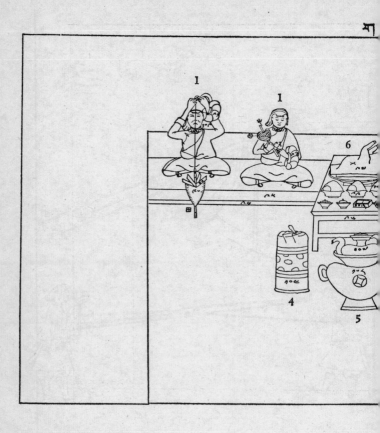

1. *Spinning yak hair into yarn*
2. *Separating hairs*
3. *Making balls of wool for the spinners*
4. *Tsampa and cheese bags*
5. *Teapot on a stove*
6. *Table with a half sheep (the forelegs) on a plate, cheesecake decorated with pats of butter, four bowls of tsampa, one loose cheese, four teacups and a box of meat seasoning.*

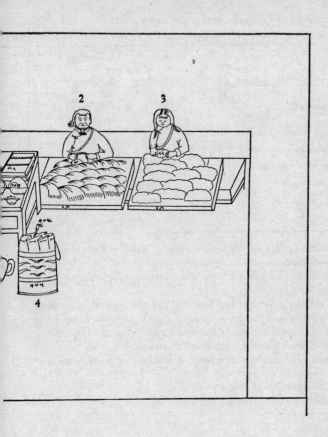

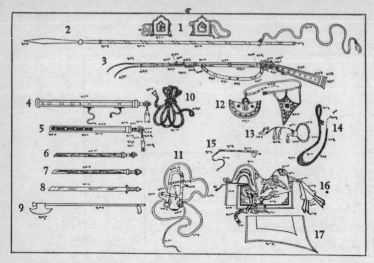

1. Charm boxes (gahu) *for holy relics, made of wood and metal and set with precious stones*

2. Fighting spear (dung) *with wrist thong and rope for retrieval when thrown from horseback*

3. Gun (menda) *for hunting and fighting. The gun support of antelope horn can be swung into position underneath, or left along the barrel when firing from the shoulder. The stock is inlaid with silver and turquoise*

4. Sword (tri) *with a wooden sheath inlaid with copper*

5. The sword of a wealthy man, with a scabbard of wood, cloth and silver

6, 7, 8. Different types of blades

   6. Dmar Gyi Gya Mtsho Phug Pa

   7. Hgu Zi

   8. Ce Rong

9. A battleaxe (tari), *also used for cutting wood*

10. Lasso (sjagba)

11. A horse bridle (thurda) *of yak hide decorated with copper and silver*

12. A container for flint and tinder (mechag) *on left; on the right, a needle box*

13. Container for gunpowder (dze re)

14. Bola (hurdo) *for hunting game*

15. Whip (tachag)

16. Saddle (ga) *for horse or yak*

17. Saddle blanket (gadan)

CHAPTER FOUR

The Waters of Pleasure

Foolish art thou who, in the midst of Life,
Ignores the coming of Death;
For all thou doest and countest as great,
Is nothing worth in that final moment.
Life's opportunity hast thou lost,
Take that which death offers thee, now it is
     nigh,
And leave not having lived in vain.
Set thy mind on the Holy Law,
Go hence with the mind so fixed.

– from BARDO THÖDOL

Lhasa is by no means the only city or town in Tibet, yet in Tibet, as in the world outside, to hear people talk you would think that Lhasa *was* Tibet. It is the one place that every Tibetan yearns to see at least once before he dies. Many walk over a thousand miles across snow-covered mountains and wind-swept plateaux to fulfil their desire, and many die in the attempt. They die happily, for they believe that the effort to achieve a goal is almost as important as the goal itself, or its achievement – in some ways more so.

I was no exception, and in fact Lhasa was the first city I ever saw, apart from the monastic city of Kumbum where I was educated. I was going to Lhasa for higher education, and the journey from Kumbum took over three months, every day bringing new experiences to me. Long before reaching the holy city, still two or more weeks away, I was met by a delegation from my younger brother, the Gyalwa Rinpoche, and with this delegation came my father. We had been separated for many years, so the reunion was a memorable occasion, remaining as clear in my mind as though it had just happened. But nothing on that trip from Kumbum, not the massive mountains nor the vast desolate stretches of plateau, nor the sight of the thousands of animals in our caravan struggling through the icy torrents that cut across our path, not even the sight of my father riding forward to meet me, upright on his horse, none of these things have for me the same quality as my memory of my first glimpse of Lhasa.

The houses and other buildings of Lhasa itself were still hidden from view by the distance, but rising boldly from the lush green valley was the stark red and white fortress, the Potala, its roofs of the purest gold seeming to set it afire. Perched on top of a great rocky mound, the two wings of the Potala are painted white, clear and clean. The buildings that make up these two wings are secular, for the housing and offices of lay members of the Potala staff and for various other non-religious functions. The central portion of the fortress, however, is the headquarters of the religious life of the Potala and accordingly is painted a rich dark red. Here are the living quarters of the Gyalwa Rinpoche, the temples and shrines, and the tombs of the Rinpoche of long ago. It is these tombs, rising from deep within the heart of the Potala, that burst into the blaze of gold on its summit.

It is a sight so beautiful that it struck me with very real shock. Here it was, still many miles away, the building I had heard of since I was a child – the centre of Tibet, the abode on earth of the earthly incarnation of Chenresig, Lord of Mercy, protector of our country. I had heard it described so many times, and in such extravagant terms, that I came over that hilltop half feeling that there was nothing new in store for me, that it could scarcely be as inspiring as the endless accounts of it. Yet there it was, and all I could do was to rein in my horse and look.

Some hours later, when passing through Lhasa on the way to my parent's home, in the Summer Palace, we passed right under the Potala. Again all I could do was to stop and gaze up at the clifflike walls, pierced by one row of windows after another, reached from the outside by twisting stone staircases rising steeply up the rock face.

This is one of the loveliest parts of the city, for just behind the Potala, at the foot of the hill, a tiny stream feeds into a perfect little lake, barely three hundred yards long, in the middle of which is the Lö Khang, or House of the Serpent. Plants and flowering shrubs seem to grow more richly here than anywhere else, and on a still day the Serpent Lake reflects the image of the Potala, towering above it. This is a place the people of Lhasa love to visit during the summer, both to worship in the little island temple and simply to enjoy themselves.

Next to Marpori, which is the name of the hill on which the Potala is built, is Chogpori, on which is housed the College of Medicine. The hill is just about as high as Marpori, and the path that skirts its base is cut in rock that has been covered with beautifully worked carvings of various deities, kept freshly painted at all times by the devout. From here there is a view of the Kyichu, a river named 'Waters of Pleasure' which runs the length of the Lhasa Valley, even passing through the southern outskirts of the city. These waters do indeed bring pleasure, for all along the banks of the Kyichu during the festive summer months, gaily coloured tents are set up and the people of Lhasa spend their time at endless picnics.

Lhasa itself is barely two miles long and not much more than half a mile wide from north to south. It is full of historic monuments, some of which, like the ancient temple of Ramoche which was built by a Chinese princess taken as wife by one of the early Tibetan kings, date back over a thousand years. Stone monuments, carved with Tibetan and Chinese characters, tell of the constant attempts made by Chinese to assert themselves in Lhasa. In the heart of the city is the old temple, the Tsulag Khang, dating back to the same king, Srontsan Gampo. Beneath this temple there was once supposed to have been a great underground lake, in which visions of the future could be seen.

Srontsan Gampo was the king who more than any other strove to bring Buddhism into Tibet. He also strove hard to establish friendly relations with Tibet's neighbours, Nepal and China. He allied himself through marriage with each country, and each of his queens helped in the introduction of Buddhism. The Tsulag Khang was founded by the Nepalese Princess as a token of friendship between the two countries. Just by the Temple stands a stone bearing details of a pact of friendship between the Tang dynasty and Tibet.

Everywhere in Lhasa there are holy shrines, and all around the outskirts are monasteries, large and small. But Lhasa is not only a religious centre, it is also a thriving economic centre, and has a large trading area with colourful bazaars right around the Temple. The buildings are all jumbled together with the houses of nobles and government officials, but among the variety of buildings and different kinds of shops and stalls, there is a conspicuous lack of hotels and restaurants. A few stalls may sell cooked food, but there are no places where you can go with friends or family, sit down and order a meal. This is so throughout Tibet, but it is most remarkable in the towns. In the country where travellers are relatively few, and where distances are great, we naturally expect to offer hospitality to anyone who asks for it. But in the cities and towns, in spite of the constant flow of traders and pilgrims, it is the same. Many people have friends, others make camp outside the city, but others simply knock on a door and ask for shelter or food. It is a custom that is seldom abused, and most Tibetans consider it an honour, as well as a pleasure, to welcome a guest.

The bazaar section is full of interest, and traders as well as pilgrims can be seen inquisitively looking over all the goods on display. The traders may have brought mules or horses bred for sale, or they may have brought in goods for use in the bazaars. Everybody is interested in what everybody else is selling, even if they don't have a thought of buying. Perhaps it is a Tibetan characteristic, for all over the country people seem to love markets and are always ready to trade just for the sake of trading. Traders themselves are really considered quite high in the social hierarchy of Lhasa. Elsewhere in Tibet we do not divide people into classes, but Lhasa is an exception, having a permanent population as well as such a large shifting population. Also in Lhasa the professional people and the craftsmen remain where they are, and everyone goes to them. Elsewhere such people travel around, seeking business as they go.

The highest ranking people are the high monastery officials such as the abbots, then the monks and government officials who form a kind of lay nobility. Then come the mule suppliers and traders, the merchant class, and then a number of specialist workers such as printers, weavers, cooks, carpenters, potters, stone and wood carvers, gold- and silver-smiths, and tailors. There are three occupations that are particularly looked down on in Lhasa: the blacksmiths and people who work iron, the butchers, and the disposers of the dead. In Lhasa there is a special problem in dealing with the bodies of the dead, the city being so crowded. Elsewhere when someone dies we usually call a monk because the most important thing is to say prayers for the dead person's

soul. Disposal of the body is no problem. But in Lhasa, for fear
of illness, the main problem is to dispose of the bodies as quickly
and completely as possible, so there is a special class of people
who do this work.

There are five ways of dealing with the dead, and usually an
astrologer is consulted to make sure that the right way is used.
Most people prefer to be cremated, though it takes a great deal of
wood to burn a body to ashes, and in many parts of Tibet wood
is either extremely scarce, or there may be no wood at all. As
burning is extremely expensive most people have their bodies
given to the birds. Burial is rare, though sometimes the birds will
not eat a body, then it has to be burned or buried. Burial is often
difficult because the ground may be stony or frozen. Another
way is to put the body in a river, but this is only for small children
or for poor people who have nobody to look after them. Sometimes the bodies of high lamas are preserved, and in very special
cases a priest-astrologer may decide that even a layman's body
should be treated this way.

A funeral is not a particularly sad occasion though relatives
may well be crying. The death is over and done with, and all that
remains is the practical matter of the disposal of the body. The
sad time is before the funeral, when the body is lying in the house
and all the relatives come to pay their respects and to say a prayer
for the dead. On the day of the feeding of the birds the body is
wrapped in a new cloth, blessed by the monk, and tied up in a
sitting position. In the country this is usually done by some
relative or friend who has done it before. Then it is carried up the
mountainside to the place where it is to be offered to the birds.
Outside Lhasa there is a special place, a large rocky outcrop,
where this is done by the specialists. In the country it would be
done by anyone who knows how, preferably by a priest who can
also say all the right prayers for the dead. The whole family come
to see the work done. If it is a man who has died, the wife's
family come if they knew him well. The flesh has to be cut in a
certain way, and as soon as it starts the birds gather, sometimes
hundreds of them. The bones have to be taken and broken,
pounded to a powder, and mixed with a little barley flour or

tsampa. This too is eaten by the birds. If they take everything, it is a good sign. If not, the remains have to be burned or buried. But everyone must stay until it is all done, the main reason again being a practical one – certain tantric sects call for the use of certain parts of the body, such as the skull or the thigh bone, for secret rituals. No family would want the bones of a relative used in this way, unless he himself so wished it, or the astrologer recommended it.

After it is over, the monks may be invited back to the house, but in any case there have to be religious services, either at the house or at the monastery, for forty-nine days following the death. A wealthy family might donate a large sum of money to a monastery, the interest from which would pay for a service for the dead to be said once a year. As well as making this donation to the monastery, however, a family will always make a contribution to the poor.

Given the doctrine of rebirth, the moment of death assumes particular importance, not as the end of a life but as the beginning of a life. It is said again and again how hard it is to win rebirth as a human. As humans we have the greatest chance for doing good and the greatest chance for doing harm, because we are endowed with will, and good or harm lie in the thought or will, rather than in the act. In Tibet there is an art to dying, and special scriptures are devoted to it. There are seven stages to *Bardo*, the intervening period between death and rebirth, and each stage is further subdivided into seven, a figure that we hold sacred, in common with all great religions. The forty-nine days of prayer, then, represent these seven-times-seven states of Bardo.

The rites should begin before the last breath leaves the body. At this moment the dying person should have last instructions whispered to him, reminding him of all he has been taught concerning death. This should be done by his teacher if possible, or a monk, but anyone who can help him direct his mind towards Truth must do so if no monk is on hand. In this way the soul leaves the body at least facing in the right direction.

The doctrine of Lei (Karma) is not a fatalistic one as taught

in Tibet. To be sure we believe that we must answer for all our
deeds, good and bad, but we are always aware of this inescapable
necessity, and we are endowed with a will that enables us consciously to offset bad deeds by good. Tibetan Buddhists believe
that faith in the Buddha, his teachings, and the monkhood is in
itself a good deed of such merit that it alone can reduce our bad
deeds to naught, if accompanied by a life of spiritual devotion
and training. Even without such a life, in an ordinary farmer or
herder, faith can wipe out bad deeds accumulated over many
lifetimes. So the first step in Bardo is of vital importance, since
consciousness is still alive.

Even after 'death', as most people think of the cessation of
breathing, the soul still exists and has awareness, and to this
awareness the rest of the forty-nine rites are directed in a supreme
effort to keep alive the faith of the deceased. Death is, in a way,
a great opportunity; it is also a time of great danger, for the soul
can slip from awareness of its true nature and from the path it
should be following.

It can even be said that to the Tibetan the right death is one
of the purposes of living. The wrong death is certainly one of the
greatest misfortunes to be guarded against. The very nature of
this belief is one reason for the existence of so large a priesthood,
and for the unswerving respect paid by all Tibetans to that monkhood. The monkhood is there at all times to help the individual
accumulate good deeds, avoid bad deeds, and to acquire the
wisdom, strength and faith required to meet his death as he
should and so safely pass through the forty-nine stages of Bardo
towards liberation. It is not an obsession; there is nothing fanatic
about the Tibetan religion; its enormous vitality and power come
from the depth of the faith of the people.

The monasteries and the monkhood are often thought of, by
those who do not know Tibet, as despotic and oppressive. Lhasa
is cited as an example of the authority wielded by the monkhood
in Tibet. Yet living in Lhasa, one is aware of the monks who live
there as one is aware of other classes of people, including the
butchers and blacksmiths and disposers of the dead. They are a
people, like others, engaged in a profession that is vital to the

welfare of the people. The people regard the monkhood as essential, and in fact it is essential, for the whole government and economy of the country depend upon it. Our lives are not so rigidly divided as elsewhere into religious and secular. Every monk and every monastery has both religious and secular duties, insofar as they can be divided, but where life itself is a religious act the difference becomes a fine one. The Gyalwa Rinpoche himself is both political and spiritual leader of the country. Every abbot is both the political and spiritual ruler of his monastery. Every monastery engages in trade and commerce as well as in performing rites for the living and the dead and praying for the welfare of the people. Above all, every monastery is a centre of education to which anyone, no matter how poor, can go for instruction. He can go for a year or for a lifetime, and nothing is asked of him except that he devote himself to his studies and progress. More than that, monks go out into the world around them, into towns and villages, and into private homes or into the camps of the nomads, to teach and to perform any services that might be asked of them.

The contact a monastery has with the people, then, is not merely as the source of authority, of government, law and order, for even in these matters it shares the responsibility with laymen elected for the purpose. There is only one time of year, and that in Lhasa alone, when a monk is expected to actively maintain law and order. During the Lhasa *Mönlam*, the Great Prayer, the entire city is placed under the control of the proctors and chosen monks of the near-by Drepung monastery. The Great Prayer lasts for about three weeks and is the main event of the New Year festival. During this time thousands of pilgrims from all over the country pour into the city, and traders likewise find it a good time to converge. During the Great Prayer the monks, numbering several thousand, also crowd into Lhasa from the near-by monasteries. The chosen body of monks from Drepung act as police to control the crowds, there being no standing police force in Tibet, even in Lhasa. They patrol the streets armed with heavy staves, which they do not hesitate to use when necessary.

This handing over of power to Drepung also acts as a check on the local administration, for during those few weeks the Drepung authorities have absolute power, including the reversal of any legislation with which it disagrees. In point of fact the local government is so well constituted that the check is a nominal one, and seldom used.

To clear the way when the Gyalwa Rinpoche leaves the Potala in procession a special guard of soldiers is used, in costumes dating back hundreds of years to the time of the Mogul invasions. It is sometimes said that nobody can ever be on a level higher than the Gyalwa Rinpoche. This is not so, though in audience he will always be seated higher than anyone else. When he makes his way through the streets of Lhasa people crowd into the windows of the houses, even climbing on to the flat roofs of the houses all along the way.

The Lhasa Mönlam, like the rest of the New Year festival, is a time for rejoicing everywhere. The prayer itself is for all peoples on this world, that peace and prosperity, or more literally abundant harvests, may be theirs. It is preceded by a series of pageants, some held in the Potala itself, which the public flock to see. They are performed in ancient costume, and every dance or play has a long tradition behind it. They are to be enjoyed just for the spectacle, but there is also a meaning that is recognized by all. There is a fire dance, to commemorate the passing of the old year, the fire being used to symbolize the driving out of evil. There is a two-day pageant in which the nobles play the part of a cavalry regiment, representing the protectors of Tibet. They dress in twelfth-century chain mail armour, and carry as weapons spears and bows and arrows. They camp outside the city, and ride about among the crowds on the first day. Then the next day they are ceremonially reviewed and ride off to much noise, out of sight, to defend their country and people. Other spectacles are directed specifically to the defence of Tibet against the enemies of Buddhism, and towards the very end of the festival, the famous State Oracle arrives from Nechung to wage such a holy war.

During the following month there is another festival, known as the Lesser Prayer, or Prayer of the Assembly. It is more concerned with the welfare of Tibet than that of the world at large, but again largely consists of pageants depicting the expulsion of the forces of evil. There are also prayers and services which the public attends no less eagerly than it does the pageants. Again Lhasa is invaded by thousands of pilgrims who were unable to attend the New Year festival. At the end of the month a long procession starts from the Temple and makes its way slowly towards the Potala. This is to symbolize the devotion of all people, lay and clergy, to the Gyalwa Rinpoche. As the procession assembles at the Potala a huge silken banner, delicately painted, is slowly unrolled until it is draped over the front face of the Potala, below the lower stories. The pictures, some fifty feet high, represent the truth of the thousand Buddhas. According to this belief a thousand Buddhas promised to come to save the world from disaster. Sakya Muni, the Gautama Buddha, was the fifth. At this moment another Buddha, Chamba, is ready, waiting to come when the time is right. The banner hangs as a symbol of perpetual security, as a reminder of the protection extended to mankind by Chenresig, incarnate in the Gyalwa Rinpoche.

The people of Lhasa no less than the pilgrims and merchants enjoy this festive season. There is no conscious effort to make the festivals religious in nature, nor to conceal their real import. By no means everyone knows the exact significance of every drama enacted, but the overall significance is known, and the festivals act as a reaffirmation of the cardinal beliefs of Buddhism. It is at this season too when the great monasteries near by hold public examinations for their highest degrees and make the awards.

The summer is sometimes regarded as a season given over to merrymaking. It is at this time that Lhasa residents flock to the banks of the Kyichu, boating and feasting. The parks are filled with holiday-makers, and the Gyalwa Rinpoche himself officially moves residence from the Potala to the North Lingka, or Summer Palace, which is in a wooded park of its own on the west side of the city. Again there are plays and dances, performed by both priests and laymen. They represent the history of Tibet from its earliest beginnings, a history in which fact intertwines with fancy, creating a whole that has a reality of its own. Fortune tellers and magicians, blatant tricksters, mingle freely with laymen and monks, plying their trade. As it does with all other festivals, the Tibetan Muslim population of Lhasa takes part as fully as any other.

It is a time of such boundless gaiety, with everyone dressing in his best clothes, putting on his finest jewellery, and setting up his best summer tent in a bold effort to outdo everyone else, it would be easy to miss the fact that no less than any other time of year this is also a time for special prayers and services and religious observances, which are attended and supported just as faithfully as are the picnics and boating parties. In particular this is a time to be charitable to the poor, so that they too can enjoy the season, though outside Lhasa, and perhaps one or two other towns, there is little real distinction between rich and poor, and life is far less full of spectacle.

It would be a mistake, however, to say that the people of Lhasa, or any other part of Tibet, are being exceptionally virtuous in attending religious services during the picnic season, or in giving alms to the poor while enjoying summer life along the Waters of Pleasure. It would also be a mistake to think that any Tibetan would see any incongruity or harm in going from a service in Lhasa Temple to the nearest house where there was a chang-drinking party being given. Nor would it be unusual to see a pleasure-seeker in a boatful of revellers, quietly counting the beads on his rosary. The essential point again is that religious activity is as much a part of our life as any other activity, and religious belief and thought is as much a part of our thinking as is our concern for where our next meal is coming from.

While not denying its spiritual aspects, Tibetan Buddhism is essentially a way of life, a way that we believe ensures, by following the middle path, a life of contentment. Pleasures and entertainments may be somewhat less plentiful and exuberant, but misfortunes are less frequent and less painful. It is engrained in our very makeup that our concern should be as much for the next life as for this, and that this life is merely a stepping-stone. One false step, a single wrong turning, can turn us into unknown paths of darkness for countless future lives. Ultimately it is our belief that everyone, that all living things, shall achieve liberation. It is up to us to hasten the process, for others as well as for ourselves. All the problems and difficulties we are likely to come across have their answer in the scriptures, and it is to them that we must turn when in need. The study of these scriptures takes from twenty to twenty-five years. All those, then, who have other work rely on the monkhood for help. It is through the Monkhood that the laymen can recognize the middle way; the monkhood guides them during life and after death. One of the most telling proofs of the system, if it can be called that, is that with the exception of the New Year festivals in Lhasa, there is no police force in Tibet – yet Tibetans are just as human as other people, subject to just the same temptations and passions. There is no police force because there is no need for it; there is no need for it because there is little crime, and virtually none that cannot be quickly and easily settled by arbitration. This is not due to any innate virtue but to the simple fact that the Tibetan people find it more agreeable and more convenient to be law-abiding. Their religion has shown them how to derive positive satisfaction from adherence to the law, and has given them a powerful incentive to right living, so there is no need of any threat of force to uphold it.

CHAPTER FIVE

The Kingless Age

When Demons noise their savage call,
Let me hear naught but the six holy sounds;*
When blinded by rain and snow, by wind and
    dark,
Let my eyes be touched with Wisdom, and
    unseeing, see.

– from BARDO THÖDOL,
'The Path of Good Wishes'

*Six sounds of the sacred Buddhist prayer:
    Aom mani padme hum.
The Bön version has eight syllables:
    Aom matre muye sale du.
In the court language of central Tibet 'padme'
would be pronounced 'peme' and is sometimes
printed this way in Western translations.

After the Monkey god and the mountain ogress gave birth to their children, the children divided and founded the six tribes, or classes of beings, which inhabit our land, from gods to demons. In the middle are the humans, and from these the present-day Tibetans are said to be descended. We know nothing about our early ancestors, except what we can tell from the time when Buddhism first reached Tibet, in the seventh Christian century. From then onward we have written records. The histories of that time, and the comments of a few earlier Chinese historians, tell us little more than that the Tibetans were a wild and fierce lot, living in tribes without any kind of kings or government. They were hunters, living up in the mountainous heights, clad only in skins.

All the earliest historic records, however, tell us that at that time there was a flourishing religion called Bön, and they describe many of its rites and beliefs. Even today, in spite of the tremendous power of Buddhism, the Bön religion is still practised in many parts of Tibet. It has changed form, in keeping with the times, but it can still tell us a certain amount about our past. So strong has been the influence of the old religion that without understanding it nobody can expect to understand the people of Tibet today, nor their practice of Buddhism.

Every traveller who has set foot in Tibet has commented on the wild countryside. But no words can ever describe it and really convey the power it has over the human mind. One has to be there, to feel the height, to breathe the air, to smell the scented valleys, and to hear the silence. It is a country that can be so still and quiet and so beautiful, that even we who have been born in it and lived there all our lives are affected strongly. We do not think of it as beautiful, until we are forced to leave it. But we somehow feel it, and feel it to be good, in those quiet moments.

Just as it can be quiet it can also be so tumultuous that it seems as though the world were coming to an end. There are earthquakes that open up the ground to swallow whole villages; there are storms that can wash away hillsides in a matter of minutes, sweeping away any beings that have no time to find shelter. The noise of wind approaching can swell and surge until there is nothing but sound all around and all through you. If the country is powerful in its quiet moments, it is something much more than powerful when it is black. It seems to threaten the very existence of everything that is not a part of its wildness.

Living in a world like this, even today, it is difficult not to become dominated by it, and in those early, early days, when man was alone in the face of such power, and still more defenceless than he is now, it is small wonder that the land itself became his ruler. Buddhism brought with it greater understanding of the world we live in, and the strength to combat it. Before Buddhism the early Tibetans had no such strength, their only way lay in submission to the forces around them. Their beliefs were simple. The forces of nature became gods; mountains and rivers, rocks and springs and trees all alike became the dwelling places for these gods. They were probably not conceived as good or bad but simply as having the power to help or to harm, to create or destroy. Religious practices grew up that were designed to secure help and to avert harm. A mountain or a tree that became recognized as the abode of one of these gods could not be passed without making an offering to secure safe passage. High mountain passes, paths crossing the faces of sheer cliffs, places where swollen rivers had to be crossed, and even insignificant mounds of rocks all became the object, not exactly of worship, but of respect. They were full of potential for good or ill.

It is not surprising then, that by the time Buddhism came and the first writers took note of these things, they found these simple beliefs had developed into a cult with elaborate practices and with specialist shamans who spent their lives in an effort to control nature. It was not yet a religion, in the proper sense, for it had no monasteries, no temples, and no brotherhood of priests; there was no central doctrine to bind people together in a common belief. But already there was a common field for action. Offerings were made that would please the gods, food in particular. Even stones and rocks were acceptable, for these would supply shelter. Today there is still hardly a pass or a river crossing without a small mound of stones, to which each traveller adds his contribution, or at which he leaves a small offering. Few Tibetans, if any, would think of washing their hands at a spring, for fear of angering the spirits there; rather will they leave a small gift of food.

In the same way that today as people we are different, no longer hunting or fighting and no longer living a wild, rough life, so are our beliefs different, although we still perform the same kind of religious acts performed by our ancestors, such as the making of offerings. Even the Bönpoba, who still follow the Bön religion, and who follow in detail the ancient rites as prescribed by the early shamans, have a different interpretation. The origin is one, however. All rites were a recognition of some power beyond human control and an attempt to come to terms with that power.

At first people made their simple offerings themselves. Some of them must have seemed to achieve better results than others, and gradually a professional class of shamans arose. At the beginning they probably worked independently of each other, but by the time Buddhism came to Tibet there was already established a vigorous cult with a common and highly elaborate ritual.

There have been a number of great teachers, or *shenrab*, among the Bönpoba, but the first of all is said to have been Shenrab Miboche. Some say he was a reincarnation of Buddha. Others say he was born at the same time as Buddha. He travelled all over Tibet, working miracles in his dealings with the gods. In particular he was famous for his powers of exorcism. The belief had already grown up that the gods were not only to be reckoned with outside the human body; they could also enter it and take possession of it. For this the only cure was exorcism according to secret rites, of which Shenrab Miboche was in possession. Disciples followed him, and slowly the cult became a religion.

Another story tells that a certain child grew up quite normally until he was thirteen years old, then he was possessed by spirits who kept him under their power for another thirteen years. At the age of twenty-six he started wandering across the country, teaching people about the gods, what manner of beings they are, where they live, how they can be appeased and how they can be angered. At this time the Bön believed in three offerings, or sacrifices. There were sacrifices to the ancestral spirits, the High Offering. There were sacrifices to the family spirits, the Middle Offering. The third, Low Offering, was to the dead. There were specific rites for each, but the most important in daily life was of course the family rite, the Middle Offering, to the God of the family hearth, Thab Lha. He had to be pleased daily by offerings of butter or tsampa and could be easily angered. In particular if the hearth became sullied in any way, if food were allowed to spill or boil over, or if dirt were allowed to enter with the fuel, this angered Thab Lha to such an extent that misfortune would settle on the household until a Bön priest was called to purify the hearth.

Bön had by this time clearly divided the world into three regions, Heaven, Earth, and the Underworld, each with its own two classes of beings: gods and demigods; humans and animals; hungry ghosts and demons, or hell-beings. Into these worlds all the early beliefs of the Bön were incorporated. The underworld is peopled with spirits who live in water, rocks, trees, and so forth. The water spirits are in the form, usually, of serpents, and they live at the bottoms of lakes, guarding secret treasures. Juniper trees are highly popular as abodes of certain spirits and the tree figures not only in Bön belief but also in its ritual practice; the berries, wood, and small branches of the juniper tree are offered in sacrifices, and the berries are used as a narcotic to help induce trance. Some spirits held the same names as the mountains or rocks or waters they were believed to inhabit; certain forms of sickness were named after other spirits who were believed to cause them. These spirits were the Bönpoba's answer to all unknowns.

Then, all around us are Lha, temporary godly spirits who again are to be propitiated. They are guardians of passes and danger-ous passages, and each such place is marked by a *Labtse*, a mound of stones to which each passer-by adds a stone or a prayer flag even today. These spirits have accumulated good deeds over the ages, and because of this are able and willing to help humans.

Some spirits appear in the form of insects, and can exert malig-nant influences when aroused. To guard against these influences the old Bön devised spirit traps. These were crossed pieces of wood around which a whole network of coloured threads was spun, forming very definite and complicated patterns. These were thought to attract the spirits and, at the same time, trap them. They are still widespread throughout Tibet.

Although the early Bönpoba had developed systematic prac-tices, they still had not really formed a single doctrine. This early stage of Bön is called *Dol Bön*. Then during the reign of one of the first kings of Tibet, the Bönpoba were challenged by the king to explain their powers. By this time the Bön had gone beyond the performance of rites designed merely to please or placate the spirit world, rites to keep the powers of nature at a safe distance. The shamans had developed beyond this and had begun to cultivate the same powers for their own use. Long aware that humans could be possessed by these powers in unguarded moments, the shamans designed rites to exorcize those spirits, spirits which caused sickness and insanity. The rites in them-selves demonstrated a power of their own, so now the shamans began to invite possession of their own bodies. Plainly this was a highly dangerous undertaking, and the ritual had to be corres-pondingly elaborate. The slightest mistake could bring disaster on the practitioner, and there are countless examples of those who have fallen victim to the power they courted, becoming insane or fatally sick. It was a logical development, however, once man began to learn how to deal with the spirit world, and properly conducted, it brought to man the powers he had formerly sought only to fight.

In answer to the king's challenge, three leading exponents arrived to demonstrate their respective powers. The story goes that the first one performed rites to the Fire God, then sitting on his sacred drum he rode into the sky where he discovered hidden things. Another performed a rite which gave him the power to cut iron with a feather. In this way he divided good from bad. The third repaired to a cemetery with evil spirits and demonstrated his mastery over them by the use of magical knives.

This formed the second of the three stages of Bön development, a stage at which Bön rites were still characterized by blood sacrifices, described in some detail by Chinese observers. Sheep, dogs and monkeys were the victims in the lesser sacrifices, but in the great sacrifice held every three years horses, donkeys and human beings were offered to the gods of the three regions. The rite involved disembowelling and the scattering of blood into the air. Details of these rites survive and they are still practised, though with symbolic sacrifice, even within the Buddhism that fought so hard to suppress them.

The original Bön concern with death lay in preventing the return of the dead, and the ritual was directed to this end. But as the notion of rebirth crept in, the burial rites took on a different significance. Unlike modern Buddhism, the Bön did not offer the bodies of the dead in sacrifice to other living beings; if anything it sought to preserve the body. Other rites began to appear (and perhaps they were as heretical then as they are now), rites that sought to prolong the life of the practitioner by extracting the life force from a living human. This almost certainly was a debasement, for however primitive the early Bönpoba may appear, their efforts were at least directed towards the safety and betterment of mankind as a whole and not just for their own benefit.

The death rite became more than a protective ritual, it became part of an elaborate ceremony to ensure proper rebirth. Buddhists today in Tibet burn effigies in ritual exorcisms such as the driving out of the gods of Evil with the passing of the old year, one of the major events of the Lhasa Mönlam, but practised throughout the country. It can only be said that it is almost identical with the Bön custom of making an effigy of the dead person using rice paper for the face. It is a rite full of symbolism and it culminates in the burning of the effigy, having first endowed it with all the bad deeds of the dead person. In this way the dead person is enabled to escape the consequences of his actions. The thought is Bön, but who borrowed the ritual from whom we do not know. When Buddhism arrived in Tibet there was a great deal of mixture of Buddhist and Bön practices. Bön was too deeply in the nature of the people for them to rid themselves of it, no matter how faithfully they took to the new religion. While Buddhism was ready to incorporate some of the old Bön practices and adopt some of their beliefs, they rejected and outlawed others. At the same time the Buddhist teachers jealously guarded certain of their own scriptures for fear of the perversion they would suffer at the hands of the Bön.

The third stage of Bön religion is marked by the emergence of a Bön sacred literature. This stage is known as *Gyur Bön*. But since writing only came to Tibet with Buddhism, it is often difficult to say which scriptures are genuinely Bön, and which are derivations of stolen Buddhist scriptures. It is possible that the bulk were taken from Buddhism, carefully disguised and adapted to suit the purposes and faith of the Bönpoba. Since Buddhism was trying so hard to suppress the Bön religion, such genuine Bön scriptures as came to be written down were written in secret and concealed. There is a tradition that many of them still remain concealed today, and from time to time they are 'discovered'. Usually the discovery is of a relatively new manuscript, alleged to have been copied from the original. This is in accordance with the Bön teachings that from time to time teachers will come back to take the teachings out of hiding and spread them once again among the people. But it also makes it easy for any unscrupulous person to try and put over whatever he wishes in the guise of being one of these teachers.

The three texts known together as the *Khar Bön*, are almost certainly translations of Buddhist texts made by the Bönpoba for their own ends. The first was a translation made by Shamtab Ngongpo. Having hidden them in an appropriate place, he then 'discovered' them and began to teach from them as though they were original Bön teachings. The second translation was made in the reign of King Trisong Detsan, a king who in his missionary

127

zeal made a law that all Tibetans must accept Buddhism. One scholar, Gyalwa Changchöb, refused, and was punished. In retaliation Gyalwa Changchöb secretly worked with the Bönpoba on further translations of Buddhist texts. These had to be hidden for the King issued an order that any person found working on such translations would be killed. These works were later known as Bön *Terma*.

The last of the three translations was in the time of a king, Lang Darma, who was himself a practising Bön, during a period of great anti-Buddhist activity. At this time Shegur Luga called together all Bönpoba to a place called Taryul Drolag, for the translations of as many texts as possible. In translation the names were changed, and so were some of the meanings. The Yum Gyeba became the Kham Chen; the Yum Nyishu Ngapa became the Kham Chung; and so with many others. These two were both hidden and later produced as genuine Bön scriptures.

Translations such as these were not so dangerous since the teaching under the Bön remained basically the same as the Buddhist original. They taught the impermanence of existence, punishment for bad deeds or thoughts, the six virtues, the six ways of salvation, the ten stages of perfection of a Changchub Sempa, and the three personal existences of a Buddha. But other teachings that came with Buddhism into Tibet, the tantric teachings of the saint, Padmasambhava, or Guru Rinpoche as we call him, were open to great abuse, and it was these teachings that the Buddhists wished to keep out of Bön hands.

Tantricism is a belief in the powers of nature that can produce life and death in all beings and things. This power is associated with the principle of male conjunction with female. But there is one school of tantricism, the *Lamèd* school, which adds the second principle of preservation and destruction. Most say this began in India as the *Kalachakra* school, but some think that it may have had its own origins in Tibet, among the Bön, for legend has it that Lamèd arose in Shambhala, a mysterious citadel somewhere in the farthest north. One of the most powerful strongholds of the Bön religion has always been Shang Shung, about a hundred miles north of Lhasa.

However that may be, the Bön certainly elaborated a system of mild and wrathful gods. These did not and still do not imply that they are good and evil gods. Tibetan Buddhists regard these gods, which they freely adopt from Hinduism as well as from Bön beliefs, merely as devices that can help the process of meditation. Whatever reality they have is in our own minds, and nowhere else. The Bön tenets developed much closer to the early animist beliefs, though, in which these gods were very real, however intangible. Even so, they were still neither good nor evil. They were powerful, and that power could, from a human point of view, either help or harm. It was common for a single deity to have two aspects. Under the one he was beneficent, under the other malignant. Which aspect showed itself depended upon the individual and his attitude to that god. Appropriate ritual could ensure the help of both aspects; in his beneficent aspect a god could help the human supplicant; in his malignant aspect the same god could continue to help that supplicant by the destruction of harmful forces. Again the rites frequently involved the possession of the priest, or shaman, by the deity. During this possession either the desired results were achieved, or it was revealed to the priest just how they would be achieved.

Probably the height of this kind of cult is best seen in a rite called *Chöd*. The place in which the shaman has to enact the rite is specified as being a place inhabited by demons. It can be a cemetery, a place where corpses are cut up, cremation grounds, or other places recognized as the haunt of demons. The rite virtually attempts a great purification in which the shaman takes into his own being all the evil around him, all the accumulated bad deeds of others as well as his own, then by offering his own life in a supreme sacrifice he purges others as well as himself. The sacrifice is symbolic (though what it used to be we cannot tell), but even so the rite courts such appalling disaster, inviting into the actor's being all the forces of evil, that the slightest hesitation or doubt on his part can bring death or insanity. Chöd must only be undertaken after long and intensive training, in which the actual steps in the rite are learned until they are second nature. The dance that is an integral part of the rite is not only symbolic; it also heightens and maintains the physical condition of the shaman at a level at which it can withstand the forces entering his body. His mind similarly has to be fortified and his whole being purified before he can attempt the rite. The rite ends when having conjured up in his mind all the demons of hell, the shaman – wielding his ritual knife, the *Phurbu* – sees his executioner approach to cut off his head and, as in the oldest of sacrifices, disembowel him and cast his entrails out and throw the blood into the air. If this final vision becomes a reality in the mind of the shaman, he is in fact liable to lose his reason, if not his life.

This ancient rite has a curious parallel as described by the traveller, the Lazarist priest M. Huc, who was making his way from Peking to Lhasa in the year 1845–6. He was passing through southern Mongolia when his party met a crowd of pilgrims making their way to the monastery of Rache Tchurin. They inquired of a monk the reason, and he expressed surprise that they did not know. The next day there was to be a great feast during which the powerful Boktè Rinpoche was 'to manifest his power; kill himself, yet not die'. Huc did not attend the ceremony, but he gives a description of it as he heard it. The similarities with the early forms of Bön are unmistakable, and this is one of the areas where the Bönpoba have survived least affected by Buddhism. His description is worth giving:

A Lama * was to cut himself open, take out his entrails, and place them before him, and then resume his previous condition. This spectacle, so cruel and disgusting, is very common in the Lamaseries of Tartary. The Boktè who is to manifest his power, as the Mongols phrase it, prepares himself for the formidable operation by many days' fasting and prayer, pending which he must abstain from all communication whatever with mankind, and observe the most absolute silence. When the appointed day is come, the multitude of pilgrims assemble in the great court of the Lamasery, where an altar is raised in front of the Temple gate. At length the Boktè appears. He advances gravely, amid the acclamations of the crowd, seats himself upon the altar, and

*The term 'lama' merely means 'teacher' – a lama need not necessarily even be a monk. The terms 'lamaism' and 'lamasery' then are meaningless, having no religious significance, and when Western writers use 'lama' they generally mean 'monk'.

takes from his girdle a large knife which he places upon his knees. At his feet, numerous Lamas, ranged in a circle, commence the terrible invocations of this frightful ceremony. As the recitation of the prayers proceeds, you see the Boktè trembling in every limb, and gradually working himself up into phrenetic convulsions. The Lamas themselves become excited; their voices are raised; their song observes no order, and at last becomes a mere confusion of yelling and outcry. Then the Boktè suddenly throws aside the scarf which envelops him, unfastens his girdle, and, seizing the sacred knife, slits open his stomach, in one long cut. While the blood flows in every direction, the multitude prostrate themselves before the terrible spectacle, and the enthusiast is interrogated about all sorts of hidden things, as to future events, as to the destiny of certain personages. The replies of the Boktè to all these questions are regarded by everybody as oracles.

When the devout curiosity of the numerous pilgrims is satisfied, the Lamas resume, but now calmly and gravely, the recitation of their prayers. The Boktè takes, in his right hand, blood from his wound, raises it to his mouth, breathes thrice upon it, and then throws it into the air with loud cries. He next passes his hand rapidly over his wound, closes it, and everything, after a while, resumes its pristine condition, no trace remaining of the diabolical operation, except extreme prostration. The Boktè once more rolls his scarf round him, recites in a low voice a short prayer; then all is over, and the multitude disperse, with the exception of a few of the especially devout, who remain to contemplate and to adore the blood-stained altar which the saint has quitted.

These horrible ceremonies are of frequent occurrence in the great Lamaseries of Tartary and Thibet, and we do not believe that there is any trick or deception about them; for, from all we have seen and heard among idolatrous nations, we are persuaded that the devil has a great deal to do with the matter; and, moreover, our impression that there is no trick in the operation is fortified by the opinion of the most intelligent and most upright Buddhists whom we have met in the numerous Lamaseries we visited.*

The essentials are there, but the purpose has changed. It is no longer held in a place inhabited by demons, for one thing, and it seems more designed as a proof of supernatural power than anything else, something far removed from the original notion of

* *M. Huc,* Travels in Tartary, Thibet, and China During the Years 1844–5-6, 2nd ed. (*London, National Illustrated Library, n.d.*), Vol. I, pp. 191–2.

self-sacrifice, the original aim of ritual in bringing the practitioner face to face with stark reality, with the raw power of life and death. In Tibet, now, Shenrab Miboche is worshipped by the Bön much as Guru Rinpoche is by the Buddhists. White Bön, which has taken pains to come as close as possible to Buddhism, even claims that Guru Rinpoche was born not of a lotus, as the Hindus claim, but as a man, and a Bön, in Shang Shung. White Bönpoba teach mystic contemplation, meditation, and the performance of correct ritual and the leading of a correct life. They also have scriptures like their *Kyeddzog* which teach tantric practices of possession and exorcism. It was tantricism that made it easy for Buddhism and the Bön religion to come to terms with each other.

There is a sect called Black Bön, however, which seeks to throw off the refinements and moderating influence of Buddhism, and which still practises rites relating to basic primal powers. During the reign of the last Gyalwa Rinpoche, the thirteenth, an edict had to be issued against the Black Bönpoba who were terrifying certain villages with their practices.

We believe that there *are* powers such as those that the Bönpoba bring into their own bodies, but we believe that such practices are not for us. They can do great harm not only to a practitioner, but to others as well, and are best left alone. If a man wants to study these scriptures and practise these rites, he must do so alone. In my own sect, the Yellow Hat or *Gelukpa* sect, anyone found practising rites of this kind would be expelled. Yet we ourselves retain a symbolic version, for there is much good in the thought that lies behind the Bön practices. While they are concerned with driving out the dark powers, however, we are concerned with seeking the help of Buddha.

We have exorcisms, symbolic ones, in which symbols are written on a piece of paper; all evil is invoked and commanded to enter the paper which is then burned. Sometimes it is done with the burning of an effigy representing evil. But we believe the power of such performances is in our minds, and the evil that exists, and must be driven out, lies there. Our faith in the Buddha and his teachings is the fire that alone can drive out that evil. The

Bön believe that fire in itself, properly conjured, has the power to destroy evil. They still practise rites, as perhaps do some tantric Buddhists, in which the priest wages war against evil, using fire as his weapon. They say that if the evil is too strong, it can take control of the fire and harm the priest. Or if the priest does not succeed in his exorcism, and the evil is not destroyed, it will later seek him out. I have known of cases where after such an unsuccessful exorcism the priest himself has sickened, or died, or fallen from his horse. Who is to know if this is because he himself had become possessed by the evil he failed to destroy, as many say, or if it is otherwise? I do not know. Nor have I actually seen such exorcisms where fire is used like this.

We Buddhists believe that the Bön religion is quite separate from our own, because however similar it seems, the Bönpoba do not recognize our Buddha, who was Gautama, or Sakya Muni. Yet our way of life is much the same; there is no way of telling whether a man is a Bönpoba or a Buddhist when you meet him. His clothes, his manner of speech, his behaviour, all are the same as our own. Inside his house the altar might be a little different. Instead of an image of Buddha there would be an image of Shenrab Miboche. Their great *ngag*, or prayer, is different from ours. Instead of 'Aom Mani Padme Hum', they pray 'Aom Matre Muye Sale Du'.

Where my home used to be, in Amdo, we did not have many Bön followers, but we offered them the same respect we would have offered to anyone. If a Bön came to our region and needed food and shelter we would give him food and shelter just as though he were a Buddhist traveller in the same need. We treat monks with more respect than laymen, but that would apply if a Bön priest were to come to our home as much as a Buddhist monk. We say our prayers in the morning and evening, so a traveller taking a midday meal with us would not be expected to join in any prayers. Nor would he be expected to join the family prayers, though if he wanted to he could. A monk might offer a prayer before a meal, but we would be just as happy if a Bön priest offered a prayer or attended our family service. When as a monk myself I was among the nomads in Chamri, I knew a Bön priest who used to come to my place and pray, and I used to visit him. He also visited many Buddhist temples, giving donations, joining in their prayers, even giving advice and help. In Yatung I visited the Bön monastery there; even the Gyalwa Rinpoche himself has visited it and given donations.

I know two Bönpoba priests, both from Amdo, in the east. They studied first at the important Bön monasteries in western Tibet: Rala Yundrun, near Rong, and Thobgyal Drutsang Gon. Bön students from all over Tibet, from two thousand miles away, come to study at these monasteries. They were founded in the early eleventh century. But these two Bön priests had also studied later at Drepung, one of the three major Gelukpa monasteries at Lhasa; yet it is the Gelukpa who more than any have tried to purge Buddhism of Bön practices. I do not think we would ever try to convert anyone, however much we disagreed with their beliefs, for we feel that true conversion can only come if the person himself wants it enough to seek it. We would not go out to seek converts, though we might hope that in our wanderings and through our teachings and by our way of life we might encourage others to join the faith.

The Bön monasteries and priesthood that exist now are certainly modelled after the Tibetan Buddhist system. Each monastery is organized in just the same way, and each monk has to take exactly the same number of vows, two hundred and fifty-three. The only difference lies in the nature of some of the vows. For one thing the vow of chastity is different since the Bön priests may marry. The Bön people are represented in the government, and the government recognizes the Bön monasteries and gives them large grants just as it does to any other monasteries.

As to the existence of spirits and powers outside our mind, I myself do not know. There are some places that seem to have a power of their own, and they affect most people the same way. Some places make you feel good, some make you feel bad. When I am in Tibet I never want to leave; I want to stay there always; I always feel good.

I once visited the oracle lake at Chu Khor gyal. It is always consulted concerning the rebirth of a Gyalwa Rinpoche and is the abode of his protectress, the Goddess Pandan Lhamo. The lake is named Lhamo Lamtso, and to reach it I had to climb up over a high pass that was covered with thick snow. It was terribly cold. Above the pass the mountains went up like giant staircases, all of red rock, too steep for snow to settle, bare even of a blade of grass. The mountains seem to close right in over you, and it is unlike any other place I have seen. Then, over the other side, is the lake. I had expected I would like it there, but when I arrived at the lakeside I found something made me feel very strange. It was not simply that I did not like being there – there was a feeling of some kind of power I did not understand. I did not feel warm and comfortable as I used to in Lhasa, when every morning I would go to the Temple and offer my butter lamps and incense.

Then there are many places I have passed when on pilgrimage which are believed to be haunted by ghosts. I was never worried about them, because I have prayers to protect me. There is one place on the trail from India, near Jelup-la, where a Mongolian monk died. It is said he haunts the place and insists that travellers get down from their horses and walk past the spot. Some travellers even make offerings of their horses to make sure they pass safely. Many people who have tried to ride past have fallen or had accidents. They say the ghost of the monk threw them from their horses. The only time anything like this happened to me was in my house at Drepung Monastery, in Lhasa. On the first floor there is a door, and as you come through it there is another door with stone steps leading down to the basement. It is believed that there is a ghost there that wants a human body. When it is dark nobody will go near the place. They say that anyone passing by after dark will be pushed down the stairs. I was just passing by, once, when all of a sudden I simply fell down the stairs. I do not know, honestly, whether I was pushed or not. All I know was that I had no reason to fall, I was not afraid of ghosts and never have been, but I fell.

If we do not understand something, we should say so. Because we cannot understand it, there is no reason to say that it does not exist. Few of us indeed reach the state of perfect knowledge;

most of us live many lives in ignorance, though with good deeds the ignorance grows less each time. We should keep our minds open and allow others their beliefs while holding to our own and all the time we should strive for knowledge. It is a long and arduous path, but every step brings fresh strength and comfort. We believe that though there are short cuts, such as tantric practice, liberation still has to be won step by step. That is the great difference perhaps, apart from the belief in the Buddha himself, between us Buddhists in Tibet and the Bönpoba. They too are striving for liberation, but they are impatient for it. They seek short cuts and they seek to escape the results of their deeds. They play with powers which they claim to exist outside their bodies but which we hold to be of no concern to us. Sometimes they only achieve their own destruction, but who is to deny that sometimes they too achieve liberation?

CHAPTER SIX

The First Light

In Khabachen they found him, in the Land of
  Snows;
Before the days of Kings,
Before the people knew the Lord Gautama:
In the mountains to the south they found him,
A man, strange and wonderful.
They asked his name.
'Tsan-po' he replied, 'The Great One' it
  seemed he said.
The people asked whence he came.
With upward pointing finger Tsan-po replied,
But his voice was mere noise,
No more could he be understood.
Four strong men made a throne of wood.
On this throne, upon their backs, they carried
  Tsan-po.
They carried him into Khabachen, as theirs.
Believing he of the upward-pointed finger to
  have been sent,
Come from the sky to be their King.

               – from BUSTON CHOSHBYUNG

We have no idea of the date from records, but since this, our first king, was followed by more than thirty other kings to the time of the great Srontsan Gampo, we can guess that he came into our land some time about the first Christian century. He was called 'Nyatri Tsanpo', meaning 'He who was carried in victory upon the back'. The stories that have been handed down say that he was fair and beautiful, but who he was, nobody knows. Some say he was a criminal who had been exiled from India. Others say he was from a branch of the royal Sakya line, the family that six or seven hundred years earlier had given birth to Gautama the Buddha. It was at a time when there were no priests in Tibet, and certainly no kings. The people were Bön, and the only other thing we are told is that Nyatri Tsanpo was made a member of the Bön faith.

It is also said that the Bön religion itself really began six generations later. There is a separate story that until this generation Nyatri Tsanpo's descendants, like himself, did not die. It is believed that he had come from the sky, using some kind of rope ladder, and by this way left the earth again. So it was that neither Nyatri Tsanpo nor the six kings who followed him left behind any mortal remains. The eighth king, Grigrum, had an argument with one of his ministers who made magic against him and caused him to cut the ladder connecting Heaven and Earth. In this way he became subject to death and had to devise other ways of effecting a safe return to Heaven following his death. It is from this time that many Bönpoba date the beginnings of a single central body of ritual, so much of which concerns death and the forces which determine it.

There was a rival king who also had heavenly origin, who came to the people of eastern Tibet, in the country of Ling. His coming is also associated with the beginnings of Bön religion, and Ling itself is not many miles from the place where the traveller Huc recorded his notes on the ancient Bön rite of symbolic death. The story of this king is contained in some of the oldest records we have in Tibet, dating from the seventh century. They make no mention of Nyatri Tsanpo, only of Pu Gye which means 'Hairy Prince'. The story is that the people of this remote district, having no king, went to their sacred mountain and invoked the gods, to ask their help. One came in the form of a great bird. The people caught the bird and refused to let him return until he made a promise that he would send his own son to be their king.

The son was duly sent, and he announced himself to the people by dancing for them day and night. But since his body was covered with hair, people thought he could not possibly be the son of their god. In despair he returned to Heaven and told his father that the people would not recognize him. Next he was sent again in the form of the son of a poor peasant woman. He soon proved himself, by fighting rather than dancing, and he has been revered ever since as one of Tibet's great heroes. Among the exploits recorded in these early documents are the wars that Pu Gye, or Kesar as he is also known, waged against China, and his great feats of exorcism, driving out the many devils he found there. It is true, it so happens, that although Buddhism came to China before it came to Tibet, China from the earliest times respected the religious teachers of Tibet. It is also true, and the story of Pu Gye reminds us of the fact, that the early Tibetans were a warlike people, feared by all their neighbours. They carried on successful wars against China up to the time of their conversion to Buddhism, when a sudden change came over the people. It must be one of the most dramatic and remarkable of historical facts for a war-loving and war-waging people to become so peace-loving in a few short years. Although the Tibetan people long ago lost the art of making war, together with the taste for it, they have never lost their love of the legends of those glorious days, however much they prefer to be the way they are.

Some time after Grigrum cut the celestial ladder, there came a mortal king whom we call Lhato Thori, King Powerful Delicate Tower. Like the other kings, he was a warrior, but also given to moments of quietness. One day he was up on the roof of his palace when out of the sky came a great casket, which landed at his feet and proved to contain religious books, a model of a golden tomb, and the six sacred syllables that make up the Tibetan prayer of everlasting truth. The king summoned his ministers, but as none of them could read they had no idea of what was contained in the books. Today we claim they were Buddhist scriptures, while the Bönpoba claim they were Bön scriptures. In any case, the king recognized that such a gift from the heavens was plainly auspicious; he put the casket away safely and worshipped the books daily, though he had no idea of their content. One legend says that he thus prolonged his life from sixty to twice sixty years. The king named the books *Nyanpo Sangba*, meaning 'hidden greatness'. We now recognize these scriptures to be the Buddhist *Dunkong Shakgyapa*.

Shortly after beginning his worship of the books, the first religious worship, we say, ever to have been offered in Tibet, King Lhato Thori had a dream. In the dream the Buddha appeared to him and told him that the secret of the books was not to be revealed to him, but in five generations time a stranger would come to the land and would explain the text to the people, and unlock the secret of the gift.

Yet another miracle was to happen, for when one of Lhato Thori's sons, born in blindness, became king, he also worshipped the books. One day he stood by a palace window, having completed his devotions, when he was suddenly blessed with sight. In front of him he saw the mountains with white sheep running across them. He is known to us by the name he then took, 'See White Mountain-Sheep'.

These kings were all centered in the southern province of Yarlung, which touches on the border of Bhutan, and they were all followers of Bön practices. Already an important new element had been brought into that faith: worship. Far from becoming less warlike, however, the kings continued to expand their realm of control until they formed the most powerful kingdom Tibet had yet known. Four generations after Lhato Thori began his worship of the scriptures, King Namri Srongtsan united the whole of Tibet, some thousand miles across, and achieved such a reputation that even the Chinese feared him for his courage and for the strength and success of his armies. Tibet was now ready to take the next step. Having welded itself into a powerful, if rude, kingdom, it was ready to open relations with neighbouring powers. The Tibetans recognized that they still lacked the developed culture that they found in China to the east and in India to the south, and they proved more than willing to learn. But while they adopted almost everything in the way of material culture from China, they turned to India for learning.

In the second decade of the seventh century there ascended to the throne the fifth successor to Lhato Thori. On accession he received the name Srontsan Gampo, meaning 'he who is powerful, just and profound'. Like his forefathers, Srontsan Gampo was a practicing Bön, but nonetheless he fulfilled the prophecy that understanding would be brought during the fifth generation. So that the *Nyanpo Sangba*, the books of 'hidden greatness', could be translated into Tibetan, he sent one of his ministers Thonmi Sambhota with sixteen students to India. The students travelled all over, studying under various great teachers both Buddhist and Hindu. Thonmi Sambhota himself worked mainly in Kashmir. In the end he was the only one left alive, the others falling sick in the low altitudes and oppressive heat of the country.

Eventually the minister returned to Tibet, and there made use of all he had learned to devise a script of thirty characters, based largely on the Kashmiri *sharada* alphabet, and on the classical *nagri* script, making changes to suit the different phonetics of the Tibetan language. Thonmi Sambhota then gathered students and scholars around him and set to work translating divers scriptures, Hindu and Buddhist, into Tibetan. The scriptures appealed to Srontsan Gampo, who studied them carefully, though he remained a Bönpoba for the time. He had meanwhile been seeing effectively to the material advancement of his country.

He proceeded with the military campaigns that had become traditional to Tibetan kings, and finding the ancestral capital in Yarlung too remote from the centre of the newly united nation, he moved to Lhasa and there built himself a comparatively modest fort on the top of the Red Hill, Marpori, the exact site of the future Potala. Until recently, in the modern Potala, there used to be a painting of Srontsan Gampo's fortress. From this central vantage point he was able to push his conquests further, and maintain control over what he already held. He was astute enough to recognize the value of a political marriage, so he allied himself in this way first with Nepal. The Princess Bhrikuti was a devout Buddhist who brought with her as part of her dowry several valuable Buddhist images. Together they built a great temple to house the images, the Tsulag Khang, which stands today in the middle of the city of Lhasa that has grown up around it, and the temple is known as the Jo Khang, the House of the Lord. Its original name meant 'House of Wisdom', perhaps a concession to the fact that the Bönpoba were already becoming a little restive at these foreign influences. Nepalese architects and builders and all the necessary craftsmen were sent from Nepal for the work on the temple, the first to be built in Tibet.

Not yet satisfied, Srontsan Gampo next turned his attention to China, which at first proved less ready to accept his request, couched more in the terms of a demand, for the hand of a Chinese princess. Angered at the refusal, Srontsan Gampo began a military campaign, the might of which quickly persuaded the Chinese Emperor T'ai Tsung to change his mind. Now Srontsan sent an envoy, called Garpa, and Garpa negotiated ably for the hand of the Princess Wong Shen Konjö from the Imperial family itself and, again, a devout Buddhist.

In his negotiations with the king of Nepal for the hand of Bhrikuti, Srontsan Gampo had stated quite plainly that he was not a Buddhist, and did not practise the ten virtues, but that if the king so desired he would adopt the ten virtues and would further the cause of Buddhism with all his might. He had already made a start with an elaborate temple-building programme, and with the translations of Buddhist scriptures. All this still did not quite convince T'ai Tsung that so valuable a princess should be given to a mere barbarian, even a powerful one. He agreed reluctantly to Garpa's insistence, in the end, on the condition

143

that Garpa himself could pass four tests, the fourth being the selection of the Princess from among a large number of beautiful girls all dressed exactly alike.

The first test involved a hundred mares and a hundred small foals. The mares and foals were kept separately, on either side of a wall. Garpa had to reassemble them, each mare with its foal. Garpa found this easy enough; he merely opened a door in the wall, and all the foals went straight to their mothers.

The next test was for Garpa to find his way back, without making a single mistake, to a room in which he had spent only one night, in a house where all the rooms looked alike. He was brought to the room in the dark and led away early in the morning. Before leaving, however, Garpa left a small stick of incense burning, and this led him back to his own room.

For the third test Srontsan's envoy was given a coral bead through which ran a twisting, crooked and tiny hole. The test was to thread it. Even this presented little difficulty to the envoy, who tied the thread to the leg of an ant and let the ant pull the thread through the coral bead.

The last test was more difficult, for Garpa had never seen the princess, and could not see how he was going to detect her. He approached a maidservant of the princess, but she said she would surely be overheard if she told him, since the Emperor's astrologers were expecting some such move. They eventually agreed to a ruse, and later on met quite openly by a stream, Garpa on one side of it, the maidservant on the other. The maidservant had discovered a way of recognizing the Princess, and Garpa had prepared himself to fool the astrologer. He wore a monkey mask, and held a long piece of bamboo to his mouth. Across the stream they talked through the bamboo tube. The Emperor saw this and thought it strange but suspected nothing. The maidservant told Garpa that all the girls would be wearing flowers in their hair, but only the princess would wear real flowers. When Garpa appeared for the test he looked to see where the bees went, and by following them found the real princess.

Like Bhrikuti, the Princess Wong Shen Konjö brought sacred images with her, at least one of which survives in Lhasa today in

the great Temple. The building of this Temple, the first place of
Buddhist worship in Tibet, is the subject of many persistent
stories that at one time there used to be a vast underground lake
beneath the site, a lake the size of an ocean. When Srontsan
Gampo and his Nepalese princess began work, every structure
that was erected collapsed long before completion for no apparent
reason. Consulting an oracle the king learned that the secret was
held by an old sage who lived somewhere in the east. On this
slender information King Srontsan sent out search parties to
cover the whole of the eastern part of Tibet. All returned having
failed but one. He himself was returning from Amdo when a
misfortune befell him; the girth of his saddle broke.

Near by was a small hut on the edge of a pond, and inside was
an old blind man. The king's messenger explained his misfortune, and the old man told him to look around, that there was
a spare strap somewhere, to which he was welcome. While
looking, but wishing to maintain his quest a secret, the messenger,
himself a lama or teacher, announced that he was a teacher from
the east, on pilgrimage. The old man said how fortunate he was,
for the finest temples were all in the east. The people westward,
in the Land of the Snows, would never be able to build such fine
monuments. Even at this moment they were trying, he said, but
they did not know that beneath the site of their temple lay a
great ocean. He hastened to swear the messenger to secrecy,
saying that an ancient spell told that as soon as a teacher from
Tibet came to know the secret, the hidden waters would leave
and flood the very site on which they stood. The tiny pond itself
was connected, he said, to that great lake.

Hearing this the messenger leaped on his horse, telling the old
man to save himself, for he had just revealed the secret to a
Tibetan teacher. He rode off towards Lhasa as fast as he could.
The old man's cries brought his son running, and in dismay the
old man told his son to pursue a stranger from Tibet and kill him,
for he had halted to repair a saddle strap and had ridden off
having stolen his secret. But the word for 'secret' is the same as
that for 'strap', and the son thought his old father had gone out
of his senses to demand the death of a man for so small an offence

as the theft of a strap. But his father was adamant, and the son rode off. Overtaking the teacher the youth apologized and explained that his father had been much upset at the loss of the strap, and had even urged him to commit murder to retrieve it, but that he must be out of his senses so would the venerable lama mind returning the strap for the comfort of the old man's mind? The teacher readily agreed, gave back the strap, and, using his own belt to fasten the saddle, continued on his way.

When the boy got back and told the old man what he had done, the old man saw that all was lost. He told the boy to fly and to save himself. He lay down on the floor of his hut and waited. At just this time the people of Lhasa were alarmed by the most dreadful noises from far below the surface of the earth and by much trembling and shaking. Soon the noises subsided and all was quiet again. But out in the east the little pond suddenly shuddered, great waves appeared, and it rapidly began to flood its banks. The old man and many others who had not heeded his warning were drowned. The waters spread for a hundred miles. They are now known as the Koko Nor, or Blue Lake.

The messenger, on returning to Lhasa and being told about the strange noise, knew that the old man had told the truth. He informed Srontsan Gampo, who once again began work on the temple. This time the ground was firm, and the Temple has stood there ever since.

The king was not content with the mere building of temples, however. He studied under Thonmi Sambhota, and became such a proficient scholar that he himself undertook the translation of a number of scriptures. He openly favoured the new teachings, and when the Bönpoba rose up in opposition, Srontsan Gampo issued an edict making adherence to the new Buddhist doctrine compulsory. The Buddha's ten Golden Precepts became law, as did a civil code of sixteen articles devised by the king in an attempt to convert his subjects not only in name, but also in spirit. Together with the new laws he began a programme of social reform. Land tenure was reorganized; Tibetans were urged to learn and master the various arts and crafts and other skills that were still in the hands of people from other countries;

agriculture, which had just begun to take hold, was encouraged; and schools were set up to teach reading and writing.

No monasteries were founded however, and, apart from the one incident of open disagreement with the Bönpoba, Buddhism and Bön managed to live side by side. The Bön objection on that particular occasion was probably because of the introduction by King Srontsan Gampo of the prohibition on the taking of life, a prohibition that would have struck at the heart of their ritual practices. Despite this favourable beginning, however, Buddhism still had no sure footing, lacking a monastic organization. But Srontsan Gampo had laid the foundations by fulfilling the prophecy made to Lhato Thori, and by unlocking the secret of the 'Hidden Greatness'. Once unlocked it was never again to be confined, but to spread from one end of Tibet to the other.

During this remarkable reign, Srontsan Gampo had by no means converted the nation to Buddhism, it was still a country where the people thought of themselves as wild and fierce, sometimes using a word meaning 'brutish' to describe themselves. A Buddhist nucleus had been founded, but it was confined largely to the Royal Family and maintained by the religious fervour of the king's two Buddhist wives. If the nation as a whole had not been converted, however, the way had been opened, and Buddhist influence was spreading, if superficially at first, to the remotest corners of the kingdom. Apart from his educational programme within Tibet, Srontsan Gampo took pains to send a number of children from important families to China. This, coupled with the influx of teachers and workers from both China and India, further cleared the way for the coming of Buddhism in its full force. Perhaps more important still, despite Srontsan Gampo's discouragement, the Bön had already begun to make use of certain Buddhist teachings for their own use, claiming some of them to be their own. In a sense, perhaps, they were not merely trying to defeat Buddhism by subverting it, as has often been suggested, but rather, recognizing it as yet another 'power' to be dealt with, they were performing a ritual of possession, attempting to take control of this new external power and use it for their own ends. This would be much more in keeping with

Bön thinking, and it is plain that despite disagreement there was no open hostility between the two religions. Rivalry was another matter. Accepting Srontsan Gampo as the founder of Buddhism in Tibet, the people later recognized him as the incarnation of Chenresig, Lord of Mercy, who came to be Tibet's protective deity.

The Buddhist influence did not deter Srontsan Gampo from continuing his military activities, and after his death they were pushed still further by those who followed him, defeating China and forcing it to pay tribute to Tibet. The army at that time has been estimated to have been about a quarter of a million strong. Three generations after the great king's death his descendant Me Agtsom imitated his illustrious ancestor by successfully demanding the hand of another princess of China. She brought with her all the religious fervour of a devout Buddhist and, once again, increased the impetus of the movement towards Buddhism as a national religion. During this reign, as before, Tibet continued to look to India for knowledge, and many new and important translations were made. Two renowned Indian sages were engaged in meditation on the holy Mount Kailas, in southern Tibet, and messengers were sent to them to persuade them to come to Lhasa and teach there. The request was refused, but the holy men taught the five Theg Chen sutras to the messengers, who learned them by heart and so brought them into the growing body of scriptures translated into Tibetan.

Buddhism had already divided into two schools of thought, largely differing in opinion as to the interpretation of the doctrine of mying di and the concept of soul. Concerning points on which the Buddha had remained silent, the Theg Man school took his silence to imply denial, whereas the Theg Chen school took it to mean that it was merely not part of the Eightfold Path; that is to say the Theg Chen school developed an esoteric system as well as the exoteric system. For the layman the all-important thing was the Path; all he had to do, or should do, was to strive to follow the way of life laid down by the Buddha in his exoteric teachings. For those devoted solely to the pursuit of religion, there was a path of higher learning, which in no way bypassed the

Eightfold Path, but was a continuation that granted higher under-standing, qualifying its followers to lead as teachers. Pursuit of questions involving the existence or non-existence of soul, or concerning afterlife, could only confuse the layman and give rise to doubts that were beyond his ability to resolve, being bound to an everyday layman's life. Hence the Buddha's silence. It was this school, the Theg Chen, which eventually made its centre in Tibet, dividing the population into monks and laymen, each following his own path, but at the same time united inextricably in pursuit of a common goal, liberation.

The fact that Tibet looked to India rather than China for spiritual and intellectual guidance was most important in one respect. North India was the centre of a flourishing school of tantricism, a school that believed rather like the Bön that man could develop supernormal powers by proper discipline. The discipline was rigid and the dangers were many if study was not carried out under qualified supervision. It was, in effect, a closed school to which members were admitted only if they were con-sidered fit and willing to devote themselves completely to the study. The aim was not the mere development of supernormal power in the individual, such powers really just came as a by-product of development towards a more truly spiritual goal. Nonetheless, these teachings were close enough to the practices, if not the teachings, of the Bönpoba, that they found a ready welcome in Tibet. In origin they were Hindu rather than Budd-hist, but in north India the two had become much mixed, and they came to Tibet as one and gave Tibetan Buddhism its particular shape when combined with the original Bön beliefs.

The tantric teachings were much more foreign to Chinese thought and did not find favour in the eyes of Me Agtsom's queen, and although the teachings were welcomed and eagerly studied by the Bönpoba, the Indian teachers and the Buddhist practitioners of tantra were considered dangerous rivals. During Me Agtsom's reign, then, there was increasing discontent with both teachers and teachings from India, on these two grounds. At this time there was a disastrous outbreak of smallpox, and the queen herself fell victim and died. The epidemic was interpreted by the Bönpoba as a sign that the ancient Gods of Tibet were displeased with the new religion and with the teachings of the foreign monks. Public opinion itself was easily aroused in this crisis, and there were renewed demands for the expulsion of all monks. Such pressure was brought upon the king that he was compelled, much against his will, to deport not only all the Indian teachers in Tibet, but also many of their Tibetan followers.

Me Agtsom's son, who became King Trisong Detsan, was himself a devout Buddhist, and determined to reverse the setback. He sent to China for further scriptures to be translated, but his uncle, who was a leading minister and had a large following, was violently opposed to any further translations and the books had to be hidden away. The young scholar Salnang who had undertaken the fetching of these books also had to be removed from the scene, so Trisong Detsan appointed him governor of a province bordering on Nepal. This was too good an opportunity to be missed, and he took advantage of it – probably as Trisong Detsan had hoped – to visit Buddhist shrines in India, where the Buddha had lived and taught. Most important of all he visited the great Buddhist university of Nalanda, and there met Shantirakshita, probably the leading Buddhist scholar of the day. Together they planned on the reintroduction of Buddhism into Tibet.

The king was much in favour, but his minister still stood in the way. He found an ally in another minister however, Gotisang. Gotisang devised a scheme whereby the State Oracle should announce that two prominent ministers should retire to a secret place and be shut in there for a period of time. The fact that Gotisang was one of the ministers allayed any suspicions that Mashang, the enemy of Buddhism, might have had when he was selected as the other. But whereas Gotisang knew his way out of the burial chamber, Mashang did not. He was walled in and left there to die.

With him out of the way there was nothing left to stop the king from openly pursuing his plan of bringing Buddhism back to Tibet. He invited Shantirakshita to come from Nalanda and to teach in Lhasa. The great man came, and in the palace on the

Red Hill he preached and taught. His teachings were not in the tantric vein at all, but were concerned with the highest moral matters, including a revival of the Ten Virtues which Srontsan Gampo had embraced on his marriage with the Nepalese princess. Perhaps the Bönpoba saw that these teachings, containing the basis of a completely new way of life founded on compassion for all living things, offered an even greater danger to the old order. When there was a violent storm and the palace on the Red Hill was struck by lightning, they immediately claimed that the gods of Tibet had been angered and that the new teacher should be sent back to India at once. Shantirakshita himself was impressed by the violence with which his teachings were received, and returned hastily to Nalanda.

When things had quietened down, Trisong Detsan, still undaunted, sent once again and invited the sage to return and continue his teachings. But Shantirakshita had had enough. In his reply he said that the forces of evil in Tibet were too strong. If Buddhism was to make any headway at all, the first thing to do was to exorcize all the demons that filled the country and controlled it with their malignant powers. He himself would not come back until that was done. To undertake such a task there was only one person who had the necessary knowledge and skill, the famous tantric monk Lopon Rinpoche, a man who in his lifetime had built up an extraordinary reputation, and was believed to have been born from a lotus.

Trisong Detsan promptly invited Lopon Rinpoche to undertake the task, and the master of tantricism accepted. With his coming to Tibet the demons were indeed expelled, and the floodgates were opened to admit the Buddhist religion in all its strength

CHAPTER SEVEN

Miracles and Darkness

First : his hand grasps the bow ;
Second : it notches the arrow ;
Third : the bow expanded,
The thumb looses the arrow.
Thus he sends the arrow straight to the chest of
  the King,
Lang Darma.
'I am the Black Devil, Ya Sher,
Sent to kill a sinful King' ;
This said, he fled.

– from BUSTON CHOSHBYUNG

The very birth of Lopon Rinpoche, as we call the saint known in India as Padmasambhava, is bound up with tantric belief and practice (*Gyud*), with man's concern with supernormal powers, their attainment and control. It seems that he was born in that part of the country which lies between Kashmir and Afghanistan, a region we call Urgyen, corresponding roughly to the modern Swat. At that time Urgyen was dominated by Mahayana Buddhism, or Theg Chen, but was very much intermixed with tantric practice. It was renowned, in fact, for the extent to which magic and sorcery were practised there, and for the secret formulas and rites by which its inhabitants were able to acquire extraordinary powers.

The history of tantricism goes back three thousand years at least; it was flourishing in northern India in the seventh century B.C. when the Gautama Buddha was born there as Prince Siddhartha, royal son of the Sakya king, Suddhodana, in the capital town of Kapilavastu. While the histories do not state explicitly that his was a 'virgin birth', the implication is plain. Queen Maha Maya had a dream that the stars opened up and from the night sky came a wonderful elephant which entered into her womb. So was the Buddha conceived. The birth itself was equally attended by all manner of auspicious omens. One day, when her time was near, the queen was walking in the Lumbini Park. A great tree bent its branches down to the ground to support her and in this bower she gave birth to the prince who was to become Buddha, from her right side. Thus Siddhartha came into the world undefiled. He was presented at the Sakya Temple, and it is said that even the images prostrated themselves before him. The priest, when he saw the child, immediately recognized him as an incarnate Changchub Sempa, returned for the benefit of mankind. Changchub Sempa are always born with a set number of discernible physical marks on the body. The priest prophesied that the young prince would remain with his people only for as long as he did not see four things. These four things were a sick man, an old man, a corpse and a renunciate. Once he had seen these four truths of life, the prophesy went, the prince would renounce his home and family forever. Other wise men, less direct in their interpretations, desiring to better please the king, interpreted the signs as meaning that Siddhartha was going to be a king of kings. Suddhodana vowed that this would be so and gave orders that whenever his son moved from the palace grounds guards were to precede him and to make sure that there were no aged, or sick, no dead and no renunciates in the streets. He set about providing his son with every possible pleasure in life, sheltering him from all pain and unhappiness.

Siddhartha grew up in this way, living life fully, tasting its every pleasure. Yet an insatiable curiosity drove him beyond these pleasures, and they quickly palled and left him listless. His teachers found his wisdom far beyond theirs, and the prince began to wander farther and farther afield in search of something new, something to fill the void that he could sense in his understanding of life.

In a final effort to keep his son closer to the protection offered by the palace and its pleasure gardens, Suddhodana arranged for the youth's marriage. Siddhartha had shown little more than passing interest in all the dancing girls given to him for his amusement, and had shown no greater interest in any of the eligible princesses except one, Yasoda. Later, when questioned as to why he agreed to marry her, the Buddha is said to have replied that they had been drawn together in a previous incarnation, and their marriage was in fulfilment of that earlier meeting. The marriage was fruitful, but soon after Yasoda gave birth to a boy, Rahula, the gods sent the four signs. Siddhartha's previous lei was now worked out; it was time for him to renounce the world. On one of his trips through Kapilavastu, on his way to the forest he loved to visit, the Prince saw first an old man, bent and all but immobile. Then he saw a man wracked with the pains of sickness. Later a corpse was carried across the road in front of him, and finally he saw a poor beggar who had renounced the world. He was sitting in calm repose, in a state of bliss, at peace with himself and with the world.

Siddhartha immediately knew what had been missing from his life, the inescapable truth of decay and suffering. He also had a glimmering of another truth, the truth of release from suffering. He determined to leave home and go in search of the ultimate truth. He took his leave of Yasoda and the infant Rahula while they still slept. He mounted his horse, and although the King had given orders that the palace gates should be opened to none, not even his son, they opened of their own accord and he rode out far into the forest. Once safely away he dismounted, sent his horse back to the palace, cut off his hair and rent his fine clothes so that he was no longer recognizable as a royal prince. There followed a period of study with various wise men, a period of increasingly severe discipline. During this time Siddhartha attracted five disciples of his own, so inspired were they by the intensity and single-mindedness of his effort. Finding further progress by way of intellectual inquiry impossible, the young man began a long series of fasts and self-mortifications until he was close to death. One day a farmer's daughter, Sujata, found him like this, emaciated and sick, beneath a great fig tree. She was bringing an offering of rice and milk to the family shrine, but instead she offered it to the dying ascetic.

At this moment Siddhartha realized that this way he would never achieve enlightenment, for both his physical and his mental strength were gone, and all that awaited him was death, to be followed by yet another rebirth in which the struggle would have to begin all over again. He accepted Sujata's offering, upon which his five disciples promptly rebuked him for weakness and left him, bitterly disappointed. The man they left bathed in the near-by river, recovered his strength, and returned to the Bodhi tree and sat there, determined never to move again until the final truth was his. He then entered into a series of temptations sent to him by the forces of evil. Thunder and lightning, fire, flood and darkness were sent to frighten him from his purpose, but he remained unswayed as the storms raged around him. The Evil

One then sent his daughters to distract the prince, but all to no avail, and finally the evil forces retreated. Then, as the night wore on, Siddhartha entered into successive stages of enlightenment, until at dawn the final truth was revealed to him, and he became the Buddha, the Perfect One, the Fully Awakened. He then sang his famous song of victory:

> *Now Housebuilder, thou art seen;*
> *No more shall thou build,*
> *Deceiving with thy artifice.*
> *The beams are shattered and rafters gone.*
> *Beneath it all have I found the truth;*
> *All cravings gone, I see only the round of birth and death,*
> *With sorrow filled.*

A final temptation was sent, for now that he had reached perfect knowledge, the Buddha could leave the round of life, the world of suffering, or he could elect to stay and teach for the benefit of the rest of mankind. He was tempted to leave, for who would understand his teachings? He was now thirty-five years old, and in his whole life he had found no one to teach him the truth . . . who then was likely to listen to him? The world, he was told, was not yet ready, and his sacrifice would be in vain. But on seeing the Buddha hesitate, it is said, the gods wept, and cried 'The world is lost'. The Buddha then determined that even if he could only teach the truth to one or two, the sacrifice would be worthwhile, and he set out for Banaras, an ancient and holy city where he could be sure of finding large numbers engaged in the same quest that had taken him so near to death.

It was near Banaras, in the deer park at Sarnath, that the Buddha set in motion the wheel of law, teaching the Truth of Suffering, the Cause of Suffering, the Truth of Release, and the Way to Release. His first five converts were the disciples who had abandoned him when he accepted Sujata's humble offering of rice and milk. Like them, many others quickly saw the truth of the Way, a middle way that eschews excess at any level, either of self-indulgence or self-mortification. The Order grew as the Buddha travelled through the country preaching. The Buddha even returned to Kapilavastu, and found that his fame had already reached his home and family, and that Yasoda had herself renounced all worldly pleasures and had been following the way of life taught by the Buddha. She sent Rahula, their son, to him, however, asking that he be given his inheritance. For Suddhodana too had been converted, and the throne was now Rahula's, with his father's blessing. The Buddha, however, responded by telling one of his disciples to administer the oath of renunciation to the boy, and Rahula received, in this way, his spiritual inheritance, like his father renouncing a kingdom.

During his teachings the Buddha carefully avoided discussion of God, and of life after death. His teachings were all directed to showing man how to live in this world so that even if he still does not reach enlightenment in this birth, he will be that much closer to it, and by constant effort the round will be shortened and finally brought to an end. To this day Buddhism has been very much a way of life, a way that can be practised by all, rich or poor, regardless of their station in life. Laws were laid down concerning the Order, the admission of initiates, their responsibilities and duties; and the same laws still pertain. The Buddha was reluctant to admit women to the order, but he could not justify their continued exclusion without denying their right and ability to achieve enlightenment as much as any other human being. On finally giving his consent to their admission, however, he prophesied that it would cause a rift in the Order sooner than such dissension would otherwise have made itself felt.

For over forty years Buddha preached his doctrine, and the Order grew and prospered in strength as well as in number. The end came when the Buddha was in his eightieth year. He announced that his body was worn out and no longer worth trying to keep alive. At that time he was travelling with some of his disciples through Kusinara. A local blacksmith, a much despised caste, offered them hospitality in his mango grove and prepared for them a meal which included fat hog's flesh. When the Buddha saw the fat meat he told Cunda to offer it only to him, and whatever he, the Buddha, did not eat was to be buried, that it was not for any others to eat. This was done, and shortly after the meal the Buddha fell ill. He then announced that his time was come and thanked Cunda for providing him with the cause for his final and supreme release. Shortly afterwards the Buddha and his disciples crossed the river, passed through Kusinara, and entered a grove of trees. Between two trees he lay down on his right side, in the 'lion's repose' posture. With a few final words of encouragement to his disciples, the Buddha passed on to Sanggye Sa, removal from all suffering. He had taught all there was to teach, keeping nothing back; the Way was clear for all to follow, if they but wanted to. His work was done.

This was the simple message brought to the world by Gautama, the Buddha. Its profound and immediate impact lay in the fact that its truth was undeniable, and that instead of merely accepting suffering as the very root of life and bemoaning the fact, or merely praying for relief, the Buddha preached a way of release. It was not a way that demanded lifelong training to the exclusion of all other worldly activities, as did most of the great Indian schools of Yoga, nor did it demand a sacrifice of all that was pleasurable in life. It was a way that was immediately practicable to all, a way that counselled moderation rather than renunciation, and a way that promised, and gave, almost immediate results. Our emotions swing like a pendulum, an equal distance to either side of the middle point of total stability, of cessation of movement. If we allow the pendulum to swing too far one way, it will swing just as far the other. If our pleasures are excessive, so will be our sufferings. This is not a statement concerning moral retribution, it is merely a recognition of the relative nature of sensation. When we say something is hot, *how* hot depends on our experience of cold. What is hot to a Tibetan nomad would be chilly to a south Indian. But far more unpleasant than mere heat or cold is a gyration from one to the other. So with emotions and sensations. What Gautama taught was the restriction of extremes, gradually narrowing them down, closer and closer to the point of absolute stability at which point alone will all suffering cease. But even the smallest progress along the path will bring a reduction in suffering.

The appeal was to the masses, not to the few, and it was directed at people who have to live ordinary lives, not at those who seek seclusion. The idea implies, however, that before ultimate stability can be reached, we have to live countless lives, each life, if properly led, bringing us closer to the goal. This was too much for the patience of many who sought a short cut to Paradise. The Buddha did not deny there was any such short cut, he merely denied that it was possible for the bulk of suffering mankind with whom he was concerned. Tantricism offers such a short cut to those who are prepared to devote their whole lives to it. It is said that when Buddha was dying one of his disciples asked him why he had taught nothing of the tantras. The Buddha replied that he had been born of man and woman, and that none born of the flesh was fitted to undertake such a task on the scale his disciples were considering, that is, bringing tantricism to the masses. It was a path full of danger and needed a teacher of absolute purity if it were to be brought to the layman without harming him. Even to be born of woman is to be touched with impurity for it is to know pain and suffering. He promised that one free from such taint would come, not to offer escape from the consequences of one's deeds, but, when the time was ripe, to show how liberation can be hastened. Before then, however, people would have to have mastered the Middle Way.

It was over a thousand years later that Lopon Rinpoche came to bring the tantric teachings to Tibet. His birth was miraculous. Somewhere in Urgyen, in the middle of the eighth century A.D., a lotus in the Indus River was seen growing to abnormal proportions. When the bud finally burst open, there, on the inside, sat a singularly beautiful boy, eight years old. The aged and childless King Indrabhuti was travelling in that region, having gone in quest of the jewel *Yishin Norbu* that grants all desires. When, armed with the jewel, he saw this wonderful boy seated in the lotus, he immediately asked that the boy be given to him as a son. In this way Lopon Rinpoche was brought up, like the Buddha, in a royal court, surrounded by luxuries. Also like the Buddha he married, but he married without the consent of the girl's parents, and they had already betrothed her to another. He finally resolved to renounce his life at the royal court, although by then his father had already abdicated in his favour and made him king, so that he himself could end his life in religious contemplation. Despite the protests of his people, the young king insisted on his own renunciation, and appeared on the palace roof to bid farewell, already dressed in rags. But as he stood there, a skull and a flaming thunderbolt appeared in one hand and a three-pronged spear in the other. As the crowd gazed at these magical emblems the sword reached out and killed a man while the three-pronged spear touched and killed a woman and child. The reverence of the crowd was turned to violent anger, and they would have killed the young king had not his old father come from seclusion to intercede. Lopon Rinpoche was then banished from the country in which he was born, and began his wanderings in quest of knowledge.

It is said that he visited all the great religious centres and teachers, including those of the Bönpoba, and received the most secret teachings from the goddesses that haunt burial places. There he learned to face the most terrible and horrifying experiences that man's mind can conjure up, and to recognize them, presented as fiendish realities, as mere conjurations. Every kind of horror was thrust upon him, but he survived them all, and so gained control of the demons.

Again by secret initiations in burial grounds he learned the mysteries of the heavens, bringing the very planets under his control, for knowledge is power. And at the more mundane religious centres and universities he learned mastery of the earthly sciences. He now began to roam the countryside, performing the most remarkable miracles, exorcizing demons wherever men's minds created them. The very display of power that is so shunned by other Buddhist schools was essential to the work of Lopon Rinpoche. If he was to defeat the evil that men created, he had to demonstrate a power equally awesome. Nowhere does he appear as a saint in the usual sense of the word, implying a person who is mild and gentle. This is not the tantric way. Lopon Rinpoche was master of the extremes, passionate and violent, but always using his passion and violence to work good. On one occasion he stopped at a tavern to drink. He drank continuously for several days without paying. Finally the woman who owned the place threatened to have him punished if he did not settle the account. He asked her if she would grant him until sundown, and she agreed. Upon this he took his magic dagger, or Phurbu, and drove it into the floor by the doorway, so that it cast a shadow. But the shadow never moved, and the sun stayed where it was for day upon day, and all the while Lopon Rinpoche continued drinking, holding the tavernkeeper to her word. When people complained, he said that if they would fill his bowl with alms, he would then pay the account and leave. They did so, he paid the account, withdrew his dagger from the floor, and the sun set. The inn-keeper became his disciple.

In Sahor he took as his wife Mandarava, daughter of the king. He made her his *shakti*, or spiritual consort, for she too was an initiate. Their behaviour outraged the king who had them burned at the stake; but the fire turned into water and the stake into a lotus, and safely seated in the lotus were Lopon Rinpoche and his shakti.

So many and so great were his miracles that none questioned his supremacy. It was he alone, Shantirakshita advised King Trisong Detsan, who could defeat the demons that controlled Tibet and bring knowledge and wisdom to the people. Guru Rinpoche, recognizing that Tibet was a challenge he had to face, accepted the king's invitation, and set out for Samye, two days' journey south-east of Lhasa. Entering Tibet from Nepal, Lopon Rinpoche made his way subduing demons all along the route. He was met outside Lhasa by an escort sent by the king to bring him to Samye, and this occasioned yet another miracle. The horses were all thirsty, and no water was to be had at the spot. Lopon Rinpoche promptly struck a rock with his stick, and water flowed from the spot. I have seen it myself, and water still flows from the solid rock from a point above the level of a man's head. We call it *Shongpa Lhachu*, or 'Horse's Water of the Gods'.

Samye had been chosen for the meeting place because it was here that the king and Shantirakshita had been attempting to build the first Buddhist monastery. But no matter how hard they worked during the daytime, laying wood and stones, during the night the demons came and threw the walls down. The king rode out to greet the Rinpoche, but when the king showed that he expected him to bow down to him, Lopon Rinpoche said that as he had come to do good for Tibet, to cast out the demons and bring knowledge, it was the king who should bow down. He pointed a finger, there was thunder and lightning, and the king's garments burst into flame. The king and the whole court bowed before Lopon Rinpoche, and perhaps it was from this moment that the real rule of religion began in Tibet.

Lopon Rinpoche proceeded to exorcize the demons that caused the ground to shake at Samye, destroying the walls as soon as they were built; the ground became firm and the monastery was built. It stood as built until not long ago when it was partly destroyed by fire. I visited it and saw a number of the books that were translated at that time, for as soon as the building was completed the work of translation of Buddhist scriptures into Tibetan began once again.

The building, perhaps the greatest in Tibet, was planned as a representation of the universe. In the centre the main temple represented Mount Rirab, while to the north, south, east and west, four other large temples represented the four worlds; smaller temples represented the islands that separate the worlds, and there were two farther temples representing the sun and the moon. The main temple was dedicated to Chenresig.

From here Lopon Rinpoche travelled all over Tibet, some say for fifty years, exorcizing demons and forcing them to work for the good of Tibet instead of against it. In this way he took the already existing beliefs of the Tibetans, beliefs that were by no means a part of the doctrine preached by Buddha, and used them to bring the people to an understanding of the truth. He showed them that evil is merely the counterbalance of what we call good and can be converted to the benefit of mankind. The many sacred paintings and prayer banners in Tibet have representations of demons and fierce deities, but their power has been converted for the welfare of man, and still in all its might it is used for the destruction of ignorance. What often seem to be different deities in fact are really different aspects of the same deity, and all are aspects, ultimately, of the one single truth. The esoteric doctrine was too elevated to expect ordinary Tibetans to grasp it, so Lopon Rinpoche used the prevailing imagery and set them on the path.

The question of the reality of demons, or evil forces, is not an easy one to answer, and many volumes of Buddhist literature are devoted to it. It might be said, though, that we believe there are various levels of reality, of which the external world is one. But the external world itself represents different things to different people (for the senses of each of us tell us different things), so that even the external world is not quite what it seems. It is in one respect a mere response to our senses, a creation of our minds. This is not to deny it, but rather to show how personal a thing the world around us is, so much of it being given colour and shape by our own imaginations.

Why then should we grant any less a degree of reality to demons, ghosts, forces of power, which again many say are mere creations of our minds? If a mind creates a demon, it exists for that mind. The self-created image is another level of reality, and the quarrel often comes in a discussion of whether it is possible to pass from one level to the other, from the physical to the mental or the other way around. There is no doubt that for the adept performing the rite of Chöd, there is a very terrible reality to the demoniacal form that advances upon him to sever his head. There is even something of the same reality in the imaginings of the person who wakes with a start in the middle of the night and strains to see a form in the darkness. A form is expected, and the attempt to see it can create it, though few would expect the form to have corporeal reality. However, in his trance, or in his semi-sleep, the individual concerned is already in the other world, and the reality of his vision is as great as the reality of this page in the waking world. Thus far Buddhists who are not tantric practitioners would have little quarrel with the tantricists. But the next step, for the tantric practitioner, is to develop the power to materialize mental images so that they have substance in the physical world and even to dematerialize physical images and relegate them to the mental world. It is rather like Bishop Berkeley's saying that a chestnut tree ceases to have existence when nobody is observing it, becoming a mere mental image at best; and if nobody is thinking of it then it does not even have that reality.*

Here there is real disagreement, but it is still relative for the Buddhist because we all believe that there is one ultimate reality, knowable only through liberation from this illusory round of birth and rebirth. Nonetheless, Lopon Rinpoche was dealing with a simple people who credited their demons with a power of their own and an existence of their own. They also believed that the demons could take material form whenever they wished, to trick the unwary who might be relying on charms effective against immaterial beings. Lopon Rinpoche was well qualified to deal with the situation, for belonging to the great tantric school, and being a master of the tantras, he was able to create, at will, images to defeat images. Also in accordance with the tantric school, he was held to have the power of materialization and dematerialization. Armed with no more than his Dorje, or symbolic thunderbolt, and the power of his mind, Lopon Rinpoche worked his miracles.

The tantricists consciously use imagery, mental and physical. During the performance of a rite the hands perform certain gestures and assume positions each of which has a hidden

---

*There is a famous limerick about this proposition:

> There was a young man who said God
> Must think it exceedingly odd,
> That this Chestnut Tree,
> Continues to be,
> When there's no one about in the Quad.

(To which the reply came –)

> Young Man, your astonishment's odd,
> For I'm always about in the Quad;
> That's why the tree,
> Continues to be
> Since observed by
>
> Yours Faithfully,
> God.

significance. But in his trancelike state, these symbols become realities to the practitioner. He may be content to leave it at that, but if there is need, he can transfer the images from the mental world to the physical world. It was in this way, it is thought, that Lopon Rinpoche brought water from the rock, or stopped the sun from setting. There are even certain tantric rites that demand such accomplishment, though they are not performed for display, but only as a necessary part of self-training and discipline. Such a rite is *Rolang*, in which a corpse is temporarily revived in order to effect a transfer of power. In effect the corpse is activated by a demon brought into it by the rite; if the practitioner loses control, then the demon is able to use the material body of the corpse to destroy the living. This is plainly different from the Chöd rite, in which all the dreadful imagery is confined to the mental world of the adept. Even so, we believe, if that adept loses control for an instant, he might unwittingly effect a transference of the creations of his mind from his mind world to the body world. Such are the dangers of tantricism, and this is the reason why the teachings are restricted to the most able and devout students.

Far from being magical or even mystical, tantricism is essentially pragmatic, and it seeks a pragmatic explanation for all phenomena. As for the assertions that it is a perverted doctrine that is contrived to permit unlicensed indulgence in sexual and other forms of debauchery, this can only be said by those who have no knowledge of tantricism. There are many of us in Tibet who disapprove of tantra, and my own Gelukpa, or Yellow Hat, sect forbids its public practice. But that is not because we do not believe the tantras are a holy and truly spiritual path – it is because we believe that this path is too dangerous, and following the teachings of the Buddha, we try to concern ourselves with humanity as a whole, not with the very few adepts for whom the tantras are suitable. Sexual energy and narcotic stimulation are recognized as being sources of power in the physical world. Sexual union in particular is considered as the greatest creative act possible in this material world, and it is thought of as embodying the whole principle of creativity. To this the Tibetan Lamèd school of tantricism have added the dual principle of preservation and destruction. The appropriate rites, to the uninitiated, read as though the participants were expected to indulge not only in sexual activity but also in an orgy of blood. In almost any temple one may see sacred figures of deities, male and female, locked in sexual embrace; and further, they and other deities may be represented in either a peaceful or fierce aspect. These images symbolize the principles involved, and help the mind to concentrate on the principles, not to induce the body to activity. The rites are performed with similar symbolism, and long before the novice is introduced to them he is expected to have attained complete mastery over his physical impulses. Any thought that the rites implied licence to indulge in actual sexual activity, or to commit actual blood sacrifice, would be considered as the greatest heresy. The power of sex cannot be denied, even by the most prudish, for they too were born by its power. The tantras try to grasp the basic principle involved and so arrive speedily at a true understanding of the nature of being.

Tantricism is based on yogic practice, and the slightest knowledge of Yoga is enough to demonstrate the extent of self-discipline demanded, for tantricism goes far beyond Yoga. It is probably the most severe self-discipline ever demanded of man in spiritual endeavour.

As sound consists of 'waves', of which only those of a certain length are audible to the human ear, so matter is only visible or tangible within a certain range of wavelengths. If the wavelength can be changed, so can the visibility or tangibility. It is stated in simple terms that might seem crude but which nonetheless have their counterpart in modern science. One of the powers that comes with yogic training is the power to alter those wavelengths.

I have studied some parts of the tantra myself, in Lhasa, and I found it very helpful. I did not study it with the idea of gaining power, or for public display, or as a way of shortening the Path, because the Gelukpa do not believe that this is what Buddha wanted. I practised it to give myself more discipline, to make myself stronger and wiser. I found it very good. In particular I studied Lamèd tantricism, but although we are allowed to study privately, if we wish, we must not practise it in public, nor must we teach it before we achieve the final goal. All I can say is that I saw nothing bad in it at all; if anything the discipline and self-control demanded is even more than with other, less secret, disciplines. I do not wish to say more because such discussion is meant only for initiates; with others we are forbidden to discuss tantra.

The most obvious and undeniable justification of Lopon Rinpoche's tantric practices lies in the results he achieved. He himself had long since renounced all the pleasures of the flesh when he left the royal court that had been his home. The wives he subsequently took were taken as *Yum*, the female principle through which the male energy is released. They were not taken to provide physical pleasure but rather to enable his spiritual force to be manifest. He was a man of the utmost purity and goodness, and for those who question his methods we can only say that it was during his stay in Tibet that the first Buddhist monastery was established, that the baser (more physical) practices of the old Bön religion were outlawed, that the Tibetan people were shown a practical path to spiritual achievement, virtually being taken in a generation from barbarism to a level of culture that, while still low on the material level, was as high as man has ever aspired to on the spiritual level. Further, although he himself was a practitioner of tantricism, he did not preach tantricism as the only way, or even recommend it for the masses. It was merely the weapon he used to combat the darkness he found, and to bring light. This is a proper use for the power that tantric practice gives one. It is the only proper use. Lopon Rinpoche brought this to Tibet in addition to the Middle Path taught by the Buddha, so that we now had the Middle Path for the mass of the people to follow, including monks, and this esoteric tantric path for the few who were strong enough to undertake it, and who could be relied on to use such powers as they acquired for the good of their fellow creatures.

When Lopon Rinpoche left we are told by the histories that it was to the great sorrow of all, and that a great multitude assembled to witness his departure. He summoned a chariot from the sky and, accompanied by his two consorts, rode off to the south, to the 'yak trail' continent (India), to deal with the demons there. Many Tibetans believe that he is still there, using his powers for the good of the people.

Not everyone was sorry to see Lopon Rinpoche leave, however, for he had demonstrated beyond doubt the superiority of Buddhism over Bön, defeating Bön priests even at their own arts. The great monastery of Samye, which he helped to found and build, became the centre for the promulgation of a form of Buddhism even more inimical to Bön than was the tantricism of the Lopon. A number of monks of the Theg Man Buddhist school, coldly intellectual, were brought there from India, and under their guidance the first seven Tibetan monks were initiated. The number was limited to seven, at first, to see how well the Tibetan people took to monastic life. All seven passed every test with ease and enthusiasm, set out to spread Buddhism even further, and to found fresh monasteries that in turn would become like centres of the new faith.

The most prominent of these Tibetans was Namnang, who went to India and studied further there, bringing back more teachings to add to the rapidly mounting body of Buddhist literature. Tibet was, in fact, to become an important repository of Buddhist scriptures. The translations were exceptionally meticulous, as we can tell by comparing them with such originals as still exist. When the Moghuls invaded India, sacking and pillaging temples and monasteries, a great deal of the original Buddhist literature was lost or destroyed. By then, however, a large amount of it had already been copied and was safely preserved in the monasteries of Tibet. Although Namnang brought back teachings to further the cause of the Theg Man sect then at Samye, he himself was a self-professed follower of Lopon Rinpoche, and he fell under criticism from all directions. The Theg Man monks regarded him as a heretic, for to them even the Theg Chen teachings were anathema, let alone the teachings of the tantra. On the other side the Bön, who had been busy learning what they could from the tantric teachings themselves, and adapting their own beliefs accordingly, suspected any Buddhist tantricist as a likely enemy and rival.

Namnang's death as a heretic was demanded, and the king had to use all his wiles to save the monk whom he respected as Lopon Rinpoche's disciple. It was his own wife who betrayed him, for the Queen was an ardent supporter of the Bönpoba. From the moment Lopon Rinpoche made her husband, the great Trisong Detsan, bow to religion, she saw the threat that this new religion held for the monarchy. Eventually the outcry was so great that the king had to exile Namnang to eastern Tibet, where he could continue his work unopposed.

Five more students who were sent to seek teachers in India, although they had received their education from the Theg Man monks at Samye, they all chose a tantric master who gave them initiation into the secret lore of the tantras. When this was learned in Tibet, their recall was demanded. Only one of them answered the call, and he was killed by a demon on his way. The king was delighted when the others finally arrived safely, and he would shut himself up with them in order to learn from them more of tantric practice. Once again it was his wife who exposed him. She did not believe his assertions that he and the monks were merely engaged in deep meditation and that was the reason for locking themselves in. She contrived to spy on them and reported on all that she had seen – human skulls and thighbones, human skins and entrails, and a sea of blood.

The king was once again forced to concede defeat, and the supporters of the Bönpoba took another step forward. They were now officially accepted on equal terms with the Buddhists, and they had monks living at Samye monastery itself, also engaged in translating Bön literature brought in from Shang Shung.

But despite the size of the monastery, quarters were too close and religious practices too different. The Buddhists were particularly offended by the Bön custom of offering animal sacrifice. For the priests, to whom all life was equally sacred, this was a horror they would not tolerate. They informed Trisong Detsan that they would leave and return to India, whereupon the king promptly issued an order prohibiting all forms of animal sacrifice.

Tibet

When Trisong Detsan died, his wife must have hoped for a more tolerant attitude towards the Bönpoba from her sons. The oldest, who succeeded his father, proved as much in favour of Buddhism as his mother was of Bön. Mune Tsanpo, as he was called, pursued a vigorous military career, for Buddhism had not yet effected the ultimate conversion of this warlike people into a people who loved peace. But at the same time he pushed forward an energetic programme of social reform. Once again land was redistributed, and it is said that Mune Tsanpo also redistributed all other forms of wealth, making the poor and the rich equal. His mother, now regarded as the embodiment of evil, poisoned her son, and made his brother king in his stead. Sena Lag, the new king, continued to favour Buddhism, however, and encouraged further translations, patronizing the Buddhists in every way he could up to the time of his death. He had two sons, one of whom, Lang Darma, followed the path of Bön. It was Ralpachen, however, who took the throne, and he was more active than ever in spreading Buddhism. He offered rewards of land and wealth, for the establishment of monasteries, to those who performed outstanding services to Buddhism, thus encouraging the expansion of the work of translation already in hand. In fact it reached such proportions and became so complex that a new standardized form of canonical literature had to be devised, which remains in use to the present day. He encouraged Tibetans to learn various arts and crafts associated with Buddhism, such as religious painting and image-making, and he standardized weights and measures. He consolidated Tibet's political position by signing a treaty of non-aggression with China, and Tibet seemed on the verge of a truly golden age when Ralpachen began to let his fervour carry him too far. His attempts to equalize the rich and poor failed for each time it was done the rich became rich again, and the poor lost what wealth had come to them. Yet Ralpachen persisted with the attempt no less than three times. Further he began oppressing the Bön, at first by insisting that every family, whether Buddhist or Bön, contribute to the upkeep of a monk, then by instigating a series of brutal punishments against any who committed offences against

Buddhists. The court around him was still largely Bön, and they now conspired against the king. Perhaps they saw the end of the monarchy in sight, for Ralpachen eventually went to the extent of allowing his hair to grow long so that when monks came to visit him he could bow to the ground and let them walk over his hair, which he could then spread out for them to sit on. This abasement of the kingship to the monkhood was too much for Lang Darma, who began to conspire with other Bönpoba. First the king's brother, who had become a priest, was forcibly banished under a pretence; then a scandal was put about that the king's wife was engaged in an affair with his chief minister, who was also his staunchest supporter in the struggle to further the cause of Buddhism. The king had the minister put to death, believing the story, and the queen killed herself. Now the time was ripe, and Lang Darma had his own brother killed by hired assassins who twisted his head off his shoulders as he slept.

Lang Darma seized the throne, and a period of darkness followed in which it seemed that Buddhism had lost all the ground it had won at such pains. Temples and libraries were destroyed; Samye itself was sacked, and it was only through the prompt action of the monks in removing sacred literature to places of hiding that all the patient work of translation was not lost. The teaching of Buddhism was forbidden, and all Buddhist monks were forced either to flee the country or to adopt Bön beliefs and take an active part in Bön practices.

Lang Darma went even further in his religious persecution than Ralpachen had done, and many of the fleeing monks were hacked to death. Before long there was not a single Buddhist monk left in the land, and all worship had been banned under pain of death. But the new faith could not be exterminated so easily, and it lay smouldering beneath this oppression, in the hearts of many laymen. After only six years, Lang Darma met his own violent death. A Buddhist monk, Palgyi Dorje, who had remained behind when the others fled, taking refuge in a cave named Trag Yarba, had a vision telling him it was time to rid Tibet of the demon incarnate, Lang Darma. The vision also showed him the means. He took a robe that was black on the

173

outside and white on the inside. He took a white horse and with charcoal he made it black. Donning the black robe, concealing its white side, he hid a bow and three arrows in the long folds of the sleeves. He made his way to Lhasa, and took part in the dance of the Black Hat dancers which the king was attending.

It is said that he twice tried to shoot the king, and each time he failed. Then with his last arrow he succeeded, and Lang Darma fell dead. Palgyi Dorje took advantage of the commotion and of the fact that nobody suspected a Black Hat dancer of this sacrilegious crime and made his escape. By the time it was realized that it was one of the dancers, and a chase was set up for the black-robed assassin, Palgyi Dorje had turned his cloak inside out, so that it showed pure white, and by riding his horse through the river he washed off the charcoal and the horse too became white. In this way he threw off pursuit and returned to his cave. Eventually the search reached him and a number of people entered the cave to see if he was there. He hid in one of the darkest recesses. One searcher, a minister, groping in that corner, felt his hand light upon a human chest. He could not see the face, but by the heavy beating of the heart he knew it was the killer. But now the thought came to him that perhaps it was not a crime to kill as evil a man as Lang Darma, and pretending he had found nothing he passed on. When the hue and cry subsided, Palgyi Dorje fled eastward to Amdo and there began a life of penance for his act.

The country fell into a state of utter disorder, and the kingship dissolved. The nation divided once more into a number of petty chiefdoms, each fighting with the next. Buddhism had been dealt a blow by the expulsion of the monks, but it still lived on in the hearts of all those who had been converted. Even the minister who felt the assassin's pounding heart was touched with compassion, and it was compassion that Tibet needed at this moment, more than ever. Lang Darma's excesses had dealt an even deadlier blow, however, at the growing power of the Bönpoba, who reaped all the blame for the period of darkness that followed. For some seventy years Khabachen, the Land of Snows, seemed once more to be a land without the religion of Buddha.

CHAPTER EIGHT

The Rebirth of Religion

The Buddha's teachings, reduced to embers,
Were fanned to life again in Domé
The monkhood reformed,
Religion spread once more throughout the land.
It spread to U and Tsang.
For this the shepherd La-chenpo,
And the keba misum, *the wise men three,*
The monks, Mar, Yo, and Tsang,
Are venerated by all the people of Khabachen.

– from DEBTHER DMARPO

With the departure of Lopon Rinpoche and the death of Shantirakshita, Chinese religious influence began to grow in strength. The Indian scholars, without a strong leader, found themselves outmatched by an influx of highly organized Chinese monks, preaching their own form of Buddhism. This was much tinged with Taoist philosophy, the basic teaching of which was non-activity. Activity of any kind is the one barrier, they claimed, that divides us from full illumination. Only by stilling our minds and bodies to a point of non-sentience can we open ourselves to divine illumination. Then it will come flooding in upon us, suddenly and completely. There are no half-measures, no gradual steps. Above all there must be no good deeds, for the activity, mental and physical, involved in good deeds, is as harmful to our spiritual progress as bad deeds.

This teaching, striking at the root of all that the Indians had worked for, caused such bitterness between the Chinese and Indian teachers that there was danger of fighting. To settle the matter the king (Trisong Detsan was still alive then) arranged for a debate between the two factions. The Indians were lucky in having been able to entice Kamlashila to become their leader. He saw the dangers of the Chinese doctrine, under which passions could never be conquered, because no effort being allowed they would quickly take over mind and body. He pointed out that according to such a doctrine a man unconscious through drink would be nearer than any to enlightenment. Before the debate, the king made both sides agree that the loser would leave the country, since they were so mutually unacceptable and opposed. The Indian victory was resounding, and the Chinese left. From that moment all Chinese hopes of exerting religious influence were lost, and by decree the Indian school, known as the Nagarjuna School, became the only lawful form of Buddhism in

Tibet. Yet in a curious way it was only through the help of two Chinese monks that the awakening from the age of darkness, which took place in the east, came to be.

Shortly after the great persecution began, three monks who lived alone in a small monastery at Palchen Chubori, and had not heard of the events that had taken place, were astounded to see a monk pass by on a hunt. They upbraided him for doing such a sinful thing, but he told them of what had happened, and said that he had been ordered to hunt, just as all other monks had been ordered to perform acts against their religious beliefs. The three monks hurriedly collected their mules and loaded them with all the sacred scriptures from their monastery and made their escape. First they fled to Ngari, in western Tibet, and from there they made the long journey eastward through Mongolia to Horyul, where they tried to preach the faith. But not knowing the language they found little success, and so descended into Amdo, where the persecution had not reached (it was to Amdo that Lang Darma's assassin, the monk Palgyi Dorje had also fled). They formed a nucleus, preaching and studying, trying to repair the harm that had been done.

Some shepherds from the Yellow River heard of these religious men, and one in particular was much attracted, even though, some say, he was a follower of the old Bön religion. He went to the three wise teachers and begged them to let him study, saying that he felt an urge he could not explain to become a monk. The three told him that to become a monk one had to study, and they doubted that he could reach the necessary level. The shepherd, La-chenpo, insisted, and the three took him in, giving him the whole of the *Dulwa*, the forbidden Vinaya scriptures, to master. They told him that if he could master that, they would indeed accept him as a monk. La-chenpo studied hard, and within one year he had mastered the Dulwa; he now sought ordination.

According to Buddhist law five monks are required to give ordination, so La-chenpo was obliged to seek out two more. The persecution had been such that most monks had fled to areas safer even than Amdo, or Domé as it was sometimes called.

La-chenpo heard that living close by was the old monk who had killed Lang Darma, and was now living in seclusion, atoning for his sin. He went to Palgyi Dorje and asked him if he would help, but the old man replied that having committed the sin of murder, even though it was to rid the country of evil and so with good intent, he was unfit to act as a monk. However, there were two Chinese monks not far away, for Amdo is on the border of China, and it was suggested that La-chenpo should seek their help. They finally agreed, and together with the three monks who had fled from the persecution, they ordained the first Tibetan monk since the calamity had fallen on the country. From this moment onward there was indeed no looking back. Word spread that ordination was once more being given in the remote province of Amdo, and laymen began flocking there. Five years after his ordination, Gonpa Rabsal, as La-chenpo became known, himself helped in the ordination of ten more Tibetan students, and since by then the political situation in Tibet had deteriorated still further, and the authority of the anti-Buddhist Bön rulers now extended no further than Lhasa, all decided that it was time to risk the danger and return to their homeland. They made their headquarters at Samye, and from there slowly began to revive the message of Buddhism, doing their utmost to purify it of the various heresies that had crept in encouraging moral laxness, even self-indulgence.

When the Lhasa Bön regime finally fell through internal dissension, one of Lang Darma's great-grandsons went to western Tibet to seek his fortunes anew there. He built up a considerable empire, and on his death it was divided into three sections, of which the land of Guge formed one. The son who inherited Guge became the second hero of the great revival of Buddhism in Tibet. He himself became a monk, as did two of his own sons. Under the name of Lha-lama Yesheho, this royal monk again invited scholars from India, and sent Tibetans to the Indian universities of Vikramashila and Nalanda for study. Like Gonpa Rabsal, Yesheho was greatly concerned by a third Buddhist movement that originated among the laymen who for two generations or more had been left without any priestly guidance. They were subject to all the most extravagant inventions of doctrine; charlatans 'discovering' scriptures and preaching a debased form of tantricism, misinterpretations of the already questionable teachings of unorthodox forms of Buddhism such as that taught by the Chinese before their expulsion, and of course an assimilation of Bön practice.

Yesheho felt that to combat this a really great teacher was needed, so he dispatched a noted translator as envoy to north India, with a gift of gold and an invitation for the great Indian pandit Dipankara Srijnana to come to Tibet. The pandit, better known in Tibet as Atisha, declined. He was of such renown and was such an important part of the University of Vikramashila that his followers there refused to allow him to go. Lhalama Yesheho was not to be discouraged, and he immediately organized a campaign throughout Tibet to raise enough money to make it possible for Atisha to leave his post. He himself was leading one such expedition in a country called Garlog, which we think was Nepal, when his party was attacked and he was captured. Such gold as he had with him was taken, and the king of Garlog held Yesheho to ransom for his weight in gold.

The royal monk's brother set about raising this enormous sum, and having amassed it he himself brought it to the capital of Garlog, where Yesheho was held in prison. The king announced that it was short by the size of Yesheho's head, and that he would not release the prisoner. He did, however, allow the two brothers to meet. Yesheho had grown old and weak through maltreatment, and he urged his brother not to try to save him, for he could not have many years left. He gave instructions that the gold already collected should be used to bring Atisha to Tibet and so do more good than his own feeble life could do. He would not be dissuaded and shortly after the departure of the party, allegedly to collect the remaining gold, he was put to death.

Eventually the party arrived at Vikramashila, and presented the gold to Atisha, telling him of the sacrifice of the royal monk, and urging him to come and help restore Buddhism in Tibet. Atisha was anxious to comply, but still his own followers at the university would not allow him to go. He used the gold to establish various schools, and sent the Tibetans who had come to him out to these and other schools. Then on the excuse of visiting them, he began to absent himself from Vikramashila for short periods, gradually allaying suspicion, until finally he was able to leave with a small party and, joining the others, make the journey into Guge. He left word that he would return to Vikramashila, but it was not to be. Atisha gave his life to Tibet, dying there some seventeen years later, in his seventies.

Like so many of the other great teachers, Atisha came from a prominent and wealthy family in Bengal. He studied in many different schools, both Mdo (sutras) and Gyud (tantras). He travelled as far as Burma in the east and Afghanistan in the west in search of knowledge, and it is said he was thirty years old before he took his vows as a monk. It was just such a man that Tibet needed. Unlike Lopon Rinpoche, who had been the right kind of man for his time, Atisha was very much a man of the world, in the sense that he had lived nearly half his life before taking vows, being a father of nine children. He was also a man of exceptional knowledge and experience, and, on top of it, evidently a man of great charm and boundless compassion. On arrival at Tholing, the monastic centre of western Tibet, Atisha soon attracted students and scholars from all over the country. He worked closely with the great translator, Rinchen Sangpo, and in his teachings he struck an ideal mean between the doctrines of the sutras and tantras. He saw the terrible state of degeneration that had come about through a misunderstanding of the tantras, but he refused to give in to those who counselled that they should be abolished. He set about teaching the tantras as only a philosopher of his stature could, elevating them to the highest spiritual level, removing them from any but symbolic connection with physical action. He himself, however, advised that only two of the four tantric initiations should generally be considered since the other two could mislead the aspirant. Even so there was considerable opinion against Atisha, and mistrust of his support for the tantric school. A number of scandals were spread about him, and still he persisted. At the same time that he supported the tantras, however, Atisha also taught the pure

Theg Chen doctrine, free of all tantric elements. One of his greatest contributions to Tibetan Buddhist literature is a discourse in pure Theg Chen tradition upon the different goals that man may set himself and their relative value. In this work he also dealt with Theg Man and tantric Buddhism, showing how each could be of use to man at different stages of his development. Here he clearly said that the tantras should only be followed by those who had passed through the previous stages of ethical training (Theg Man) and philosophical reflection (Theg Chen), and that the actual practice of tantra was a purely spiritual affair, in no way calling for a female counterpart or the use of intoxicants, and in no way permissible for the selfish goal of self-advancement.

Despite his work at Tholing teaching monastic students, translating, and generally systematizing anew the basic teachings of Tibetan Buddhism, Atisha found time to travel among the laymen of the country, preaching and giving whatever help he could. Always he strove to avoid extremes; if an intellectually ambitious student asked him for personal guidance, instead of taking him into the heights of Theg Chen philosophy, Atisha would teach him about purity and love. A devotee brimming over with the emotional desire to worship would be given food for the intellect. What Atisha taught was a thorough development of the whole being of man, physical, emotional and mental – all there together, and only together, making for genuine spiritual advancement.

This synthetic approach he elaborated in his private teachings given to his chief disciple, Dromton. It was in effect a reform of the old teachings, introducing a much tighter discipline and guarding against intellectual as well as physical extremism. It was also the beginning of sectarianism, and the reform sect so founded became known as Kadampa, and was to lead directly to the great reform sect later instituted by Tsong Khapa the Gelukpa.

More monasteries were established throughout the country, and soon after Atisha's arrival in Tholing Buddhism in Tibet had not only revived but had attracted more followers than ever. After a number of years in western Tibet, Atisha travelled to

Lhasa and worked on the many books that had been re-established in the library of Samye. He was surprised to find there many Sanskrit works that were not even available in India. He continued teaching, constantly striving to raise Buddhism to the highest possible plane, even for the layman. It is said that Chenresig, Lord of Compassion, appeared to him twice, declaring that he was going to make Tibet his abode, but Atisha's life was singularly free of visions and miracles. Yet his teaching, however intellectually profound, was touched with a true Buddhist love for all living things, and Atisha perhaps more than anyone gave Tibetan Buddhism, and the Tibetan people, the character they have today.

By the time Atisha died, in the middle of the eleventh century A.D., Buddhism in Tibet had grown to such proportions that there were serious problems of organization. No longer was there any central king who could carry out reforms on a national scale, and the rulers of the petty chiefdoms were still subject to the power of the Bön nobility. There was an equal lack of religious centralization. The Kadampa sect founded by Atisha and Dromton was not the only one. Two other disciples of Atisha, finding the severe discipline not to their taste, and wishing to reintroduce at least some of the old familiar deities, founded the Kargyupa and Sakyapa sects. Those who had not been convinced at all by the teachings of Atisha and followed the old belief became known as the Nyingmapa, the Old Sect. The Bön beliefs and practices found a ready home there, for this Old Sect was weakened by the number and quality of all those who had followed Atisha's teachings. The Nyingmapa strengthened their position from time to time by 'discovering' still further scriptures, or Terma, hidden in remote places, allegedly writings of Lopon Rinpoche. In this way they reintroduced, as Buddhism, many old Bön rites, and the Bön of today consider themselves closer to the Nyingmapa than to any other Buddhist sect.

Again and again the great tantric teachings were perverted and abused, yet still there were those who, recognizing their spiritual potential, felt that Atisha had gone too far in subordinating them. One of his followers, Marpa, in particular felt the need to settle once and for all the disputes that constantly arose around these teachings. He had visited India three times, studying under various masters, including Naropa, disciple of the famous Tilopa who had been initiated into the highest mysteries of the patronage of Nagarjuna himself, and through the medium of a sorceress. Not one story recounts Tilopa as having studied under any earthly teacher. Even though his disciples – Naropa, and Marpa after him – had all, unlike Tilopa, studied long and hard, their eventual initiation was similarly mystic, and the tradition has continued to the present day. The power conveyed by the initiation is so great that it has never been set down in writing but has been passed on by purely oral tradition, from master to disciple, protected by oaths of secrecy.

The secret initiation comes only after the longest and most arduous period of training, physical and moral, demanded by any discipline. Once acquired, however, this extreme asceticism need not necessarily be continued. In this way our knowledge of Marpa as a teacher in Tibet gives us a picture of an apparently worldly man. He was married and fond of good living. He is frequently depicted as excessively corpulent, not always sober, and given to bad temper. This does not prevent him from being, even today, a greatly revered figure. Each holder of this secret teaching has the responsibility for passing it on to one who has been tested to the utmost. It is up to each one to devise his own ways of establishing the worthiness of his disciples and of selecting only the highest. Marpa's way was to assume as unsaintly a form as he could and behave not only in an unsaintly manner but on occasions even to go against the most fundamental Buddhist laws. It is clear, after the fact, that never did he actually do any harm, but at the time only a disciple who had the most unquestioning faith in his master would have ever stayed with him. Such a disciple there was, and only one. He became one of Tibet's most loved and respected figures of all time, the saint and poet Milarepa.

With his other disciples Marpa had equally effective though less drastic methods of training, for they were not destined to hold the secret but rather to become scholars and teachers of the

Kargyupa sect. This sect attached much less importance to the nontantric scriptures than had been recommended by Atisha, and also it relied much less on the rigid monastic discipline that had been a cardinal point of Atisha's reform. On the other hand it is no less firm in advocating the most rigorous moral training before the commencement of any tantric instruction or practice. The instruction, under Marpa's guidance, combined the highest forms of tantricism as taught in different schools, and ordered them into four successive stages. The first is the method of acquiring an illusory body and the ability to transfer consciousness, the basis of the art of dying and acquiring a good rebirth. The second stage teaches the method by which the illusory nature of all phenomena, of all existence, is directly realized, rather than merely reasoned, and by which the aspirant acquires the power to control his subconscious when in the dream state. This again is directed towards securing a better rebirth, for during the dream state of Bardo, between death and rebirth, the subconscious is subject to many illusory temptations to which it may succumb, if not specially prepared. The third stage of Marpa's four successive orders gives the method of realization of the absolute emptiness of all self, subjective and objective. Practised together with the method for obtaining an illusory body, this grants the aspirant the 'Triple Body of Enlightenment'. The fourth and final stage concerns the much-discussed, and abused, inner source of mystic power in man, the *Tummo-me*. This is the direct path to the realization of the Supreme Truth, and can only be undertaken after mastery of the other three stages.

In order to ensure that both the preservation of knowledge and the continuation of spiritual practice should be guaranteed, Marpa set disciples aside for the one or the other. He himself worked ardently as a translator and continued to appear, to those whose inclinations were intellectual rather than spiritual, as a more than worldly man. It is perhaps because of the excessiveness of this aspect that he revealed his spiritual powers to certain of his closest disciples by demonstrating the power of Entering the Dead. Otherwise his life and example must have seemed unremarkable to all but a few. However much he may have been respected for his intellectual ability, there was little or nothing of an outward nature to attract the spiritual aspirant. Milarepa proved just the exception to the lack of interest in Marpa by aspirants that Marpa was looking for. He saw and knew the *real* Marpa.

The name given him at birth was Töbaga, meaning 'delightful to hear', his father's reaction to the news of the boy's birth. The name proved apt, for Töbaga grew up with a fine voice and a great talent for singing. When he was only seven years old, however, his father died, and the uncle to whom the family were entrusted stole from them all their property and land and left them destitute. The widow was filled with an insatiable desire for revenge, which she managed to instill into her young son. She eventually told him that the only way the wrong done them could be avenged was by Mila going out to seek a sorcerer from whom he could learn the spells and acquire the power that would bring destruction to his uncle's household, just as destruction had been brought to theirs.

Mila set out, and was accepted by a great tantric sorcerer only when he offered his life, having nothing else to offer a man accustomed to being paid the highest fees for his instruction. Mila learned well, and put his learning to use, as he had promised his mother, by bringing destruction and death to his uncle's household. He conjured up a giant scorpion which pulled away the main housepost, bringing the house down and killing all who were assembled inside for a wedding feast. His uncle and aunt both escaped to suffer the full brunt of the tragedy. Mila further brought a violent hailstorm down on their fields, destroying their crops and reducing them to poverty.

The deed pleased Mila's mother, but it did not please Mila. He was stricken with horror at what he had done and now gave himself up entirely to a life of penance. He studied for a while with a Nyingmapa teacher but was always restless, moving on in search of greater solace. He heard of Marpa, and it is said that at once he felt certain that it was from him that the way to purification could be found. It must have been an act of faith from the outset, for Mila was not seeking for intellectual enlightenment, and there was little else about Marpa, outwardly, to attract the aspirant. Yet as far as we can see there was no doubt in Milarepa's mind.

Marpa agreed to take Mila as his student, but refused to have anything to do with him until he had first atoned for his crimes. Mila was more than willing, and when Marpa instructed him to go to a certain place and fetch stones (carrying them on his back) with which to build a house, he did not hesitate. Marpa specified exactly what kind of a house was to be built, and slowly Mila erected it, stone by stone. When it was finally done Marpa, instead of giving the promised instruction, denied that this was the kind of house he had asked for and made Mila return the stones to the place where he had found them and start all over again. The next time Marpa said the house was in the wrong place, so once again Mila set about his task, not for a moment questioning his master. Even when Mila's back was raw and bleeding, Marpa would allow no respite.

To further test his pupil, Marpa feigned drunkenness and anger and was quite unnecessarily harsh and cruel. Once or twice Mila tried to run away, but always he came back. Marpa even made him use the sorcery he had learned to kill some people that Marpa said were his enemies. Once again the disciple did not flinch, though he was well aware of the kind of rebirth he could expect following a repetition of his former act of violence . . . if Marpa were a false teacher. He carried out the wishes of his master, and only by his unquestioning faith did he win the goal he sought. Having tried every means he could, at the expense of his own reputation, to discourage his disciple, Marpa was finally convinced of Mila's sincerity and initiated him into the secret doctrine, and gave him the responsibility for carrying it forward. Together, it is said, they drank wine from the symbol of impermanence, a cup made from a human skull, a symbol still used in tantric rites today.

Mila now spent some six years in self-purification, making use of the secrets he had won. They were six years spent in solitude and meditation in a near-by cave. Then Mila decided to return home, having had a vision in which he saw his mother dead, the house in ruins, and his sister in rags. It was all as he had foreseen, and overcome by grief, he resolved to spend the rest of his life as a hermit and, by pursuing the ascetic path, find final liberation. The idea was in no way a selfish one but one designed to enable him to help others on the way, by his own sacrifice. It was a path not only not taught by the Buddha, but one against which the Buddha had specifically preached in advocating the Middle Way. However, there have always been those who have said that the Buddha's teaching did not rule out such practices in exceptional instances.

Mila went up into the mountains and there began a life of the severest asceticism, for he realized that death could come at any time, depriving him of his goal of liberation. Every minute of every hour that he could stay awake had to be given to his meditative search. Even in sleep his inner self continued the search. To begin with he used to gather wild fruits around the cave in which he lived, but then he began to worry that that too might cost him his goal, and he ended by eating only the nettles that grew in abundance all around him. For clothes he only wore a light cotton robe, even in the winter when he was shut off from the few pilgrims who used to come and bring him offerings of food. It is for this reason that he became known as Mila-Repa, Cotton-clad Mila.

His sister and the woman to whom he had once been be-trothed, and who had never married, followed him, begging him to give up this terrible life of hardship. When he persisted, they did what they could to help, bringing food and clothing such as they could spare. Often it was rejected or abused, for Milarepa well knew how easy it was to become earthbound by attachment to luxuries. For him even a rough blanket was a luxury, and when his sister brought him one so that he could cover his naked body, he cut it into little strips. In this way he taught her and all others who came to him. Yet his gift for song and poetry never left him, and his verses were written down and preserved to become the common property of all Tibetans today. It would be rare to find a farmer or a nomad who could not quote from the Hundred Thousand Songs of Milarepa. Despite his asceticism he was a man keenly aware of beauty, and he describes with love and reverence the countryside all around him, from one season to the next, so full of life. Animals, birds, insects, even plants were all alive to him, yet they also served only to remind him further of the impermanence of all things, the illusory nature of all existence. Once when he was going from one cave to another, ever in search of greater solitude, his clay food bowl broke. He at once burst into song and praised it, saying that now it had become a great teacher, for it had again reminded him of the transitory nature of all things.

He was a gentle man, with none of the passion shown by his own master. Yet he was firm. When a scholar, too proud of his learning, came to him Milarepa sang the following song: –

Accustomed long to meditating on the Whispered Chosen Truths,
I have forgot all that is said in written and in printed books.
Accustomed, as I've been, to study of the Common Science,
Knowledge of erring Ignorance I've lost.

Accustomed long to keep my mind in the Uncreated State of Freedom,
I have forgot conventional and artificial usages.

Accustomed long to know the meaning of the Wordless,
I have forgot the way to trace the roots of verbs and source of words and phrases;
May thou, O Learned One, trace out these things in standard books.*

Milarepa achieved liberation, and died, as he wished, in lonely isolation. The love that he felt for all living things is reflected in the devotion Tibetans have shown to the saint ever since. Some of his followers found the asceticism too much, and moving back towards the old Nyingmapa sect they founded subdivisions of the Kargyupa known as Karmapa, Dikungpa, and Dugpa. Needless to say, despite the simplicity of his life and teachings, numerous stories grew up around Milarepa telling of miracles performed.

* *From W. Y. Evans-Wentz,* The Tibetan Book of the Great Liberation, (*London, Oxford University Press, 1954), pp. 20–21.*

A Christian priest, a member of a mission that had been working
in Tibet during the seventeenth and eighteenth centuries, was
horrified at the stories told of Milarepa, considering that such
works could only be the works of the devil. Nonetheless so great
was the devotion of the people to the memory of Mila, that the
priest was forced to confess shame in the fact that 'I did not
honour, love and serve Jesus, sole master, sole and true teacher,
as well as this people loved and served a traitor, a deceiver who
brought them a false religion.' As for the miracles, we believe
that, like everything else, they occur in men's minds and so have
that degree of reality. But Mila himself would have had us look
further, to the reality beyond.

The story is told that when Milarepa died clouds formed mystic symbols in the sky, gods descended to earth and walked
among men, and Heaven wept tears of blossoms. These things
may or may not have happened, but the belief that they did
happen is an act of reverence for the truth and beauty and goodness of Mila's life, and as such can only enrich our understanding.

CHAPTER NINE

The Foundation of the Order

*He who would harm another is no seeker after
truth;
He who would act wrongly toward another is no
monk.
From all wrong abstain,
Live in goodness, in purity of mind as well as
body;
Such is the Word of the Buddha.
Do not scorn, nor do harm;
Live in the law of the Order,
Take but little food, seek not overly the
company of others,
By meditation keep control of every thought;
Such is the Word of the Buddha.*

— from DHAMMAPADA

The period of anarchy that followed Lang Darma's death was broken by the revival of Buddhism, rather than by the emergence of another line of kings. Politically, Tibet remained divided amongst rival petty chiefs, whose fortunes waxed and waned in a manner that led, inevitably, to an increase in the political importance of the monasteries. For one thing the monasteries were fast accumulating wealth and land, and to guard against raids in those lawless times they were built like fortresses, surrounded by high stone walls many feet thick. They became a symbol of stability as well as being places of refuge.

Whereas Samye had risen to a position of pre-eminence in both scholarly and spiritual endeavour, the younger monastery of Sakya* was the first to achieve and wield truly political authority. It must not be thought, however, that it deliberately aimed itself towards this goal, nor that its political activities were allowed to overshadow its religious life. The founder of the school was Drokmi, a great scholar and translator who had studied at the University of Vikramashila, in India, for a number of years. He rejected the old tantras, following the new school of Atisha, and establishing a monastery of his own in the province of Tsang. To this monastery came a certain Koncho Gyepo, who was to be the effective founder of the great Sakya Monastery. Koncho Gyepo was a member of the old school, the Nyingmapa, which kept to the old translations of the tantras before their expurgation by Atisha. This school allowed its members to marry, and Koncho Gyepo himself was married. But those who married were only aspirants, not monks. Neither Nyingmapa nor Gelukpa monks are allowed to marry. Koncho Gyepo felt a great dissatisfaction with the way in which some Nyingmapa

* *The name does not indicate any connection with the Sakya royal family from which came the Buddha.*

deviated from the strict order of secrecy, performing secret rites in public. He could see such relaxation of the rule leading to further corruption.

Koncho Gyepo wandered from teacher to teacher in search of a higher discipline and fell under the influence of Drokmi. Around the year 1071 he founded Sakya Monastery, so called because it was built on a site where the earth was coloured grey (*sa-kya*). There he taught that too much reliance on meditation could lead the aspirant into thinking that he had achieved a realization of the ultimate truth, whereas in fact all that might have been achieved was a mere development of physical and mental faculties. To guard against such a mistake, which would lead one only further into ignorance and delusion, he laid great stress on a systematic study of the Buddhist scriptures. Sakya quickly became famous for both its scholarship and its spiritual advancement, a combination that was all too rare.

Koncho Gyepo's son followed his father, and since Koncho Gyepo had never seen cause for advocating celibacy among monks, it became an established custom, at Sakya, for the post of abbot to pass from father to son, or uncle to nephew. In this way there arose an ecclesiastical dynasty which has continued up to the present day, though the political and economic status of Sakya has diminished considerably from its position of ascendancy in the thirteenth century.

Koncho Gyepo's grandson, Kunga Gyaltsan, who became known as Sakya Pandita, or the Sakya Grand Lama, again showed that rare combination of academic and spiritual attainment, and undertook a careful study of non-Buddhist scriptures which enabled him to establish more firmly than ever the preeminence of Buddhism in Tibet. One famous incident in his life was the defeat he inflicted on a renowned Brahman philosopher in a debate on Vedanta, or Brahmanic thought. Acknowledging defeat, the Brahman became converted and took holy orders as a Buddhist monk. His hair, cut off for the ordination, was used to decorate a black banner erected by Kunga Gyaltsan, a practice still followed today.

It was in Kunga Gyaltsan's time that the political ascendancy of the Sakya dynasty was established. So great was his learning and his reputation for spiritual attainment that he received an invitation from the Mongolian chief Godan, a descendant of the great Genghis Khan. While at the Mongol court, the Sakya Grand Lama won ready recognition by the force of his personality and the power of his teaching. The court was still further impressed when the Lama managed to cure Godan of a serious illness. With the Lama was his nephew, Phakpa, and together they adapted the Uighur script so that the Scriptures could be translated into Mongolian, which at that time was an unwritten language. The establishment of friendly relations with their powerful northern neighbours put Sakya's supremacy beyond question, for no other monastery or sect could command such support. The militant spirit that was so much a part of Tibetan character was by no means dead, and it was not unknown for one monastery to carry out a raid and sack another, so great was the rivalry.

When the Mongol domination of China was secured, and Kublai Khan became emperor, Phakpa was invited to the Imperial Court. Kublai had an inquiring mind, and he had seen enough of the world to realize that despite its military superiority, Mongolia lacked the sophistication of its neighbours, particularly in religion. He had interested himself in Christianity and Islam, as well as the Chinese school of Tao. Phakpa won him over to Tibetan Buddhism, not once admitting that he was anything but the Emperor's equal. His insistence on the fact caused a historical debate, in which Phakpa, backed by Chinese records, showed how Tibet had once defeated China. Kublai accepted Phakpa as his teacher, accorded him a number of highly honorific titles, and established him as the political ruler of Tibet. This was no empty honour for by then the Mongol armies had effectively subdued the last vestiges of power among the Tibetan chiefs and had unified the country under Mongol control. The administrative centre was established now at Sakya, with the Sakya Lama as nominal and effective head of state. The Emperor wanted to go even further and issue an edict making the Sakya sect the only lawful Buddhist sect in Tibet.

Phakpa, however, insisted that there should be complete religious freedom.

The wealth that was showered on Phakpa by the Imperial Court was used to enlarge and enrich the monastery of Sakya, and it became the greatest repository for religious treasures in all the country. The main temple contained a golden statue of Gautama no less than thirty-five feet high, and innumerable other golden figures. The walls and pillars were hung with the richest gold brocade. Such was the importance of Tibetan religious leadership to the Imperial Court. The Mongol army could be relied on, at the same time, to defend its protégé, and its not infrequent incursions into Tibet on this account caused growing dissatisfaction with Sakya rule. As Mongol power waned, however, so did that of the Sakya dynasty. Other monasteries and sects had been building up their own followings and now began to challenge seriously the political authority of Sakya. Even within the Sakya sect there was dissension, and on one occasion the Lama was assassinated by his own ministers.

Other monasteries began to send their own delegations to the Imperial Court, seeking its patronage in return for their religious and spiritual guidance. This further undermined Sakya supremacy, and in the middle of the fourteenth century its overlordship came to an end. Although it had a relatively short life, Sakya overlordship accomplished several important things. It united Tibet under a joint political and religious leadership; it set the example of such leadership being hereditary; it organized a central administrative machinery in which the country was divided into thirteen provinces, each with a lay governor who did not have to belong to the Sakya sect; and finally, in the political realm, it established a mutually acceptable basis for international relations with its two powerful neighbours, China and Mongolia. It was a basis of political equality, with Tibet supplying religious teachers and counsel in return for protection. The protection was a necessity, for already Buddhism with its emphasis on the sanctity of life, was beginning to erase the last traces of militarism among the Tibetan people.

Sakya, during the same period, had given a new impetus to

Buddhism, not only raising the academic standards and establishing new monasteries throughout the country, but broadening the scope of Tibetan Buddhism while fighting the tendencies to degeneration within it by stressing spiritual as well as academic achievement. It kept alive and furthered the work of reform begun by Atisha, preparing the ground for the great reform that was yet to come and for the final establishment of a theocratic state that would come at the same time.

Buddhism had spread throughout the country, but as long as it remained divided into rival sects and independent monasteries it could effect no firm control over either clergy or laymen. Influence from India was still strong, particularly the lower forms of tantricism which found a ready appeal among the less educated mass of the population. Among the clergy too there were those who, pretending that these tantric writings were the authentic word of the Buddha, used them as an excuse for the grossest self-indulgence. Others who practised a more austere life only did so for self-gain, to acquire magical powers. Even today you can see *Nagpa*, ascetic magicians, decorated with necklaces made of human bones and using human skulls as drinking cups. They are not monks, but have taken the tantric teachings and followed them for the sake of power alone. Regardless of the fact that most of them use their power in a harmless way, being little more than soothsayers, they have done a great injury to themselves by concentrating on the development of power, for this blinds them to the higher attainments yet to be sought.

At the time of the disintegration of Sakya rule there was a great need for a spiritual force that could not only restate the reforms introduced by Atisha, but also could compel adherence to monastic discipline. Such a need was fulfilled in the person of Tsong Khapa, who was responsible for the whole edifice of Buddhist rule in Tibet as it has existed up to the present day. He was born in Amdo province, of a nomad couple who had long been childless. The couple had set up their tent near a convenient watering place and in this tent the wonder child was born. That spot is now in the middle of the great monastery of Kumbum, where I myself was educated, and where later I became abbot. There is a great tree growing there which, it is said, sprang up from the spot where the mother's blood fell to the ground.

The boy began his religious studies when only a few years old and learned to read and write at the monastery of Shardzong. While he was there a learned scholar from central Tibet passed by and took a great interest in Tsong Khapa. Quickly seeing the exceptional qualities of the boy who urgently begged to be given the vows of monkhood, the visiting priest, Rolpai Dorje, cut the boy's hair as a sign of renunciation of the world, and Tsong Khapa took the first five vows: not to kill, commit adultery, steal, lie or drink intoxicating liquor. When the hair was cut the priest cast it down on the rock beside the cave in which Tsong Khapa was living. From the rock sprang a juniper tree, which today is still strangely scented like human hair. By the time he was sixteen years old Tsong Khapa's intellect had developed to a point where he had outstripped his teachers in Amdo, and at this early age he was sent for higher studies at the great monasteries of central Tibet.

He had a wide education, including the tantras, but since tantric initiations are kept secret it is impossible to know to what extent Tsong Khapa, or any other teacher, practised tantric rites. But in all disciplines he quickly proved himself a master in debate as in exposition, and he wrote numerous important works that restated the basic teachings of the various systems, shorn of the accumulated overgrowth that represented the desire of less idealistic followers to suit the teachings to their own tastes. As was Atisha, so was Tsong Khapa fully aware of the value of the tantras, but he was perhaps even more aware of the danger they represent to monastic discipline. Tsong Khapa believed that tantric practice is something between an individual teacher and an individual pupil. The teacher initiated the pupil only when he was convinced that the pupil was fully prepared, often after many years of arduous self-discipline and rigid asceticism. He then passed on to his pupil the secret teachings, many of which have never been written down, but have been communicated from teacher to disciple by word of mouth. The highest teachings are only passed on to one disciple, who holds them in trust and, before his death, passes them on again to one other. In this way the highest teachings never become common knowledge or subject to abuse. They exist so that there may at all times be one who, by making proper use of them, can make the maximum use of his present life as a teacher.

Even the lesser initiations are very much a personal matter, and an initiate is generally not only forbidden to pass on what he has learned, without the express instruction to do so from his teacher, but he may not even reveal that he has been initiated. The purpose of the initiation is only incidentally the self-development of the initiate. It has a much higher ultimate purpose, for the initiate consequently develops various faculties with a view to helping others towards liberation. The years spent in solitude, working towards such development, are not selfish years. On the contrary, they demand the utmost self-denial. Many aspirants in order to free themselves from distractions have themselves shut up in tiny cells, or walled up in caves with only a tiny aperture left for ventilation and through which the bare minimum of food can be passed. Some even have elaborate traps in which food can be placed without disturbing the aspirant, without even letting light into his cell, thus ensuring perfect solitude. It is said that this rigid training and renunciation of all worldly things, to the utmost possible extent, can alone, within a single brief lifetime, guarantee arrival at the knowledge of the impermanence of material things, of the illusory nature of existence. With this realization comes the power of release, so that even in their lifetime, that is while the body continues to breathe, the now-perfected master can leave his body at will and pass out of his cell, through the tiny vent or even through the walls, and roam at will, manifesting himself to others either in his habitual bodily form, or in other forms, or even by entering other bodies. This would only be done, however, for some urgent purpose, such as the transmission of knowledge.

Sometimes aspirants die while still in seclusion, but even so their effort has not been wasted, according to Buddhist belief. A single man striving to achieve perfection radiates perfection.

Even the hearsay knowledge that there is such an individual, perhaps thousands of miles away, will serve to inspire others towards similar ideals. In dying he dies having achieved a higher level and will consequently be reborn closer to perfection and will thus be able in his next life to be of greater value to his fellow beings.

The tantras, which teach the means by which enlightenment may be reached by this short path, plainly demand the utmost sacrifice and devotion. Tsong Khapa, therefore, saw that they could not be a part of monastic life, for a monastery is a community and works as such, for the same goal but by a different method. A monastery serves the lay populace, by its worship, its religious services, its teaching, and in many other ways. Even in Tsong Khapa's time the more truly Buddhist monasteries deliberately extended their influence far beyond the monastery walls, helping in the maintenance of law and order, helping with the distribution of land among the farmers ... quite apart from the religious aid offered by monks who travelled amongst the lay people, preaching and teaching and performing necessary rites.

As Tsong Khapa saw it, the tantric teachings, if they are to be properly applied towards the highest goal, which is the only legitimate one, demand a way of life exactly opposed to that of a monastery, where one is surrounded by hundreds or even thousands of others. A monastery, if it is to survive, must have a common discipline followed by all whereas the tantras demand that each individual make his own way under the personal supervision of his teacher to begin with, then in absolute solitude – preferably, it is so often stated, in places unfrequented by man. The fact that Tsong Khapa devoted his life to monastic reform, forbidding tantric teaching and practice within his own monastery, is only a recognition of the incompatibility of the two ways, not a judgement that one is superior to the other. It is more than likely that he was himself a tantric initiate. His stress on discipline does not mean, as many have said, that he was a mere intellectual and administrative genius, without spiritual power. He could hardly have achieved what he did, nor attracted the immense following he had in his lifetime, had he not matched his intellect with spiritual development.

Looking back to the degeneration that had taken place since Atisha came to Tibet, however, he saw what damage could be done by lowering tantric standards, by opening this essentially esoteric teaching to all, even to the point of giving classroom instruction. Having undertaken tantric studies himself he must have been well aware that in the initial stages of self-development by use of tantric practice, various changes take place in the physical and mental being of the aspirant that can mislead him into thinking he has achieved a much higher level of perfection than the first step, which is all he has taken. This danger is particularly acute if he is not secluded and so is still in a position to make comparisons with others around him. Tantric practice ultimately demands the complete negation of self-consciousness, and this can only be achieved by first obliterating consciousness of the outside world. It would be a superhuman task for anyone to accomplish without the help given by seclusion from that world, so far as it is possible.

Tsong Khapa's teaching along these lines attracted many followers who were, like himself, dismayed at the abuse into which these great teachings had fallen. Tantric practice, unaccompanied by self-denial and even self-removal, can only lead to greater delusion and ignorance at best, and at worst can easily lead to abandonment of the self to all its desires and passions. Monasteries everywhere were permitting and even encouraging such practices and were thus failing in their duties to both the individual practitioners and to the lay public, to whom they were meant to be bringing help and knowledge. Rather than try to introduce reform into any of these monasteries, Tsong Khapa founded his own, known as Ganden, meaning Place of Joy (in the sense of perfection), and from this his followers came to be known as Gelukpa, or 'those who follow the path of perfect virtue'. Here, at Ganden, Tsong Khapa was able to establish at the outset, without having to compromise with any old order, the pattern of monastic discipline that he deemed fit.

The course of study was eclectic, and a proficient knowledge of non-Buddhist philosophical systems was demanded equally with a knowledge of the various Buddhist schools. Tantras appeared in the course of studies not with a view to practice, but rather with a view to right understanding. In this way the symbol of sexual union was emphatically declared to be a symbol of the union of knowledge and activity, leading to the right application of knowledge, or power. It in no way licensed sexual activity as a practice leading to spiritual advancement, as some of the old sects now taught. To reinforce this, Tsong Khapa exacted absolute celibacy from all the monks who joined the Gelukpa order, from the lowest to the highest, whereas most other orders permitted (and some still do) marriage or intercourse for the lower orders of monks. The Sakyapa sect, as we have seen, not only permitted their abbot to marry but demanded it, as a means of ensuring succession of wisdom as well as succession of leadership, in distinction from the master/disciple system of succession practised by the mystics.

The use of liquor and narcotics was equally forbidden to all Gelukpa, and once again Tsong Khapa saw that it was best to stress the symbolic meaning of intoxication and of meat eating (another practice which some old sects said had spiritual value). To simply deny them any value would only achieve a limited end within his own following. By offering a symbolic interpretation he hoped to be able to slowly introduce reform into the other sects. Similarly he took the old gods and demons, images and paintings of which filled the temples and monasteries of the day and nearly all of which had non-Buddhist origins, and he taught the symbolic meaning of each. In this way, to all outward appearances, the Gelukpa even today do not differ all that much from the Nyingmapa, or unreformed sect. The difference is in the way followed by the monks.

While Tsong Khapa stressed the highest academic standards as an absolute prerequisite to advanced spiritual practice, involving the use of meditation for personal spiritual advancement, he equally stressed the need for a spiritual goal to be held above all others. He insisted on a period of retreat in a hermitage for all members of his order to remind them forcibly of their spiritual goal and to further the order's achievement. He further introduced a series of vows, numbering two hundred and fifty-three, taken by monks as they pass from one grade to another, each grade demanding a higher level of renunciation. The four main vows, or *Tsawa Shi*, were to refrain from killing, stealing, having sexual intercourse, and lying. His teachings were similarly graded so that the novice entering the order knew that before him lay many years of sheer hard work and severe discipline, the fruits of which would not be the sudden blinding revelation of truth promised by the short path but rather a gradual, infinitely safer and more sure advancement of his whole being, mental, physical and spiritual. His attention was always directed, by the monastic discipline, to the needs of others so that he could never lose sight of the Changchub Sempa ideal, the ideal by which the ultimate sacrifice is made, the sacrifice of one's own liberation for the sake of others. Here lies the basis for the theory of the reincarnation of teachers which has come to provide Tibet with spiritual dynasties such as those of the Gyalwa and Panchen Rinpoche. It was in Tsong Khapa's time that the foundations of these dynasties were laid.

The great reformer himself eschewed the policy of attracting followers by the performance of miracles, just as he refrained from promising the novice any startling development of supernormal powers. Consequently the Gelukpa sect has always seemed rather austere to some Tibetans as well as to those foreigners who associate our country and religion with miraculous and mystic powers. Yet the force of Tsong Khapa's arguments was so great that he rapidly attracted a large following, and the other sects sought various ways of stemming the rise of the Gelukpa. His fame reached even to China, and the reformer received a pressing invitation to visit the Imperial Court. This would, of course, have been an ideal opportunity for him to seek the secular power and backing to give his reformed sect a dominant and controlling position in Tibet. Tsong Khapa refused the invitation, however. He made the excuse that if he came with the large retinue that would be demanded by the occasion, it would cause much hardship among all the villages along the route, where people would be taxed and made to contribute food they could ill afford in order to provide him with a fitting reception. In the end he sent a representative, but only with the purpose of expounding his teachings, not to seek for the material support he so badly needed at the time.

Both religious sects and secular chiefs were afraid of Tsong Khapa's reform movement because of its undeniable validity. During his own lifetime his following grew to such an extent that his disciples had to found two other major monasteries, also near Lhasa, to house the ever-growing number of monks. These monasteries were known as Sera and Drepung, and like Ganden they differed even outwardly from the older monasteries, being built down in the valleys, rather than as fortresses perched on mountain tops. Tsong Khapa also began the practice of combining the New Year festival with the Great Prayer, in which the welfare of the whole world, Buddhist and non-Buddhist, is prayed for. On this occasion thousands of Gelukpa monks came from the three new monasteries to fill the great temple in Lhasa and to offer the prayer.

The greatest strength of Tsong Khapa lay in his own blameless life, the perfection of the example he set others, and his own absolute reliance on the teachings of Buddha. This has been the strength of the Gelukpa sect ever since. The discipline is still too severe for some who prefer the less austere but perhaps less perfect way of the Nyingmapa. Within this strength lies still more strength, for the discipline demanded by the reformer includes the ideal of service to others. Tsong Khapa, like Atisha, allowed for the fact that different people have different opportunities and different abilities, and therefore that even laymen should have differently graded paths to follow. All paths must rest, however, on the word of Buddha. It is the duty of the monkhood to expound the word, having first qualified themselves by those long years of study and sacrifice. In this way the monkhood makes itself indispensable, so long as it remains true to its own teachings and to the precepts of the Buddha. The moment it departs from those precepts it sows the seeds of its own destruction. The Three Precious Truths: the Buddha, His

Word, and the Monkhood are the foundation not only of the Buddhist church, but of all Buddhist practice. By making the Three Precious Truths a central part of Gelukpa doctrine, Tsong Khapa ensured at once the success of the sect and the success of the doctrine.

Had he set out to subvert or even to reform the older sects, it is unlikely that he would have succeeded. Success only came through his living example. As a further result, the other sects have gradually come closer to the Gelukpa ideal, while still maintaining their own traditions, so that today there is no discord between them, and even the Bön religion persists, though now much influenced by Buddhism, in harmony with the Buddhist sects.

The terms 'Red Hat' and 'Yellow Hat' which have found such common use outside Tibet confuse the situation, giving the appearance of sectarian rivalry on the one hand, and the impression, on the other hand, that one sect indulges in diabolical practices while the other alone is lofty and pure. The essential difference is that the one follows the old translations, and the other follows the later translations, from which most of the non-Buddhist influence has been expunged. The more significant translation of the sectarian names would, then, be Old Translation School and New Translation School. Before Tsong Khapa it was the custom for all monks to wear red hats, and the reformer, wishing to set his followers apart, to emphasize their break with the old school, introduced the use of a yellow hat, possibly because yellow is a colour associated in Tibet with the notion of purity and with the idea of growth, or increase. Red is associated with physical strength and power, or authority. Black is force, connected with warfare, and white is thought of as having to do with peace. Some people use colours in this way to achieve special results. If a monk wanted to subdue unbelievers and bring them under his control, he might, in his meditations, wear a red hat and a red robe, use a red rosary and sit on a red carpet, and perhaps decorate his shrine with red flowers. Black hats are used in some dances that represent the fight against evil. The white hat of the Sakyapa sect is said to enhance the spiritual state of the wearer, and so is associated with inner peace. Not only the colours but also the shapes of the hats all have symbolic significance.

Because a monk or priest belongs to one sect does not mean he is divided from the other. There is nothing to stop a Gelukpa monk from wearing a red hat, if for some reason he thinks it will benefit his progress.

I often used to visit Nyingmapa monasteries. They are much like our own, though sometimes instead of being painted plain red, as ours are, the walls are painted with vertical stripes in different colours, like red, white and black. When I first saw this I felt very strange, but perhaps that was just because I was so used to the plain dark red of my own monastery. Then there were little differences in the ritual, the way the Nyingmapa make their offerings and the way they chant. There is more tantric practice with the Nyingmapa too, and if you are not used to that it may make you feel uncomfortable. Certain tantric rites demand the use of human bones, and in a Gelukpa monastery we are not allowed to use these, except perhaps in certain very special services and in places that are set aside for them. Certain initiations demand their use, or an individual may have a protective deity whose offerings have to be made with their use. But they are never in general use, as some people seem to think. There are many ridiculous stories about human flesh being eaten and blood drunk from cups made of skulls. This is just a reflection of the people who think these things.

For instance our protective deity in Tibet is Chenresig, Lord of Compassion. But he has another form, which we call Gonpo. Whereas Chenresig is gentle, Gonpo is fierce. In his fierce form Chenresig destroys evil. He is pictured as being a giant, black, carrying a skull in one hand, wearing a necklace of skulls, and usually trampling on a corpse. The ritual offering to Gonpo has to be made in a skull cup. We actually put holy water in it, but what you see depends on what is in your heart. Someone who is pure sees milk and believes that an offering of milk has been made. Someone who has accumulated many bad deeds thinks it is blood. Some are themselves so evil that they see parts of the body, a heart or an eye, and think that this is the offering. If we take the initiation of Gonpo, then we may eat meat, but we do so with the thought in our minds of the destruction of evil. The eating of meat in itself is not bad, what is bad is the thought in your mind. If you take pleasure in it, you are taking pleasure in the taking of life, and that is bad. If you eat meat merely because, as is usual in Tibet, there is no other food, or not enough to keep you alive without meat, then that is not bad, but neither is it good, and you must eat it with the thought in your mind that perhaps the animal whose life was taken to give *you* life will, by this sacrifice, acquire a better rebirth. You must have compassion. We Gelukpa allow the eating of meat as a necessity, though some prefer to abstain. Some, who want to, take the initiation of Chenresig in his gentle aspect, and during this initiation all our offerings are of fruits and rice and milk, and that is what we ourselves live on; we are forbidden to even touch meat. Nor can we use any spices, for the food must be soft and gentle, and instead of thinking of Chenresig as Gonpo, destroying evil, we think of him in his other aspect as having come to help us from our misery.

Compassion is everything to us in our religion. We can live our lives in perfect celibacy, without touching meat, worshipping in the temple every day, teaching in our monastery or meditating in our cell, but if we do not actively feel compassion for all living creatures and work towards their relief, our lives are empty. A golden temple is worth nothing if the gold is not offered with devotion and if the worship within the golden walls or in front of a golden image is without compassion. If you have a seed of barley you need water, and then you still need sunshine before it will grow. You can lead a blameless life full of good deeds, but if you have lived it without compassion your life will bear no fruit, your deeds are empty.

People sometimes think we are hypocrites because we claim to have so much respect for life, yet we eat meat. We never kill animals ourselves, yet we allow the Muslim butchers to slaughter hundreds right in the middle of Lhasa every day. We know this, and we wish it were otherwise, for eating meat involves taking life. Yet if we do not eat meat we die. Some of us think that we are born into this unhappy lot because of past misdeeds, and it means, we say, that we have to work twice as hard to wipe out all this demerit by good deeds coupled with compassion. If, through the eating of meat, we increase our compassion for all forms of life and redouble our attempts to help relieve the suffering we see around us, then we to some extent at least have atoned for the sin of eating meat, and we have also turned the animal's death into a sacrifice to itself. This is not just a convenient rationalization, for from what I have seen it *can* be beneficial. Unfortunately it is not always so, and the same argument is used by some to excuse their own gluttony. We are sorry for them, as we are for those whose lot is even worse than ours and who have to kill the animals. We all pray for a rebirth where we do not have to take life in order to live.

The early part of my life was spent just exactly where Tsong Khapa spent his. I learned to read and write at the same tiny mountainside monastery of Shardzong where he was taught, and I used to visit the tomb of his Karmapa teacher, Rolbai Dorje. I was taught to write probably much as he was, for we had no pens or pencils or paper even when I was there. I used a wooden slate that was covered with chalk so that the writing showed up dark when the surface was scratched with a sharpened wooden stick. I used to sit by the rock from which the juniper tree sprouted and wonder at how strangely it smelled of human hair. At Kumbum too, where I was sent for further studies and to take up my position as head of the Tagtser Labrang, there was the great temple to honour the place where Tsong Khapa was born. Its walls outside were of green glaze, and the roof was gilded; inside stood a *Chörten*, or pagoda, three storeys high, made of silver and decorated with turquoise and other precious stones. The walls inside are painted to show scenes from the lives of the famous scholars who have studied at Kumbum, and balconies run around so that you can look at the pagoda at different levels.

The chörten is surrounded by images and relics, the ashes of old abbots of Kumbum are also kept in special miniature chörten-like shrines there, and there are butter lamps of silver and gold burning all the time. Off the balcony on the first floor are the rooms of the temple keeper, and on the second floor is a large room for special religious studies. On the top floor there are no rooms, just the balcony encircling the top of the silver chörten. In this chörten grows the sacred tree which sprang from the ground where Tsong Khapa's mother shed the blood of birth. Until a hundred years or so ago the tree stood in the open and had many marvellous characteristics. There was said to be no counterpart anywhere, and efforts to grow like trees from cuttings or seeds all failed. Perhaps its most famous and remarkable characteristic was that its leaves each bore mystic symbols and distinct letters of the Tibetan alphabet. The bark too was covered with similar writing, and travellers were given to peeling off the outer bark to see if the work had been done by human agency but even the inner bark bore similar writing. The same famous Lazarist priest, the Abbé Huc, visited the monastery in the middle of the nineteenth century and, with some scepticism asked to see the tree. It was then merely enclosed by four walls and had erected over it a silver canopy presented by the Emperor Khang Hsi. The Abbé subjected the tree to every test he could, even tearing off some of the bark. Huc tells about having heard of the tree, and of Kumbum as a place of pilgrimage on its account, then says:

It will here be naturally expected that we say something about this tree itself. Does it exist? Have we seen it? Has it any peculiar attributes? What about its marvellous leaves? All these questions our readers are entitled to put to us. We will endeavour to answer as categorically as possible.

Yes, this tree does exist, and we had heard of it too often during our journey not to feel somewhat eager to visit it. At the foot of the mountain on which the Lamasery stands, and not far from the principal Buddhist temple, is a great square enclosure, formed by brick walls. Upon entering this we were able to examine at leisure the marvellous tree, some of the branches of which had already manifested themselves above the wall. Our eyes were first directed with earnest curiosity to the leaves, and we were filled with an absolute consternation of astonishment at finding that, in point of fact, there were upon each of the leaves well-formed Thibetian characters, all of a green colour, some darker, some lighter than the leaf itself. Our first impression was a suspicion of fraud on the part of the Lamas; but after a minute examination of every detail, we could not discover the least deception. The characters all appeared to us portions of the leaf itself, equally with its veins and nerves; the position was not the same in all; in one leaf they would be at the top of the leaf; in another, in the middle; in a third, at the base, or at the side; the younger leaves represented the characters only in a partial state of formation. The bark of the tree and its branches, which resemble that of the plane tree, are also covered with these characters. When you remove a piece of old bark, the young bark under it exhibits the indistinct outlines of characters in a germinating state, and, what is very singular, these new characters are not infrequently different from those which they replace. We examined everything with the closest attention, in order to detect some trace of trickery, but we could discern nothing of the sort, and the perspiration absolutely trickled down our faces under the influence of the sensations which this most amazing spectacle created. More profound intellects than ours may, perhaps, be able to supply a satisfactory explanation of the mysteries of this singular tree; but as to us, we altogether give it up. Our readers possibly may smile at our ignorance; but we care not, so that the sincerity and truth of our statement be not suspected.

The Tree of the Ten Thousand Images seemed to us of great age. Its trunk, which three men could scarcely embrace with outstretched arms, is not more than eight feet high; the branches, instead of shooting up, spread out in the shape of a plume of feathers, and are extremely bushy; few of them are dead. The leaves are always green, and the wood, which is of a reddish tint, has an exquisite odour, something like that of cinnamon. The Lamas informed us that in summer, towards the eighth moon, the tree produces large red flowers of an extremely beautiful character. They informed us also that there nowhere else exists another such tree; that many attempts have been made in various Lamaseries of Tartary and Thibet to propagate it by seeds and cuttings, but that all these attempts have been fruitless.[*]

Unfortunately the constant attentions of souvenir hunters must have threatened the tree, and caused its enclosure. There

[*] *M. Huc,* op. cit., *Vol. II, pp. 52, 54.*

is a door at the bottom of the Chörten, but this was sealed at the time the work was completed and has only been opened once since. Even if, as abbot, I had wished to break the seal, I could not have done so without the consent of the entire governing body of the monastery. It was opened some seventy years ago for cleaning, and when the monk who had been given the task came out, he found one leaf that had fallen on his shoulder. It had the lettering, still firmly marked. He took the leaf and kept it, and it was seen by many.

All this of course gave me a feeling of closeness to and great respect for Tsong Khapa – so perhaps it is natural that I should feel so strongly in my support of the reformed school that he founded and to which I belong. It was in Kumbum too that I had my first contact with the old sect's concepts of fierce deities and tantric practices and with their interpretation by Tsong Khapa. When the great reformer was born, on the site where the chörten now stands, close by there were two small buildings that constituted all there was of Kumbum Monastery in those days. The huge monastic town that has grown up around that spot has done so in honour of Tsong Khapa, so it stresses his teachings. All monasteries have one special temple in which there are no windows and which is kept dark. This is the temple of the Guardian of the Law, and the approaches to it, along dark passages, and the shrine itself, are decorated with pictures of deities in their most fearsome aspects. There are scenes of death and destruction, of corpses and parts of bodies like the heart or eyes, of flesh and blood – all the things that the lesser tantrists, by taking them literally instead of symbolically, have abused, misleading themselves and others. It is an awesome experience to stand inside such a temple, and it reminds one of how much destruction and misery and suffering there is in the world. It also serves to remind one of how much misery one faces in future lives if the path to liberation is not constantly sought and followed. But in our temple of the Guardian of the Law, at Kumbum, we were not content to leave it thinking only of the terrible aspect of existence. We were taught to view such scenes not with fear, nor with thoughts of evil, but with the thought that truth is all around us, and can be found, if earnestly sought, wherever we look. Destruction is an inevitable part of existence in the world as we know it, and there is no sense trying to hide from it. In itself it teaches us the lessons of impermanence and of suffering. The force of destruction itself can be turned to good ends when it is directed against evil, against ignorance. We should leave such a temple filled only with compassion for all suffering. That is its purpose. It was this spirit of compassion that Tsong Khapa sought to reintroduce by his reforms, and it is this spirit that we still try to make the centrepiece of Buddhism in Tibet today.

CHAPTER TEN

A Celestial Dynasty

Great Lord,
The people are empty of knowledge,
Empty of Spirit.
To bring them to holiness is hard,
Demanding an ocean of wisdom.
May victory be accomplished through my actions.

— BSODNAMS RGYAMTSO,
third Gyalwa Rinpoche

When Tsong Khapa died, his place as abbot of Ganden Monastery, and as leader of the reformed sect, the Gelukpa, was taken first by Gyal Tsab and then by Khadrub. These two, having once been his strongest opponents had become his most diligent disciples. Khadrub was almost as great a scholar as Tsong Khapa himself, and was given the job of teaching the great reformer's youngest disciple, Gedundrub. Like Tsong Khapa himself, Gedundrub came from a nomadic family of eastern Tibet. The night he was born, in a cattle pen, the small homestead was attacked but the newborn infant was miraculously guarded from all danger by a large raven. At seven years of age he entered the monastery of Nartang and quickly won the attention of Gelukpa scholars. In twelve years he passed the twelve grades of monkhood and took the highest vows. Tsong Khapa himself taught Gedundrub, but he came mainly under the teaching of Khadrub. When the latter died and young Gedundrub became leader of the reformed sect, one of his first acts was to set about building a monastery in honour of his late teacher. He took the double precaution of not only laying deep foundations for the monastery buildings and the surrounding walls, but also taking care to propitiate the local gods, for even the reformed Gelukpa still did not dare to flaunt the old Bön beliefs too openly. In five years the great new monastery was completed and given the name Tashi Lhunpo, Mountain of Blessings. It was later to become the seat of the Panchen Rinpoche, second only in rank to the Gyalwa Rinpoche.

During his long lifetime Gedundrub extended the teachings of Tsong Khapa far beyond the bounds of Lhasa. The building of Tashi Lhunpo near Shigatse, in the province of Tsang, was just one step in the expansion of Gelukpa influence. He continued the reformer's insistence on monastic discipline, so that by the time of his death, around the year 1475, the new sect presented more of a threat than ever to those struggling for secular power. The Phakmodru family, which had ousted the Sakya monastic dynasty, was at this time itself falling apart due to internal strife, the power eventually being wrested from them by their ministers. One minister took control of Shigatse, close by Tashi Lhunpo, and from there began his conquest of Tsang, founding the anti-Gelukpa dynasty of Tsangpa kings. It was vital, under such hostile conditions, for the sect to remain firmly united, and through their own insistence on celibacy they were denied the possibility of hereditary succession such as had been employed by the Sakya Lamas. Further, the Gelukpa doctrine not being secret, it was impossible to maintain continuity of leadership in the way it was achieved by sects like the Kargyupa, in which the highest teachings are handed down as a secret and sacred trust from master to disciple, by word of mouth alone.

The Gelukpa found the answer in the theory of reincarnation, an answer that was to ensure their own position of supremacy for the centuries to follow, and that at the same time was to bring about the fusion of temporal and spiritual leadership and authority, converting Tibet from a land torn by political and religious strife into a single nation united under a central theocratic government. The notion that gods from time to time took birth in human form was already an old one, and of course it was already a central part of the Buddhist doctrine that all living things are subject to rebirth until they achieve liberation. When Gedundrub's successor, known as Gedun Gyatso, was chosen, the notion of successive reincarnation was for the first time introduced at a purely human level, the claim being made that Gedun Gyatso was the reincarnation of Gedundrub, returned to continue his work as a lama, or teacher.

In this way Gedun Gyatso was accorded all the loyalty and devotion that had been shown to Gedundrub, and the new sect remained as firmly united as ever. During the intervening period, while the boy was growing up, an older monk who had been very close to Gedundrub during his lifetime acted as regent. He was elected to the office by the monks of Tashi Lhunpo. Meanwhile the young Gedun Gyatso was being prepared for his role, undergoing the rigorous training and discipline expected of any Gelukpa novice. He studied mainly at Drepung, and eventually became known as Drepung Lama, moving the centre of religious authority back from Tashi Lhunpo to Lhasa. During his life the Gelukpa sect continued to grow in size and influence, and a special official had to be appointed to supervise the internal administration. Although the sect still wielded no political power, it was nonetheless developing an internal administrative machinery, the director of which, the Depa, could even be a layman.

When Gedundrub was dying, he told his disciples that it was not necessary for them to pray for him; he had already reached the state of enlightenment, or Buddhahood which brings release from the round of rebirth. Yet he chose to come back, in the body of Gedun Gyatso, to continue his work, helping others to achieve the same goal. When Gedun Gyatso was dying, some seventy years later, he was even more specific. He expressed the wish to return with a new body so that his long life's work could be carried even further forward. According to the Buddhist belief, following death the soul remains for forty-nine days in the 'in-between' state of Bardo; it may take its rebirth any time after that period is over. One year following Gedun Gyato's death a boy was born bearing the physical signs of greatness and quickly attracted attention. He began to claim that he was Gedun Gyatso, and was readily able to recall events from his previous life and recognize people he had known then and objects he himself had possessed. Without hesitation he was officially established as Gedun Gyatso's incarnation, and given the name Sonam Gyatso.

The new incarnation quickly excelled his teachers in knowledge and wisdom and developed extraordinary powers. He was careful not to be sidetracked into a merely academic or administrative life, and like his predecessors he frequently retired for periods of solitude and meditation. It is sometimes said that the Gelukpa way is moral and intellectual rather than spiritual, but this is not so; from these earliest days, from the days of its very inspiration under the teachings of Atisha and Dromton, it has stressed the need for the two to go hand in hand, the mind and the spirit, together with the body.

His own personal reputation, and the ever-increasing strength of the sect he ruled, soon brought Sonam Gyatso an invitation to visit the court of the great Mongolian ruler, Altan Khan. Although Kublai Khan had been converted by the Sakya Lama, after his death the court and country reverted to the old animistic religion, much like the Tibetan Bön. Altan Khan was a shrewd statesman, and perhaps his original motives were far more political than religious, but his invitation was to result not only in his own conversion but that of the whole of Mongolia, the people of which were to become almost as ardent Buddhists as the Tibetans.

At first Sonam Gyatso, perhaps not wishing to be made a political pawn, refused to go and sent a disciple instead. From this disciple he learned the true state of affairs, and seeing the enormous opportunity for spreading the religion throughout Mongolia, when Altan Khan sent a second invitation Sonam Gyatso accepted. Recognizing the strength of the existing religious beliefs of the Mongolians, Sonam Gyatso made use of the long and arduous journey to demonstrate his powers and his superiority over local demons. Altan Khan, already considerably influenced by the teachings of the great lama's disciple, had ordered all his chiefs to pay homage to the holy man as he passed through their lands. They did so, but without any belief in or respect for this new religion. It is said that to convince some of them Sonam Gyatso had not only to stop the flow of a raging torrent but also to turn it around and make it flow briefly back up the precipitous mountainside. It would not be right to say that the people were converted by these miracles, as such acts seemed to them. A mere display of physical power cannot win a man's heart. True conversion to Buddhism can only come through a knowledge and understanding of the words of Buddha. All that Sonam Gyatso's feats achieved was to show that he, and his religion, were powers to be reckoned with and worth listening to. This was all that was necessary, for no power is as great as that of the *Chö*, the Law of the Word. Once a man's mind is opened to that, his heart is as good as won. Sonam Gyatso used his powers, and Altan Khan's influence, to open the whole of Mongolia to the Dhamma, even though it is a law that runs counter to all that the great Khan stood for, insisting as it does on non-violence.

Mongolia, at this time, was by far the greatest political force in the East. In China the Ming dynasty was becoming weaker and weaker and could offer little resistance to the continual invasions of their land by the Mongol armies. The Mongols were a people much like the Tibetans had been before Buddhism came to Tibet. There was little room in their lives for compassion for fellow human beings, let alone for animals. Such feelings would have been considered almost criminal weaknesses. Yet the message that Sonam Gyatso brought was undiluted, uncompromised and uncompromising. He announced that the time had come for Mongolia to accept the Buddhist religion and that from that moment onward there must be no further animal sacrifice, all images of the old gods were to be destroyed, customs such as the immolation of women on their husbands' funeral pyres were to be discontinued, there must be no taking of life, animal or human, for any reason, and military exploits must be abandoned. The latter command was of no small importance to Tibet, as well as China, for Tibet had been suffering for many years from the invasion of its northern territories by Mongol armies.

It is not easy to see why such an apparently unattractive message was even listened to with respect, yet it was not only heard, it was heeded. Altan Khan himself embraced Buddhism and officially proclaimed that it should be the national religion of Mongolia from thenceforth. Sonam Gyatso said that Altan Khan, in an earlier life, had been the great Kublai who had been converted to Buddhism by the Sakya, and that his destiny and that of Mongolia were thus inevitably bound to that of Buddhism. Sonam further enhanced his own position as Altan Khan's spiritual mentor by saying that he himself had been the Sakya Lama who had converted Kublai more than three hundred years earlier. Altan Khan, to show his recognition, bestowed on Sonam Gyatso the title of *Dalai Lama*, 'Dalai' being a Mongolian translation of the Tibetan 'Gyatso', meaning ocean, and the title therefore meaning Ocean of Wisdom. This is the title by which the leader of the Gelukpa sect has been known ever since, in China and in the Western world, but most Tibetans would not even know what it meant. In Tibet each head of the Gelukpa sect has 'Gyatso' added to his name, and is most often referred to as Gyalwa Rinpoche, or 'Victorious One', or Kyabngon Rinpoche, 'Precious Protector'.

The Chinese managed to persuade Sonam Gyatso to visit the Imperial Court. He did so on his way back from Mongolia, establishing a special official to maintain friendly relations between the Gelukpa and the Chinese court. It was also an opportunity to further the Gelukpa cause in eastern Tibet, which had always been under the sway of the unreformed Nyingmapa sect and of the old Bönpoba. It was at this time that the great monastery of Kumbum was founded, to mark the birthplace of the new sect's founder, Tsong Khapa.

The Gelukpa sect was still far from having any political power nor did it at this time have any political interests. Its sole concern was the spread of its teachings, the uprooting of old animistic worship and the purging of Buddhism of many of the foreign practices that continued to creep in and degrade it. Sonam Gyatso was particularly concerned with the work he had begun in Mongolia, where monasteries were established with remarkable rapidity. To this end he made a second visit, and it must have given him much satisfaction to see how completely the Mongolians had taken to the new religion. It had already begun to have its political effect in lessening, if not altogether stopping, Mongolian raids on Tibetan and Chinese territory. Altan Khan had died, but his son continued giving vigorous support to the Buddhist cause. During his second journey to Mongolia Sonam Gyatso was called on to adjudicate on a minor border dispute between Chinese and Mongolians, and this was perhaps the first instance in which the Gyalwa Rinpoche, or Dalai Lama, exercised purely political authority. It may have been recognition of the political potential of the Gelukpa sect that caused China to issue yet another invitation for the religious leader to visit the Ming court. The Emperor himself sent many gifts, but Sonam Gyatso had fallen ill and was to die while still in Mongolia.

Surrounded by his converts he was urged by them not to leave them just when they needed continued religious leadership, and he promised them that indeed he would not leave them but would take his next birth as one of them. The year after he died, a son was born to the Mongol king bearing all the signs of being an incarnation, and he was eventually recognized as Sonam Gyatso's reincarnation and given the name of Yönten Gyatso. After preliminary studies in the Mongolian monasteries, however, the young Gyalwa Rinpoche had to leave his home country and take up his duties in Lhasa. A representative was sent in his place, founding a dynasty of Mongolian incarnations to exercise authority over the Mongolian Church.

The growing friendship between the Mongolian kings and Tibetan lamas was not at all to the liking of the Chinese, hard-pressed as they already were by the Mongols to the north and still mindful of the barely dormant fighting zeal and skill of the Tibetans to their west. While the Mongols supported the Gelukpa during the reign of Yönten Gyatso, even to the extent of attempting to forcibly convert some Nyingmapa monasteries to the reformed faith, the Ming dynasty gave what support it could, weak as it was, to the Tsangpa kings who were the most powerful of any of the Tibetan petty chiefs at that time. The Tsangpa were of lowly origin and ardent supporters of the old Karmapa (Black Hat) sect. For both religious and political reasons they were bitterly opposed to the Gelukpa. They even entertained Christian missionaries, probably in the hope of finding a religious force to combat that of the Gelukpa; their own priests, however, were antagonistic to the Christians from the start and the mission never really succeeded in establishing itself. When the Tsangpa rulers extended their influence to include the whole of central Tibet they carried their war into the heart of their Gelukpa enemies, raiding the monasteries of Drepung, Sera and Kumbum.

During the reign of Yönten Gyatso's successor, the Ming were to succumb to the Manchus. With that the power of the Tsangpa was to come to an end, and the Gelukpa were to take over temporal as well as spiritual authority, extending that authority over the whole of Tibet and exercising enormous political as well as religious influence beyond, in China and in Mongolia. For the moment, however, although the sect was being recognized everywhere more and more as a political factor, within itself its major concerns and goals were purely religious. Perhaps it was the care and attention they paid to internal order and discipline that, despite its religious motivation, made the sect into so potent a political entity.

Out of religious belief, too, the Gelukpa had established a system of succession that was to have equal success as a political system of succession, ensuring against all the possible evils of a hereditary system, particularly that of nepotism, by introducing a judicious element of uncertainty. There is never any way of predicting who the next Gyalwa Rinpoche will be. It can only be determined by long and painstaking search, following the death of the previous Rinpoche, under the supervision of a carefully constituted body of monks. There have been fourteen such incarnations to date, and only one, the grandson of Altan Khan, has come from a family of any consequence. All the others have been born in humble and utterly unconnected families. Attempts at fraud are not unknown, and the Chinese have attempted to influence the choice on more than one occasion, to their own political advantage. But so tight is the system of checks and counterchecks that such attempts are readily discovered, and so great is the faith of ordinary Tibetans that they would be incapable of accepting any candidate who had not passed all the tests.

This faith, and the whole system, rests on the Buddhist doctrine of the threefold form of Buddha – two manifest forms (one earthly and one subtle) and one unmanifest. The Tibetan Buddhists in particular believe that the manifest forms are manifest countless numbers of times for the salvation of all living things. The Buddha, at the moment of enlightenment, made the supreme sacrifice by vowing to forgo release until suffering was ended in the world. Thus was established the Changchub Sempa (bodhisattva) ideal, the highest goal for which a monk can strive, the achievement of enlightenment and a return to the round of rebirth, subject to all its laws, out of compassion for the world. Just as there are forms of the Buddha, so are there three forms of the Changchub Sempa: Compassion Wisdom and Power. Each Buddhist sect in Tibet recognizes a series of incarnations of one or other of these Changchub Sempa.

The Gelukpa recognized Chenresig, the Lord of Compassion, and the system as formally and finally established under Yönten's successor established the Gyalwa Rinpoche, or Dalai Lamas, as incarnate manifestations of Chenresig, come for the express purpose of the deliverance of all from suffering. Although Sonam Gyatso had been the first to actually hold the title, Gedundrub being the first of the line was at this point recognized as being the first Gyalwa Rinpoche, making Sonam Gyatso the third. The Buddha himself prophesied that he would return in this way, beyond the mountains to the north of India, which accounts for the particular reverence paid by all Tibetan Buddhists to the Gyalwa Rinpoche.

Chenresig is usually represented in paintings and sculpture as ineffably beautiful and having four arms. In this form he is thought of in Tibet as a herdsman whose flock includes all the living things of the world. Like a herdsman he leads and guides his flock, bringing it surely back to the safety of the fold. He himself does not seek the shelter of the fold until the very last of his flock has entered. Only then is his work done and may he enter. Sometimes, however, Chenresig is shown in a different form, having eleven heads. This is a form used to illustrate in another way the boundless compassion of the Changchub sempa. As such he is perfected and incapable of sin although in incarnate form his body is subject to all the suffering of earthly bodies. Yet also as a perfected one, he always has the option of release from the world of suffering. When the Buddha first manifested himself as Chenresig, for the deliverance of all living things, so great was the compassion he felt for the suffering he saw all around him that his head split into a thousand fragments and he returned to mying di. There, his head restored to him, dismayed at having abandoned his self-appointed charge, he returned once again, and again his head was sundered in a thousand directions. This happened eleven times before his compassion was strong enough to absorb all the suffering of the world, giving him the strength to stay to fulfil his task.

Although the term 'Gyalwa' means 'victory', it is in a defensive sense rather than aggressive. As a title it is generally translated as 'Protector'; the Tibetan notion of protection is such that a better translation might be 'Refuge'. A man who seeks protection from his enemies does not expect them to be magically turned away from him, but rather seeks the means to repel them. Having repelled them or been conquered, regardless of the outcome, his goal then is to find a way of preventing further enmity from arising, this being the surest protection of all. Protection does not come from outside intervention, but rather from inner action.

Although the Gyalwa Rinpoche is thought of as the great protector of the Tibetan people, this in no way means that he is believed to have the power to save people by such simple means as the laying on of hands or even by the conferring of holy secrets, of prayers the incessant repetition of which will bring enlightenment. Such possibilities are completely out of line with Tibetan thought, for we believe, as Buddhists, that there is no escape from the consequences of our deeds, from the law of Lei. The incarnate Changchub Sempa's task is a much harder one. He can only achieve the release of the whole of mankind, and hence his own, by bringing mankind to right action through a recognition of the Truth, through the teaching of the Three Precious Ones: the Buddha, His Word, and the Order of Monks.

Because he is an incarnate Changchub Sempa the Gyalwa Rinpoche is able to impart special force and vigour to the teachings of the Buddha's word, by which man is saved. His very presence is beneficial, embodying all possible human virtues and therefore acting as a living example of perfection. Salvation comes to man through hard work and conscious effort, not by escape. Tibetan Buddhists believe that sincere good intent is of the greatest importance, and the presence of the Gyalwa Rinpoche is a constant inspiration for all to make the attempt to follow the teachings of the Buddha. During the attempt we shed the effects of our previous bad deeds, one by one, while by the good deed of good intent alone we work towards a higher rebirth in our next life, and towards ultimate liberation.

The complete devotion and loyalty felt for the Gyalwa Rinpoche by the Tibetan people is founded in their recognition of the sacrifice he has made on their behalf, voluntarily re-entering the world of suffering, binding himself to it until he has ultimately brought them all to the state of bliss he had won for himself.

CHAPTER ELEVEN

Incarnation and Succession

As long as any living thing draws breath,
Wherever he shall be,
There, in compassion, shall the Buddha appear;
Incarnate.

– from MNGON RTOG RGYAN

In Tibet the Gyalwa Rinpoche, or Dalai Lama, is the highest but by no means the only incarnate Changchub Sempa. The highest ideal for every monk is to achieve his own liberation only to renounce it and to return for the benefit of others. Sometimes, as with the Gyalwa Rinpoche, the return becomes a regular and recognizable series of rebirths in human form. Nearly every monastery in Tibet is the home of such an incarnate lama, or teacher, often descended from the original founder of the monastery. These incarnations, or *Trülku*, are divided into four grades from the highest of which are chosen candidates for the regency of Tibet during a Gyalwa Rinpoche's minority. While the more fortunate incarnations are supported by large estates and often considerable wealth, other *Trülku* may find themselves impoverished, yet still with onerous responsibilities. In all cases, however, Gelukpa incarnations leave the effective control of their inheritance to specified officials of their monastery.

Among the lesser incarnations succession is largely determined by common consent within the local community, local oracles being consulted and omens followed and divine assistance invoked. The name is then submitted to the Gyalwa Rinpoche for approval, and if there is any question as between two or more candidates he must make the final decision. But even at this level the issue is a solemn one and is considered a spiritual matter, not political.

When it comes to the choice of a new Gyalwa Rinpoche, however, the issue becomes of the highest spiritual importance. The fact that the office accords the holder both spiritual and temporal authority over Tibet in no way gives a political colouring to the succession, as far as the Tibetan people are concerned, though the Chinese have long attempted to manipulate the succession to their own political ends. For the Tibetan people it is only a political issue insofar as, for them, their political welfare is synonymous with their spiritual welfare. The fact that the incarnation is of Chenresig himself, the protective deity, or refuge, of Tibet, calls for every possible care and precaution against mistake, fraud or intrigue. There is an elaborate system of safeguards, but the greatest safeguard of all is the prayer of the people who at this time pray day and night that divine guidance may be given to those in charge of the discovery. For a discovery it is, often taking many years to achieve.

When the Gyalwa Rinpoche dies, it is usual for him to reappear as a newborn child within a year. The search begins almost at once, for the Tibetan people feel lost without their spiritual leader. Somewhere, in the whole of Tibet, there is a boy who bears unmistakable signs of his real identity and who is capable of offering irrefutable proof. Even the shape and form of his body must conform to an established pattern; so must the shape of the head, the shape and size of the ears, and marks showing the rudimentary form of Chenresig's second pair of arms. Whereas lesser incarnations are not necessarily expected to have any memory of their previous existence, in order to prove his identity as the new Gyalwa Rinpoche, a young boy, only a few years old, must pass severe tests and display a thorough familiarity with his earlier lives.

Sometimes the search is aided by a dying Rinpoche indicating where he is likely to take rebirth. Sometimes a boy is born with such unmistakable signs of greatness that word reaches the authorities who immediately send delegates to investigate the claim. It has been known for boys to come forward on their own and demand to be returned to their monastery and recognized. One that I know, reincarnation of Shidé and head of Redreng, one of the most important of all Tibet's great monasteries, became recognized quickly because of his strange powers as a child. He did not claim to be that particular incarnation, but he was always showing knowledge of events that were yet to happen. He came of a poor family and certainly not one accustomed to receiving important visitors. But one day the boy became very excited and told his parents to prepare tea and put on their best clothes, and then he ran out into the courtyard and drove a wooden peg into a rock for the as yet unknown guest to use for tethering his horse. The visitor was from Redreng Monastery and had come to investigate stories he had heard of the boy, who quickly convinced him that he was indeed the reincarnation. He was a man of quite outstanding ability, and when the thirteenth Gyalwa Rinpoche died, before my brother was chosen as the fourteenth, he acted as regent even though he was not quite twenty years old.

Especially when in search for the reincarnation of the Gyalwa Rinpoche, the search is conducted in the greatest secrecy, numerous parties being sent out to different parts of the country, all in disguise. Some may go to investigate claims or rumours of wonder children, others may concentrate on an area which various oracles and omens have indicated as being likely. One oracle in particular, a lake high up in the mountains, is always consulted for guidance concerning the location of a new Gyalwa Rinpoche, for its guardian is his patron deity, the Goddess Pandan Lhamo, who in a vision appeared to Gedundrub, the first Gyalwa Rinpoche, shortly before his death. In this vision she promised him that she would continue to watch over all his successors. The lake, Lhamo Latso, is frequently visited by the Rinpoche during his lifetime, and on his death the regent goes there for guidance. In the depths of the waters can be seen wonderful sights. To the regent the lake sometimes reveals the exact location of the infant successor, or it provides clues or evidence that will help in the identification. On the death of the thirteenth Gyalwa Rinpoche the regent, Redreng Rinpoche, saw countryside which clearly indicated eastern Tibet and then was granted a vision of the actual homestead, my own home, where the boy would be found. When the mission that was already investigating in that area returned, having on their own decided that my younger brother was almost certainly the new reincarnation, they gave a description of the house that tallied exactly with what the regent had seen, even to the colour of our dog – mottled brown and white.

The mission was, of course, disguised, and the abbot of Sera, who headed the mission, took the role of servant. I was at Kumbum at the time, and neither I nor my parents had any thought even that the boy might be chosen as the new Gyalwa Rinpoche. The strangers who asked for lodging were accepted and welcomed as pilgrims. My parents even took pains to keep the young boy out of the way of the visitors so that they would not be troubled. On the second day, however, he came into the room where they were and immediately showed the greatest delight as though he were meeting old friends. He identified some of them, particularly the abbot of Sera disguised, as he was, in servants' dress. For an ordinary incarnation this would have been proof enough, but for a Gyalwa Rinpoche it was only the beginning.

My brother was then engaged in conversation and surprised everyone by showing a knowledge of the official court language, which nobody else in the family knew. Then came the test on which so many candidates fail. Each mission engaged in the search for the new incarnation takes with it a number of articles that had belonged to the recent Gyalwa Rinpoche together with a number of replicas or similar objects. If a candidate shows promise, the objects are offered to him, and he must, to be successful, unhesitatingly select only those which had belonged to the last Rinpoche. When the Sera abbot produced two rosaries, my brother did not even wait to be asked but immediately snatched the correct one, claiming it was his, and wanting to know why the abbot had it. So it was with all other manner of articles. The mission was convinced beyond doubt and sent a report back to Lhasa and left to wait for further instructions.

Rumours began to spread in the neighbourhood, but my parents were simple folk, and it still never entered their heads that such an honour could be theirs. The State Oracle of Nechung, the protective deity of Drepung Monastery, confirmed the opinion of the mission, however. Yet another test was applied, a number of names being entered in a lottery, consecrated by a special ceremony and drawn in front of a number of high incarnate lamas, and again it was my brother's name that came out. There were almost certainly many other tests, too, that I do not know about.

It must not be thought that these tests are merely mechanical. The whole process of selection depends on the prayers not only of the priests but of all the people. Throughout the whole country prayers are held and special services offered to secure the spiritual guidance necessary to make the correct choice.

The consultation of oracles is similarly a spiritual matter. Each of the three great seats of learning, Ganden, Sera and Drepung, have their oracle, but that of Drepung, known as Nechung, is considered the most powerful. Like the Goddess Pandan Lhamo, Nechung promised to help the line of Gyalwa Rinpoche. This oracle, like many others, is in fact a monk who acts as a medium, being able to communicate with Nechung when in a trance. He has to live a very carefully regulated life, with special restrictions on the food he eats, so that he is constantly ready and fit to communicate with Nechung, should the Gyalwa Rinpoche want it.

There are many oracles in Tibet; almost every village has one. In the village, even though the oracle speaks through the person of an ordinary villager, perhaps the local carpenter or a farmer, yet everyone believes that it is the voice of the god or spirit speaking. The person who acts as medium, or as the oracle, has to undergo special training and take initiation. When he is asked for help he puts on his robes, usually bright and colourful, and his attendants begin chanting, asking the god or spirit to come down and enter into the oracle and speak. The person who wants help burns incense and makes offerings of butter lamps and perhaps of food. Then the oracle begins to shake and tremble and falls into a trance. While in this trance any questions asked will be answered by the god. The voice is very strange, quite unlike that of the medium, and often his whole appearance changes so much that you could not recognize him as the same person you also know as your neighbour, or as a local farmer, or whatever he might be. Among the nomads I have seen an oracle always consulted before a hunt. He holds a heavy sword, which quivers and shakes and finally points in the direction the hunt should go.

Of course there are some frauds just as there are with astrologers and soothsayers many of whom are merely beggars. But for the most part the people who act as oracles believe in what they are doing, as do the people who consult them, and this is what really matters. If a question is asked in the faith that it will be answered and with the proper reverence, then we believe that it will be answered, even without an oracle.

When the state oracle or the sacred lake is consulted concerning the birth of a new Gyalwa Rinpoche, the regent is accompanied by a number of high ranking officials from the main Gelukpa monasteries. They often engage in several days' prayer before even putting the question to the oracle. Sometimes the oracle itself may be put to the test and made to prove that it is indeed speaking with the authority it claims and not just pretending. For instance questions may be written down and sealed in scrolls and handed in silence to the oracle who, without opening the scrolls to read the contents must nonetheless answer the questions. This was done when my brother's succession was disputed by a rival claimant.

The idea of a number of people taking part is not merely a way of preventing a single person from manipulating the results for his own good, though we are perfectly aware of this danger, but it is also because their combined prayers can bring far better results by bringing greatly increased spiritual force to bear on the oracle. Some oracles, such as the lake, reveal different secrets to each person, so again a number of people all concentrating to the same end are likely to get a more complete answer to their single question: where may the new Gyalwa Rinpoche be found.

When the sacred lake is consulted the regent is accompanied by government officials and representatives from the National Assembly. So also when the search parties are chosen they always include a cross-section of the people, both monks and laymen. The state oracles may even be consulted as to who should be sent. Such care is taken that it may be three or four years before the missions return and even then, sometimes, they return with more than one candidate. After such careful preparation it is unlikely that any of the final selections are frauds. They may possibly be other incarnations, or else it may be that for some reason the previous Gyalwa Rinpoche divided his rebirth among two or three bodies, appearing in the body of one, the speech of another, and the mind of a third, for we believe that these three are separate entities that together make up the complete person. In a case such as this the boy manifesting the mind of the previous incarnation is unhesitatingly chosen, for the mind rules speech and body and will be able to bring his own speech and body into conformity.

The Gyalwa Rinpoche is head of the Gelukpa sect, but he is also spiritual and temporal head of the whole of Tibet and is recognized as such by all sects. The sects are not mutually exclusive in any way; the difference between them is more like the difference between different academic schools, each of which may stress a different aspect of the same discipline. While not denying the validity of the other school, each believes that its own emphasis is the most important. People who are temperamentally or spiritually or academically suited to one school, or sect, rather than another are naturally drawn in that direction, and certainly it is there that they belong. That does not bar them from entering or learning from the other schools, however. A Gyalwa Rinpoche may perfectly well even be born into a Nyingmapa family. He will be brought to Lhasa as soon as he is old enough, around six or seven years old as a rule, and will begin his training in the Gelukpa colleges there, for his first responsibility is to master the reformed doctrine. But it must be remembered that all the great reformers themselves studied all the scriptures, including the tantras; the reform was based on what they believed was good for the people as a whole, not on what was good for individual monks. Each individual monk must find his own path. So with each Gyalwa Rinpoche. Some lean in one direction, some in another. The fifth, in some ways the greatest of all, himself leaned strongly in the direction of the Nyingmapa teachings yet for the general public body of laymen he continued to advocate, as firmly as ever, the teachings of the reformed sect. He is usually shown as carrying the phurbu, even, the mystic dagger, one of the major tantric symbols and one which Gelukpa members are forbidden to carry or use in public, though if they wish to take the necessary initiations and practice the tantras in private, they may do so after they have completed the last of the Gelukpa initiations.

The training prescribed for all Gyalwa Rinpoche recommends that he take these other initiations as soon as he has completed his Gelukpa training so that he is fitted to understand and lead all religious communities, and the country, as a whole. Our belief is that this system gives Tibet the most truly spiritual rule that we can hope for. It is not the Gyalwa Rinpoche as an individual who rules, it is religion itself. During both the Great Prayer and the Lesser Prayer, marking the beginning of the Tibetan New Year, all control of law and order, all administration in Lhasa, is taken over by the two highest lamas of Drepung Monastery. During the Great Prayer monks take their examinations for the highest degrees; during the Lesser Prayer others take examinations for the second highest degrees. During all this time the prayers for peace for the whole world, and for Tibet, are continuously said, and even the Gyalwa Rinpoche subordinates himself to the rule of religion as represented by the two Drepung monks, who for this period have absolute power.

It is often thought, outside Tibet, that we Tibetans regard the Gyalwa Rinpoche as a God, holy and untouchable. This is not so. The Gyalwa Rinpoche is two things. He is the reincarnation of Chenresig, and he is a human being like anyone else. It is the spirit of Chenresig which animates his body that we revere. We give thanks that Chenresig has entered human form so that he can more effectively give us the guidance we need. It is the Buddha, through his manifest form as Chenresig, whom we worship, not the body or being of a human. We believe that the body, the form of the Gyalwa Rinpoche, while likely to be in many respects superior to others, is still esentially human. That is the whole point of Chenresig's sacrifice. The body he enters, for our sake, is subject to decay, as are all things. It is subject to illness and suffering; it is subject to weakness; and death will come to it in the normal course of time, just as it comes to all human bodies.

There is nothing to be gained from trying to touch the body

of the Gyalwa Rinpoche as though the mere contact would convey some kind of benefit. The only way that benefit can be had by physical contact is if the Gyalwa Rinpoche consciously conveys his blessing, communicating something of the essence of Chenresig to the person paying homage. Souvenirs of the clothing or body of the Gyalwa Rinpoche are valueless, or nearly so, unless they have been given with the Rinpoche's blessing. They are not entirely valueless, however, if they are unwittingly the cause of good thoughts, which are good deeds. It depends on what the possessor of the souvenir himself imparts to the shred of cloth or the strand of hair. If it leads his thoughts to Chenresig he will be rewarded for his devotion, however mistaken it may seem to us. If he thinks that by touching the relic to an injury he can cure it, the cure depends on the extent of his faith and on whether it is centered in the relic itself or in Chenresig. If, however, he thinks that the relic has some power in itself, which he can use for his own ends, he will only increase his own suffering.

The body of the Gyalwa Rinpoche may well show signs of weakness and suffering, and this is in no way thought to indicate that perhaps he has wrongly chosen. It is not expected that his body should be any more perfect than anyone else's. It *is* expected that his actions will be perfect, for he being the incarnation of Chenresig, his deeds, governed by Chenresig's spirit, cannot help being good. I have known it said of lesser incarnations who displayed tendencies to wrong action that they must have been wrongly chosen, and this can happen. It is also said sometimes that there is collusion, that a child has been given all the answers beforehand so that he can display the necessary recollection of his previous existence. There was such a case when the mission in Amdo province was looking for the successor to the thirteenth Gyalwa Rinpoche. I am not sure whether or not they had already visited my family at Tengtser for I was at Kumbum Monastery then and had no idea that my brother was a candidate. Near by, however, there was a family I did know who had a boy of the right age, and they put him forward as a candidate, claiming that he had shown all sorts of signs and performed all sorts of miracles. Every such claim, however weak, must be investigated, and the mission visited this family. The parents had carefully coached the child for it was they who wanted preferment for themselves, not the child. He had apparently learned his lesson well, but when the mission began to ask him questions he burst into tears and ran away. Far from being attracted to the mission, as he should have been, he seemed driven away from them in terror, and everyone laughed at the family for having made such fools of themselves.

The boy was a good boy, however, and had no knowing part in the attempted fraud. He eventually became a monk and was a student at Kumbum when I was abbot. I used to see quite a lot of him, and he often came to take meals with me, not because of what had happened – we never even mentioned that, I think – but simply because he was one of the leading students and represented his class. There was certainly no feeling against him for what had happened.

In Lhasa too there was a false claimant, a very important family trying to establish their young son as the new Gyalwa Rinpoche. They even manipulated omens, such as causing horses belonging to the thirteenth Rinpoche to stampede and run away to the family's own stables as though that were where they belonged. Because of the importance of this family it was thought not impossible that they might even have bribed the state oracle, which suspicion was subjected to a most rigorous test, and my brother's case was re-examined with minute care and verified by additional means.

Perhaps we should be more criticized than others for such attempts at fraud and personal advancement, since we think and talk so much about religion. But we never claim to be any better than any other people. Our own belief is that Chenreisig was sent to us, on the contrary, because we were such a wild and barbarous people. We are still far from perfect, but that does not make it wrong for us to rule our lives by religion as far as we can, and we can at least claim that we are consciously trying to improve ourselves. I am particularly aware of this since I was, myself, chosen (or 'recognized', as we say) as a spiritual reincarnation and as such am meant to be a spiritual guide to my people. Yet I have no recollection of my previous existences and can only think of how unfitted I am, with all my imperfections, for the task I have been given. I am certainly very conscious of having a human body.

My own recognition, being only one of the Middle Incarnations, was not so important, and if I was being tested at any time I did not notice it. When the previous reincarnation of Tagtser died it was indicated that he would be reborn somewhere in my neighbourhood, and so the monks of his monastery, at Kumbum, made a list of all the boys born within a year or two of his death and sent it to the thirteenth Gyalwa Rinpoche. For some reason they had not included my name. Perhaps they already had indications that I was the most likely candidate, and this was my test; I do not know. Anyway, the Gyalwa Rinpoche looked at the list of some twenty or thirty names and said that the right name was not on the list. It is often within his powers to know the identity of lesser incarnations, through prayer and with the help of the oracles, and if he makes a decision, then that is considered enough. The priests of Tagtser Labrang again made up a list, adding some names, but still not including mine, and again it was sent back to them. When on the third occasion, my name was included, the Gyalwa Rinpoche put his seal on my name and sent the list back to the monastery. Calling all the priests of Tagtser Labrang together they opened the Gyalwa Rinpoche's letter, saw that the seal had been placed on my name, and at once set out for the village of Tengtser with presents.

I was six or seven years old at the time, and I remember very well how I was playing in the fields at the time, down by a little stream. My sister came running out to tell me that some monks had come to visit our home and that they wanted to see me. She took me to the house and there in the courtyard I saw a lot of fine big horses and inside were the monks. They gave me beautiful clothes to wear, finely cut and made of silk, better than anything I had ever seen, let alone worn. Then they told me that I was the reincarnation of the monk Tagtser, and that I would have to leave home and go to Shardzong Monastery to study. I don't know whether they expected me to cry at the thought of leaving home, but I did not cry at all, not then. I was overcome with delight and wanted to leave right away. For a long time I had wanted to run away to the monastery; it used to be my favourite game and favourite dream.

My parents too were very happy, for it was a great honour for them. The monks stayed several days and gave a reception for all our friends from the village, giving everyone presents and announcing that I was the reincarnation of Tagtser. For the next two years, nearly, we continued receiving visits and presents, and occasionally priests would come to teach me prayers, and my mother also took extra time to teach me more prayers. Then the astrologers fixed the date that would be most auspicious for me to leave for Shardzong, and the monks came to take me, with my whole family, to the monastery. I remember how beautiful it looked, high up on a cliff face and that I could not think how our horses would ever reach it. It was even more beautiful when we got there, with its view over the wooded valleys below. There were only a few buildings, trim and clean, and some of them overgrown with climbing flowers. Parts of the monastery could only be reached by a narrow wooden plank running across a sheer face, and I was terrified that I might shame my parents by showing how scared I was. Then someone took my hand, and soon I was able to run back and forth across that rickety bridge as though it were a wide, firm street.

Then, after two or three days, my parents left. My mother left first, and I thought she was coming back. Then the next morning when I awoke I found my father had left also, and I began to realize that I was going to have to stay in the monastery on my own, that I had left my home and my family for good. I did not like that at all, and I cried for the first time. My early longing to join a monastery had been a genuine one, however, and soon I was excitedly beginning to take part in monastery life, making new friends, and starting a few simple lessons, learning how to read and write. Most of my time was spent playing however. There were a number of other boys a little older than I was, and although they had certain duties to perform, cleaning their quarters, going out to collect yak dung from the mountainside and so forth, we spent a lot of time together. I had no duties myself, since being an incarnation from a wealthy monastery I had a servant appointed to look after me and to do all the cleaning and prepare my food. It was he who first taught me how to write, and he became my closest friend.

I was so pleased and happy with all the attention that was shown to me, and with the fine clothes I was given to wear, that I still did not think much about what it all meant. Life seemed like one long happy game for those first few months. I do remember, though, thinking how good it was to be there, learning to read and write at the very same place where the great Tsong Khapa was given his first lessons. Young as I was I knew of Tsong Khapa and of at least some of the things he stood for, and it made me feel even happier to be there.

After a number of months, the time came when the astrologers said I must leave for my own monastery of Tagtser Labrang, in the greater monastery of Kumbum, and be installed as the new reincarnation. Again I was too excited to feel sorry to be leaving Shardzong, happy as I had been there, and too young to realize that I was, at the age of eight years, about to leave behind a carefree childhood. A great cavalcade led me in procession to Tengtser where the whole village turned out to greet me and where to my great joy we stayed for several days at my parent's home. Then we moved on, the procession getting bigger all the time, towards the huge monastery-town of Kumbum.

About half a mile away all sorts of things seemed to happen at once. A further escort of monks arrived on horseback while others lined the route wearing all sorts of different robes I had never seen before, carrying banners and sheltered by brightly coloured umbrellas. Some were making music, blowing noisily into trumpets and immense long horns, perhaps ten feet long, made of copper and richly wrought with silver and inlaid with turquoise. Altogether there must have been about three thousand monks, come to welcome the new Tagtser Lama, apart from the fact that not only my family but most of Tengtser village had come along with the procession.

Inside I was taken to the Tagtser Labrang, a fine spacious place, and carried to a throne in the assembly hall. This is the chair on which Tagtser himself sat and on which his reincarnations have sat ever since, and only they. Even a regent may not sit on the throne. There was a small step to help me climb up, and once I was seated people began to come and to present me with the white scarves that are our traditional greeting. A special prayer was offered by the monks for me, that I might have a long life and forever stay in good health.

When that was all over I was taken to my quarters where friends came to visit me and a number of boys of my own age were brought to meet me. I had a wonderful time with them; they took me all around and showed me things I had never seen or heard of before, like cuckoo clocks and music boxes. There was a visit from the abbot of Kumbum to welcome me, and of course the next day I had to pay a formal visit to him and other high-ranking officers of the monastery, myself bringing scarves to present to them. There were pilgrimages to make to the temples and particularly to the birthplace of Tsong Khapa, and again life was far too busy for me to really stop and think of what was happening to me. I had a little more studying to do, but there was still plenty of time for playing, and life seemed, if anything, better than ever.

Even some first-rank incarnations are not well endowed, and hardly have enough wealth to provide them with food let alone to care properly for their monasteries. The grade of an incarnation does not depend on wealth but on the reputation for wisdom and virtue shown by the whole line of successors. Although Tagtser was only in the middle grade, it happened to be one of the wealthiest, having had many wealthy patrons. The money is by no means squandered in luxury, even an incarnation has to live according to the prescribed standards of simplicity once he has taken holy orders. As yet, however, I was unordained and could be spoiled.

Other incarnations might have to go to their teachers' quarters for instruction, but Tagtser Labrang could well afford to offer food and private quarters for a personal tutor, and this too made life easier and more agreeable. My tutor was a wonderful man who treated me like his own child. Every morning, before dawn, he came to me and read prayers with me and we studied until about nine o'clock. In the winter we worked in the same room in which I slept because although my quarters had several rooms, we never kept more than one warm. Then we used to have breakfast together, tea with butter and yak cheese. After we had eaten he went off to continue his own studies, and I could go out to play with the other children. We used to run about the monastery and hide from each other, or else we would make statues or build houses of mud. In the summer time we were free to go out and play on the mountainside so long as five or six of us went together.

There was a light mid-day snack, and then the main meal of the day came in the mid-afternoon, with meat, tea and tsampa. After that there was not much time left for playing because at five o'clock my studies and prayers began again and continued until it was time to go to bed, around eight or nine o'clock. I was not even expected to attend temple services though sometimes on my own I used to like to visit the temple and pray, and on special days, like the fifteenth of each month, I would sometimes attend with my teacher. As yet I was still not a monk, not having taken any vows. That was the next step.

After I had been at Kumbum Monastery for six or seven months – I suppose I must have been nearly ten years old then – I was told that the astrologers had said the time was right for me to take my first vows. Of course I could have refused if I had wanted to, but I was so anxious that I asked if I could not take the first two sets of vows together, and this was agreed upon. One other boy from Tagtser Labrang was to take vows with me, and three days before the ceremony our heads were shaven, all but for a small lock left on the crown.

On the appointed day the other boy and I were taken to the temple to wait for the incarnate lama who was to give us our vows. He was Cheshö Rinpoche, an old blind man. He arrived with his servant, and was joined by four other monks. He lit his butter lamps in front of the image of Buddha and sat there and prayed for about an hour. Then myself and the other boy were called in. We went in and bowed to the old Rinpoche, and he blessed us with holy water. He asked us a few questions to make sure that we really wanted to take the vows and knew perfectly well what we were doing; then with a pair of scissors he cut from each of our heads the last lock of hair that bound us to the world.

He then asked us again if we really wanted to take the vows, and when we said yes, he read each vow out to us, one after the other, and to each one we had to give our assent. While in prep-aration, we were already Rapjung, or novices who are entered on the path, but are not yet full monks. After our first thirty-six vows we were Getsul, or junior monks. Then we went on to take the rest of the two hundred and fifty-three vows to become Gelong, or full monks. From this moment on we were allowed to wear the simple clothing of the monk, which to me seemed so much more attractive than all the fine silks I had been wearing. And the long, long years of study began in earnest. It would be seven years of hard work before either of us would be ready to take the examinations that would qualify us to enter the monks' assembly, which was our next goal, and then many more years after that until we could hope to reach the end of our training in the Gelukpa school. Beyond that it would be up to us to take what further instruction we wanted or felt we needed, but that was far too far ahead to think of at the moment.

I had other things to think of, because at last it was beginning to come to me just what it meant to be recognized as an incarna-tion. At Shardzong some of the monks had talked to me about it, but I never really understood. I kept asking where Tagtser was, and when he would be coming back. They tried to tell me that he had died, and that I understood, until they tried to tell me he had returned in my body.

Then at Kumbum everyone showing me around used to point places out and say, 'This was where you used to sit,' and show me objects and say, 'You used this in such-and-such a life.' Then

I began to understand that all this part of Kumbum, the Tagtser Labrang, was mine, and so had been Shardzong, for it is one of Tagtser Labrang's branch monasteries. Some say it is founded on the spot where Tagtser himself used to meditate. I had already understood, in a very simple childish way, that these places and this wealth and in a sense, even, these people all belonged to me, and I to them, but only now, at Kumbum, did I realize that it was all mine not because, in some strange way, it had all been given to me as a present, but because in a far stranger way it had been mine even before I was born, that I actually *was* Tagtser.

Then I quickly saw that as people pointed out all my previous possessions they eagerly looked at me to see if I showed any signs of recognition. Not that it is expected, or even usual, for incarnations to remember their previous lives, but somehow it is always hoped for. I began to hope for it myself, but no one single object looked familiar, not one place brought back any memories. In the heart of Tagtser Labrang itself, on the very throne of Tagtser, nothing stirred inside me except a growing realization of the responsibility that had been bestowed on me. All these people were looking up to me, an uneducated child from a peasant family, for spiritual guidance, all of them hoping, secretly, for some miracle. And out in the countryside, on the lands owned by my monastery, peasant folk like my own family, were depending on me to help them and guide them, using my knowledge and power and wealth for their good. It would have helped me if I had been able to recall even one event from my previous life, but I, who can often not even remember what happened yesterday, what chance is there of my remembering back to another existence?

I suppose it would be strange if I did not wonder, as I do, if I really *am* Tagtser's reincarnation. The Gyalwa Rinpoche believed it; everyone else believes it; but I myself, I just do not know. I can only suppose that if it *is* so, then in my last life I must have laid up bad deeds that have prevented me from having even one memory. And if, by some strange chance, I was wrongly recognized and am not Tagtser, then I must be thankful that in my previous existence, whatever it was, I was fortunate enough to store up the good deeds that brought me to Tagtser Labrang, even if mistakenly. The mission may have made a mistake, even the Gyalwa Rinpoche may have made a mistake, but deeds never make a mistake, and I could not imagine a greater blessing to have befallen me than to have been brought, so early in this life, into contact with all those holy and truly religious people who have meant so much to me ever since.

I have had to accept their belief in me as Tagtser, and do everything I could to fill the role. Perhaps my doubt in myself is sent to me as the suffering that I have to endure in this life; for other than that, life, however hard at times, has staunchly continued to fill me with the same joy that it did when, as a boy, I used to play at running away and becoming a monk.

CHAPTER TWELVE

Monastic Rule

The Potala is the Paradise of Buddhas,
Palace of Chenresig.
To east, west, south and north,
There is a Potala on this earth;
From the Land of Snows to the Lho Potala,
Potala of the Southern Seas.

– Tibetan saying

Ngawong Gyatso, the fifth Gyalwa Rinpoche (1617–82), is known to Tibetans as 'The Great Fifth' and for many different reasons. He is renowned for his military exploits in the seventeenth century, leading to the secular unification of Tibet, and he is equally renowned for his political astuteness by which the independence of Tibet was maintained despite the manoeuvres of the Mongols on the one hand and the Chinese on the other. He left behind him a monument which he conceived and built and which has, even outside Tibet, long been regarded as a symbol of the country's greatness – the vast Potala palace, named after the spiritual home of Chenresig. To Tibetans the Potala is the centre of spiritual as well as of political life, and so also to Tibetans is the fifth Gyalwa Rinpoche renowned for his spiritual as well as for his secular greatness.

It was under the rule of Ngawong Gyatso that the rule of religion was finally established, and even to the layman, to the nomad or to the farmer in his fields, Ngawong Gyatso can have no more deserving claim to greatness than this. It was not merely the ascendancy of the Gelukpa sect that was established, nor only the victory of Buddhism over the old Bön beliefs. It was a dedication of an entire nation to a religious principle, and it has been the constant attempt to put that principle into practice that has always been Tibet's greatest source of strength. There has never been any police force in Tibet, no means of enforcing laws by the use of physical strength. The rule of religion has always depended solely on the religious fervour of the people themselves, and this is something that cannot be imposed from outside. In following the laws of the country, in accepting the rule of religion, the Tibetan is only following his own religious inclinations, and in so doing he sees that benefit will follow both for the nation as a whole and for himself as an individual. To be a good, patriotic

249

citizen, a Tibetan has only to be a good Buddhist, no more and no less is demanded of him.

Yet when Ngawong Gyatso came into power the situation was by no means as simple. There was both secular and sectarian rivalry, and the old Bön religion was again making a bid for supremacy over Buddhism. Themselves long persecuted, the Bönpoba of northeastern Tibet had been steadily gaining in strength, and now took control of the province of Beri, imprisoning or driving out all Buddhist monks. Making use of the strong ties already forged with the Mongols, Ngawong Gyatso called on Gushri Khan who promptly sent an army to Beri and subjugated the rebellious Bönpoba. They never regained power, but right to the present day this area has been a stronghold of Bön belief.

Not far to the west the young Gyalwa Rinpoche had an even more powerful enemy, the king of Tsang. By far the strongest secular leader in the whole of Tibet, this king belonged to the Nyingmapa sect, and was bitterly opposed to the Gelukpa on religious grounds. He also feared their potential rivalry and in his own province did his best to completely suppress them. He even attempted to have the young Gelukpa leader assassinated. Once again Ngawong Gyatso appealed to Gushri Khan, who this time sent an even larger army which entered central Tibet, sacking and pillaging and forcibly restoring dispossessed Gelukpa monks to their monasteries. The armies of Tsang were engaged and defeated, the king and his nobility exiled.

Gushri Khan consolidated his position and soon established control over virtually the entire country. Retaining only an honorific title for himself, he formally handed over this control to Ngawong Gyatso, and from this moment onward the Gyalwa Rinpoche has been the undisputed secular leader as well as spiritual head of the country. The Mongol prince had intervened so willingly and effectively partly out of personal friendship for the young incarnate lama but also partly because of his own hostility to the Nyingmapa sect and his desire to see the Gelukpa sect flourish in Tibet as it did in his own country. Had Ngawong Gyatso wished, he could have used the Mongol military strength to destroy the Nyingmapa as a sect. As it was, while making sure that their political, secular authority was crushed, he went to extraordinary lengths to incorporate Nyingmapa teachings and practices in his own ecclesiastical court.

He underwent all the training demanded of any leader of the Gelukpa sect and proved himself to be an exceptional scholar. He went on, however, to study the Nyingmapa teachings, and some say he took Nyingmapa initiations and in fact became a member of the Nyingmapa sect. As such, unless he had not become a full monk, he would have still been bound by the vow of celibacy, yet it is further said that the man he appointed as regent, and to whom he handed over most of his secular authority, was in fact his son. Others deny this, claiming that he did in fact take full vows and maintain a celibate life. However that may be, it is certain that whereas he could with ease have established the complete subjection of the Nyingmapa to the Gelukpa, he established rather their spiritual and religious equality. It is certain also that whereas he could have kept the secular authority firmly in his own hands, as Gyalwa Rinpoche, he preferred to turn it over to the office of regent, a practice followed by nearly all his successors.

It was during Ngawong Gyatso's reign that the centralized form of government was established, which lasted with little change right up to the present. Under this system the government, while always subject to the ultimate authority of the Gyalwa Rinpoche, was divided equally between monks (both Gelukpa and Nyingmapa) and laymen. Both were included in equal numbers and acted as an effective balance to each other in the governmental deliberations. Part of the purpose of the great New Year festival, also instituted by the fifth Gyalwa Rinpoche, is to remind everyone, clerics and lay alike, that the government of Tibet and the welfare of its people rest on our religious belief and practice. It was Ngawong Gyatso who ordered that at this time the senior proctors from Drepung Monastery, near Lhasa, should take over absolute control of the government. The formal ceremony includes speeches, made in public, admonishing nobility and clerics alike to heed the rule of religion.

Ngawong Gyatso was an able politician, and throughout his

life he maintained his close friendship with the powerful Mongol prince Gushri Khan, at the same time establishing cordial relations with the new Manchu dynasty in China. He visited the Imperial Court at Peking and won for Tibet all the concessions granted by the previous Ming dynasty and for the office of Gyalwa Rinpoche recognition of its absolute independence and authority.

Partly because of the need for a physical home for the new central government, and partly, perhaps, because of the desire to avoid its being regarded as an exclusively Gelukpa monopoly, Ngawong Gyatso decided to move from his quarters at the Gelukpa monastery of Drepung and establish the new court of the Gyalwa Rinpoche, as spiritual and secular head of Tibet, on the site of the palace built long before by Srontsan Gampo, on Lhasa's Red Hill. Few men have left behind such a monument as the Potala, yet because of this and because of his many other secular accomplishments, the fifth Gyalwa Rinpoche is often thought of outside Tibet, primarily, or even solely, as a states-man and politician or as a scholar. In Tibet, however, we think of him with equal respect for his spiritual greatness, as the man who gave us, among other things, the Lhasa Mönlam, the Great Prayer of Lhasa which commemorates the beginning of every new year. We think of him as the man who allowed us to dream of paradise and tell the world of our dreams in the joyous butter-tower festival. He himself had such a dream, showing the infinite beauty of the world of the Buddhas, and had the scenes re-created in giant models made of hard butter for all to see and wonder at. Once a year we still do this, and my own monastery of Kumbum is most famous of all for the beauty and excellence of its butter towers. We work hard at our creations, which are kept secret until the evening of the fifteenth day of the twelfth month when they are paraded in the streets for everyone to enjoy. Then, as a poignant reminder of the transitory nature of all things, before the sun rises on the sixteenth day our dreams in butter are dissolved in flames.

Erudite as he was, Ngawong Gyatso recognized the limitations of mere academic learning and increasingly retreated into a life of spiritual contemplation. While looking down from the Potala once he saw an old man making his circuit of the sacred city, followed by the figure of a woman whom he instantly recognized as Dolma, the heavenly consort of Chenresig. Every day at the same time the old man appeared on his pilgrimage, and every day he was followed by the image of Dolma. Ngawong Gyatso asked for the old man to be brought to him and then questioned him. The man knew nothing of Dolma following him and amused the court by his ignorance and apparent stupidity. He was merely making the prescribed pilgrimage, he said, and reciting the holy *ngag*, or prayer, as he had been taught. When he recited the prayer for all to hear he was ridiculed for the number of mistakes he had made, and he was carefully taught how to recite it correctly.

The next day Ngawong Gyatso watched from the roof of the Potala with members of his court but when the old man appeared as usual, he was alone. There was no sign of the goddess Dolma. Once more the Gyalwa Rinpoche had the old man brought to him. There, in front of everyone, he told the old man that he was more fortunate than those who had presumed to try to correct him for his faulty recitation, for in his ignorance he nonetheless had the protection of Dolma, whereas in his newfound learning he had lost it. He told the old man to return to his pilgrimage and to continue as he had begun, with his mind and heart fixed on their purpose, for it was devotion and not learning that brought such blessings. The old man did as he was told and was once again seen making his round of the city, mumbling his faulty prayer, but with Dolma once again following and protecting him.

To Tibetans the Potala is a symbol of the spiritual rather than the temporal greatness of the fifth Gyalwa Rinpoche, and it is open to all, Buddhist or otherwise, as a place of spiritual pilgrimage. Its very name refers to the celestial home of Chenresig, so we generally refer to the Potala in Lhasa as Phobrang, meaning the palace of the earthly incarnation of Chenresig. There are said to be other Potalas too – homes for other earthly incarnations. The Lho Potala, that of the Southern Seas, is supposed to be near Shanghai. In Shengshi province is the Rio Tsen ga, or 'palace of the five mountain peaks', the eastern home of Chenresig. To the west is the land of Urgyen, which we think may include Kashmir, and there lies the western Potala, and to the north is Shambhala, which some say is in Tibet and others even think may be Moscow.

We do not know exactly where these four Pótalas are, but we believe that somewhere in this world they exist, and in each of them Chenresig has incarnated himself in a Changchub Sempa for the welfare of mankind. For us, in Tibet, the Potala in Lhasa is the home of Chenresig, incarnate in the body of the Gyalwa Rinpoche, and that is its importance for us rather than that it is the centre of our government or for its historic importance. Some even say that it was the earthly abode of Chenresig himself, before Tibet was inhabited.

Pilgrims must leave their horses, if they have come by horse-back, at the foot of the Red Hill. Then they have quite a stiff climb, up the rock face, along paths and up steps cut into the rock face. Above towers the White Palace, and behind and even higher stands the Red Palace. The Red Palace contains the temples and monastic apartments and the private monastery of the Gyalwa Rinpoche. His private apartments are the highest of all. The White Palace is for secular offices and for the residence of all secular members of the Potala staff. Here also is a school for government officials.

After climbing up the steps on the rock face, the pilgrim enters the building itself. It is nearly a thousand feet long and thirteen storeys high, filled with a maze of corridors and staircases. When I first visited the Potala I went in by the pilgrim's main entrance, going from the bright sunlight outside into a chamber that was so dark I could see nothing at first. In this chamber there is a huge prayer wheel, twenty or more feet high, about eight feet in diameter. From one side of it there is a wooden stick, and when anyone turns the prayer wheel the stick comes around and sounds a deep-toned bell. Every pilgrim visiting the Potala must turn this wheel. From there I climbed up inside the Potala, going along dark corridors lit by butter lamps or by small open sky-lights and climbing all the time. Sometimes I came out into the open, such as by the huge courtyard under the Red Palace where many of the festivals take place, particularly the religious dances and plays.

There are temples and shrines to see, and towards the back are the tombs of all the Gyalwa Rinpoche from the fifth onward, excepting the sixth, whose death was as strange as his life. The tombs, particularly that of Ngawong Gyatso, are highly revered. His reaches up for over sixty feet through three storeys inside the Potala, bursting out into a golden canopy on the roof, beside the canopies of the other tombs. Inside, if the weather is clear, the shutters are opened and there is plenty of light to see the chörton, enshrining the Rinpoche's remains, standing in the centre. When the shutters have to be closed, the tomb is lit by butter lamps, but you can still clearly see the chörton, covered with gold and inlaid with many kinds of precious stones. The relics are buried inside, and are not kept out for viewing, as some people say, and certainly there are no mummified bodies. The notion of the Potala as a mysterious place, filled with secret passages and chambers, is completely foreign to us, as is the notion that we forbid any but Tibetan Buddhists to visit the Potala. We have ourselves never had any interest in preventing other peoples from coming to Tibet, and any visitor to Lhasa, regardless of his religion, has been welcome to make the pilgrimage to the Potala. During the past century both the Chinese and the British have seen it in their interest to refuse admission to foreigners wishing to enter Tibet, but we have never had any reason to do so.

Only one of the temples in the Potala is really dark, and that is the temple to Chenresig himself. The image is small, not much more than eighteen inches high, and is on a long altar with many other images around it. In front is a single golden butter lamp, always burning, just showing that the temple is also decorated with umbrella-like canopies and with religious banners.

There is so much to see that a pilgrim can spend a whole day there and still not see everything. Most of us bring food with us and have a picnic on the rooftops, for as well as being a pilgrimage this is an occasion for rejoicing and for being happy. Those who live in the Potala sometimes have mixed feelings about the number of pilgrims, for the toilets, although numerous, are only openings that drop down to the rocks below, and unless rain comes to wash the refuse away it can make living in some of the rooms uncomfortable.

Those who have friends or relatives living there are free to visit them, and they may be entertained to meals and offered hospitality, or if a pilgrim is really struck by hunger or thirst he can ask any of the monks and will be given something. Even during the highest religious festivals the Potala is open to the public, so that we truly think of it as belonging to us and not to some remote, disinterested autocrat. We have always believed that the Gyalwa Rinpoche, as Chenresig's incarnation, is here for our well-being, and our trust in him has never once been ill-founded.

Some people seem to think that the rule of religion in Tibet is the same as the rule of Church, the rule of this sect or that. They also seem to think of the Church as something exclusive. Far from it. Anyone, from any family, can enter a monastery at any time of his life and take the vows of monkhood. He can be young or old, rich or poor. Depending on his ability and his inclination he may become a scholar monk, devoted to learning and teaching, or he may offer his life in service of the monastery for even the most menial work is done by monks. Probably one out of every six people in Tibet enters a monastery. Yet it is by no means a parasitical existence, nor is it a life for the lazy. From the lowest to the highest in the hierarchy, monastic discipline is rigid and severe, enough so to frighten away most weaklings. Monks, like monasteries, do not exist and live for themselves; they live in the service of others. However menial the work of a monk may be, the act of service is considered as deserving of the highest respect, equal to that accorded a scholar. Similarly, a monastery is respected for its service to the people and is the centre of every community in Tibet, however rural and remote and humble.

The word 'monastery' might perhaps mislead some people. Some monasteries in Tibet are like Shardzong, the first monastery to which I was sent as a child incarnation. They are small, perhaps only four or five buildings clustered together, with a temple and an assembly hall and with living quarters for the monks. They are places of retreat, for meditation and for study, and for the holding of regular services for the benefit of mankind. Others, like my own Kumbum Monastery, for instance, even though far out in the open countryside, are more like towns or even cities. Kumbum is built where a number of valleys from the mountains above it fall down and come together. Where they meet there is a cluster of high hills, and spread over these hills are the buildings of the monastery, some three thousand of them. The buildings are separated by streets, many of them busy and bustling and at certain times of the day crowded to capacity. The buildings are of all shapes and sizes, covering the entire area without any apparent uniformity. This is not surprising, for within a monastic town of this kind there are many semi-independent monasteries, each separately endowed and correspondingly different in size and splendour. Some monastic towns, such as Drepung, near Lhasa, are even larger. Drepung holds some ten thousand monks whereas the population of Kumbum is only about four thousand. The population in Gelukpa monasteries like these consists exclusively of monks; there are no nuns and no laymen, though visitors are always made welcome.

A monastic town has its main buildings, particularly its temple and assembly hall, large enough to admit the entire congregation. From here the monastery as a whole is guided by the abbot and his staff, and it is here that the unity of the monastery is established. But it has never been the way of Buddhism, least of all in Tibet, to establish unity through uniformity, and the rest of a monastic town is made up of what effectively are smaller independent units, sometimes regional and sometimes religious. For instance, at Kumbum there were many smaller monasteries contained within the town, including my own Tagtser Labrang.

The small but wealthy monastery of which I was born to be

the head is high up, at the top of the northernmost hill in Kumbum. It is almost a quarter of a mile long and narrow. It is really a series of courtyards, each running into the next and each surrounded on all four sides by two-storeyed buildings. You enter by the first courtyard, around which are stables for the horses and mules and a barn for our few cows. Off the same courtyard are rooms for storing straw and fodder for the animals, and quarters for the monks whose job it is to look after them. Visitors arriving leave their horses in this courtyard and then go through another gateway at the far end into the middle court. Here you have the main kitchen in which food is cooked for all the monks living in the Labrang and the rooms of the chief steward, or butler. Nearby, on the other side of the entrance, is the storage house and a small dairy in which milk products are prepared—yogurt, butter and cheese. In this middle courtyard also is the granary, where we keep the wheat, barley and oats we get from our fields, and a few dried vegetables. Each Labrang in Kumbum has to look after its own needs in this way, and although my own Labrang has bigger and better-stocked granaries than many, our wealth being greater, it does not mean that we live much differently. No monk may indulge in any form of excess or luxury, food included, and according to Buddhist belief we are obliged to share. Even the poorest Labrang must contribute part of its wealth to the central treasury of Kumbum, and of course Tagtser Labrang contributes quite heavily. From this central treasury the wealth, money and food alike, is redistributed to ensure that everyone gets a fair share.

In the far corner of the middle courtyard are the guest apartments, so spacious that the main room can be used as an assembly hall for the prayers we hold on our feast days the ninth day of our eleventh month, and the fifteenth day of the first month. In these apartments we lodge our visitors, laymen and monks alike. They come to us from all over Tibet and Mongolia, and we like to be able to make them comfortable after they have travelled so far. But if my own parents were to come, as they used to, then just being a small party from not far away they would stay in the first courtyard.

Just across from these apartments, in the other corner, are the quarters of my teacher and servant, and here we might sometimes put an especially important visitor. Within the same corner is a small inner courtyard, about thirty feet long, with two small rooms on each side. This is where I stay, and where I have my own small kitchen. From here, if I want to, I can go directly into the third courtyard without going out into the middle court, and in the third courtyard on the east side is our temple and treasury. The temple is on the first floor, and there we keep all our sacred images and our scriptures. Beside it is the assembly hall, large enough to hold five or six hundred monks. On the second floor is the treasury proper with our most precious belongings and valuable gems. On the north side is more storage space, for meat on the second floor, and grains, below. From this grain supply we can let grain out to those who need it for planting. In one corner we keep a supply of wood and materials for maintenance and repair of the Labrang buildings, and in the other corner is our fuel supply. On the west side are my official quarters where I must stay if I have guests and where I must receive visitors. There are just three rooms, one is my bedroom, one is the reception room, and the other is a kind of waiting room. Above my quarters are more guest apartments. Near the entrance from the middle courtyard is another small court, much like my own, where the monks live who take care of the temple, the lighting of the butter lamps, and the performance of our daily services.

The outside walls are all made of brick and stone; the inner walls are wood and the roof is sometimes tiled and sometimes just covered with baked mud. On the ground floor no windows look out onto the street, only into the courtyards, as protection against thieves, but the upper floor has windows on both sides, and the rooms are bright and airy. The windows are large and made of latticed wood, and we cover ours with either a fine white cloth or with translucent paper. The walls are plastered and usually covered with brightly coloured paintings. In the guest apartments the paintings tell the story of how the monastery came to be built, or they may show scenes from the life of Buddha. In the temple and assembly hall the paintings, all done by monks, show religious scenes, tell the story of the Buddha's renunciation or of his attainment of enlightenment, and in the assembly hall we have pictures of the eight Buddhist symbols: the wheel, the fish and the conch shell, the vase and the flower, the umbrella, the prayer banner, and the woven symbol of eight, the *Palbu*.

Palbu

Every year, in the ninth month, just before the snows come, the first fifteen days of the month are given over to whitewashing all the buildings in Kumbum. The rains have ended by then, and for the rest of the year we have lovely clean white monasteries, shining in the sun, with their bright and colourful interiors. This is how we live.

It was in the time of the fifth Gyalwa Rinpoche that monastic communities such as this really began to have a single organization, binding them together in a common discipline. The Gelukpa have always encouraged intensive academic study of the scriptures, and insist on a monk attaining a certain very high level before he is permitted to branch out into tantric studies. For instance, a Gelukpa monk wishing to study at either Gyume or Gyuto, the two most famous centres of esoteric learning in Tibet, must first graduate from one of the three Gelukpa academies, Ganden, Drepung and Sera, with his doctorate, or *Geshi*, degree. Only then is he considered fit for occult study and practice. Consequently Gelukpa monasteries of any size are also to be considered as universities, organized along the lines instituted by Ngawong Gyatso in the seventeenth century.

At the apex of the organization is the Lachi, an academic council consisting of the heads of all the various colleges within the university, together with a treasurer and one or two other officials. Their offices are generally near the main assembly hall, in the very heart of the monastic town. The Lachi is, in a way, a coordinating committee, existing to maintain a certain uniformity of academic standards, for each college is allowed a great deal of freedom in arranging its curriculum. Some colleges, or *Dratsang*, specialize in certain scriptures, and they may further differ from each other by having different rules of discipline. While a student can to a large extent choose whichever Dratsang he thinks will suit him best, he is given his place of residence, or *Khamtsan*, according to his place of birth. The Khamtsan are all regional, although in different monasteries, according to their size, the regions may be grouped together somewhat differently. In his own Khamtsan a young student will find people from his own country or part of Tibet, speaking his own dialect. He will almost certainly find relatives there. Membership in a certain regional residence in no way restricts the student however, for in his daily studies at the college he will meet others from all over Tibet, and eventually he will meet students from other colleges within the same monastic town and so broaden his intellectual horizon as well.

A boy may join a monastery when he is only seven years old, or a man when he is seventy. In either case the procedure is the same. He must find a friend or relative who will sponsor him and arrange for a teacher and for residence. Usually a boy's parents will do all this, and once it is done the boy is brought to the monastery and submitted for acceptance. Unless there is some very good reason for rejecting him, there will be no question. Even if a boy runs away from home and comes to the monastery on his own, the officials themselves will find someone to act as his sponsor and guardian. He is admitted to a college, or Dratsang, and given a place to sleep in his proper Khamtsan. This is where he will eat and sleep and do most of his studying, and for nearly everyone this is where he will spend the rest of his life.

The Khamtsan buildings are just like the others; in some areas where wood is plentiful that is used, but in most places the walls and floors and even the roofs are made of stone, and wood is only used for the main beams and crossbeams and for doors and windows. Stones are crushed and laid on top of straw, mixed with dirt and more straw and all pounded up with water. When it sets it is like cement, and we rub it and rub it with oil until it has a high sheen, which we like to see. These buildings may be five or six storeys high, and on each floor are rooms for students and teachers, all members of the same Khamtsan, and the kitchens. Each student has his own room, maybe as small as seven or eight feet square, perhaps twice as large, and behind it will be his kitchen, for everyone must do his own cooking. In the room there is a mattress for sleeping at night and sitting during the day and in front of it a small low table which can be used as a desk. A small chest is enough for the few personal belongings a monk will have, and the top of this chest is used as an altar. The only other furniture is a little charcoal stove or a fireplace for keeping the tea warm.

In the kitchen there is a water pot where water must be kept for all cooking and washing needs, a few cooking utensils, and a stove on which yak dung and wood are burned. The stoves are built of bricks, quite high, and the ashes are carefully kept underneath since we use them on the fields. Every three days or so the ashes are taken out and thrown down the toilet. Each floor has its own toilet which is simple, since there is no running water, but which the students and teachers take great care to keep clean. It is usually a small room built out beyond the outside wall, with a chute to take all the refuse down into a covered pit dug into the ground below. The ashes from the fire help to keep the smell down, and waste water is used to clean the toilet and the chute, so it is not bad at all. The villagers come every few months to dig out the pits and take the sewage away for use as manure.

Every building has an official we call Rakor Gonpa, who makes sure that people are clean in all their habits, and he can fine any student who does not keep his room clean or who makes too many cooking smells. Otherwise students are free to cook whatever foods they want and can afford. Poor students can usually make money to buy food by performing extra services for those who are more fortunate, for every student has certain compulsory duties, often very menial. He is allocated these duties as his

contribution to the monastery, but this is primarily a way of ensuring that all the necessary work gets done. If a student's time is
so taken up with his studies that he has no time for his duties,
and if he can find some way of paying another student to do the
work for him, this is considered perfectly alright. For instance a
student working for his examinations would almost certainly try
to find someone to clean his room for him and attend to other
chores and in return would be only too glad to share his food.
Sometimes the monastery distributes alms to the monks in the
form of money, and this is used for the purchase of food outside
the monastery compound, in a near-by village or town. Some
prefer to save this money to buy off their duties.

More often, alms are distributed in the form of food itself.
Even a small monastery will do this on ten or fifteen days of every
month, others for as many as twenty days or more. These are
days on which we honour the patrons who have made donations
to the monastery, and all monks assemble in the main hall and
attend a religious service during which the food is distributed and
eaten. We all carry our wooden bowls under the folds in our
robes, and the junior monks serve us with tea and tsampa and
perhaps some sweet cakes or other delicacies. Some monks live
on this almost entirely, never buying food on their own for the
days on which there is no patron's feast.

The year is divided into semesters, and in between there are
vacations we call *chötsham*. During these vacations the student
monks are free to leave the monastery, and most of them go to
work in neighbouring villages and farms. Whatever they get paid
they use to buy food or whatever else they need for the next term,
or to make a contribution to their teachers. They have not yet
taken full vows, so they can do this. Monks do not have to study,
however, and those who are neither students nor full monks, but
but who merely offer their service to the monastery, are expected
to provide for themselves in this way.

Everyone entering a monastery, however, is expected to take
the first vows and become Rapjung. This is the first of three
grades of monks, the other two being Getsul and then Gelong.
All are equally considered as *Trapa*, or monks, and among the

Gelukpa are bound by an oath to celibacy. The non-student monks may be trained as craftsmen or artisans; they may take care of the monastery farmlands, and they generally supply the officials who take care of all financial and business arrangements. Others with less talent work in the monastery kitchens as servants. They are by no means divorced from religious life, and many are specially trained in the performance of religious rites and are sent out to minister to the needs of the local population, taking back to the monastery any alms they might be given in return for their services.

Those who decide to stay as Rapjung and not take any further vows may do so simply because they feel they will not be able to lead the more rigidly disciplined life of Getsul or Gelong, in which for instance no food may be eaten after midday, except tea. Or else they may stay as Rapjung because the *Khanpo*, or abbot, advises against their proceeding further, at least for the moment. Before taking the additional vows, a Rapjung monk should go first to his teacher, who will then take him to the abbot's private quarters for approval and for initiation. Before each additional vow is administered the abbot closely questions the applicant as to whether he really knows what it means and is taking it of his own free will and in the conviction that he can and will uphold it. To become Rapjung sixteen vows must be taken, including avoidance of certain sins and the adherence to certain rules. Getsul involves the taking of twenty additional vows, and for Gelong the full two hundred and fifty-three must be taken.

There is no particular time limit, the only rule being that you must be over twenty years old before you can take Gelong. If you enter the monastery after this age, and if you wish it and the abbot approves, you could take all the vows of the three grades in the same day, but generally people wait. Older men joining a monastery may want to take all the vows at once, for if they stay as Rapjung they will find themselves living and studying mainly with younger boys, and they may feel self-conscious. By taking all the vows, they are entitled to the privileges that belong to the older men and can mix with them more freely though they are still just students. They wear the special Gelong robes, sit in the more honoured place in assembly, and eat at special times; these are the main differences between their life as Gelong and their life as Rapjung. When there is a patron's feast day in the assembly, the Rapjung must wait on the other monks and serve them their tea and food.

Every fifteenth and thirtieth day of each month there are special services that the different grades attend at different times, with the Gelong entering the assembly hall first. The idea is that during this service each monk should consider how well or how poorly he has upheld his vows during the past two weeks. If he has failed, he must speak up in front of all the others and confess his fault. The abbot, or whoever is in charge of the service, may say nothing, but if it is a serious or repeated fault he is likely to comment on it and ask for everyone to pray for the offender so that he may have the strength not to fail again. There is no giving of penance, only prayer. Only if the fault is exceptionally bad, amounting to a sacrilege or a complete desecration of the Buddhist faith, such as murder, is action then taken and the monk expelled.

Studies fall into five groups, each one taking several years to complete. First is Namdrel, which is the study of logic. It comes first because the most important thing for the student, right at the beginning, is for him to learn how to think properly, in an orderly and reasonable manner. Then comes Parchin, a comparative study of the Buddhist scriptures, introducing the student to the different schools of thought. At Lhasa Namdrel and Parchin each take five years to complete. They are followed by Oumah, which teaches the avoidance of extremes and leads the student into the difficult two-year study of the Tong pa nid, better known in the west as Sunyata, or the study of nothingness, non-existence. We Tibetan Buddhists do not, like some, avow that death is an end to everything, nor do we conceive of Sanggye Sa as being the entire destruction of existence, though we certainly can say that it is not existence as we recognize it. Then comes Dzö, the study of metaphysics, for one year. After that is a time for complete revision of all that has gone before, and the final course of study which is Dulwa. Here the Vinaya philosophy is expounded, laying the basis for all monastic discipline. At least nine years have to be spent on Dulwa and the overall review before the higher degrees can be taken. Even then many years of further study remain for those so inclined.

About halfway through, when you have completed Parchin, you can take the degree of *Rabgyemba*, for which you have to come before the assembly and give an account of all you have learned so far, and you can be questioned up to that point. Then when you complete Oumah you can take the degree of *Kaju*, and in the last stages of your studies you can take the three highest degrees of Lharampa, Tsogrampa, and Dorampa. The first two are given only to those who complete at Lhasa and take part in the Mönlam festivities. Dorampa, a lesser degree, may be awarded by monastic universities outside Lhasa but is not so exacting and does not carry the same weight or prestige.

From the beginning students are expected to study on their own to a very large extent. Each chooses his own teacher, who suggests appropriate readings and who discusses the scriptures under study with a student. One of the main features of academic study at a monastery is the use of debate. Every day all classes assemble in the courtyard outside the assembly hall, and each in turn comes before the abbot. The abbot gives the class some words of advice and encouragement, a hint as to the general direction they should take, and then the class retreats to its allotted space in the courtyard and its members begin loudly debating with each other. As they do so, senior students may come over to join them, mainly to brush up their own earlier studies but also to give some help to their juniors by friendly criticism. Any contestants who attract and hold a large crowd are considered to be doing particularly well, and this is everyone's aim. All sorts of tricks are used, particularly wild and threatening gestures for the debate takes place in a prescribed open space within which the two opponents can sit or stride up and down as they like. Sitting impassively can be just as disconcerting as the wildest gymnastics, but nothing can conceal from the critical ears of the onlooking crowd the discordant sounds of ignorance.

This is the way we go through our studies, learning to be learned without being proud, and at the same time learning the meaning of discipline. In the same way that our minds are disciplined, gradually, so are our bodies. For this, as well as for our whole monastic system and for the rule of religion in our country, we have to thank the fifth Gyalwa Rinpoche, Ngawong Gyatso.

CHAPTER THIRTEEN

The Seed of Dissension

Lhasa is densely populated, not only by natives, but by a large number of foreigners of divers nations, such as Tartars, Chinese, Muscovites, Armenians, people from Cascimir, Hindustan and Nepal, all established there as merchants; and who have made large fortunes.

– FR. IPPOLITO DESIDERI (C. 1714)

Writing from Lhasa during the first quarter of the eighteenth century, Fr. Desideri was not the first Christian missionary to live there, and as can be seen from his own account he was far from being the only foreigner. It is circumstance rather than the Tibetan people that has isolated the country from the rest of the world, and the ban on travel has been imposed by foreign governments, not by the Tibetans. On the contrary, we have always welcomed foreigners, and the great fifth Gyalwa Rinpoche himself invited Christian missionaries to come to Lhasa to discuss their religion, with freedom to both teach and practise. There had for a long time been Muslims in Lhasa, but during the time of Ngawong Gyatso there came to Lhasa a very renowned holy Muslim. He used to visit the Gyalwa Rinpoche and they would have long talks together and would even eat their meals together. One day when up on the roof of the Potala, the holy man said that he very much wanted a quiet place of his own where he could practise his religion. The Gyalwa Rinpoche called for bow and arrow and said that wherever the arrow dropped would become a place for all Muslims to worship in their own way. He fired the bow, and the arrow fell in a place called Gyangdrag Lingka, near by. There to this day stands a mosque where generations of Muslims have followed their religion in Lhasa since the seventeenth century. Many of the costumes worn during our festival plays tell of the long contact we have had with the Muslim peoples from the West.

Even stranger, perhaps, is the story of the Christians in Tibet. It is said that at Hemis, until recently, there was a document telling of how Jesus Christ, following an argument with his parents, ran away and spent some years in India, studying the scriptures and finally residing at Hemis Monastery in Ladakh, and embraced Buddhism before he returned to his own country to preach a new religion. A Russian traveller named Notwitch took away the manuscript, and later sent a translation to the monastery, but this in turn was taken away by some foreign traveller.

There is no further evidence concerning this story, which may or may not be true. There is, however, much similarity between the teachings of the two religions and even in their ecclesiastical organization. This cannot in any way be accounted for by the presence of the Christian missionaries in the seventeenth century for the earliest of these themselves remarked on the same similarity.

Christian missionaries were already spreading through Asia in the seventh century, and by the thirteenth century they were established not far from the northern and eastern borders of Tibet. There is a curious legend attached to the early life of Tsong Khapa, who above all others established the principles on which the Gelukpa order is founded and in which many similarities are seen with the Christian teachings and the Christian Church. When Tsong Khapa was a child he renounced the world, to seek for truth, and entered a period of fastings in the mountain wilds of his homeland, in Amdo. It is said that at that time an extraordinary lama, or teacher, from the far west arrived in Amdo. The young boy, much struck by the wisdom and goodness of the stranger begged to be taught by him. The lama from the West instructed Tsong Khapa, and after teaching him all that he knew, he died, high up in his mountain retreat. The lama achieved fame not only through the greatness of his teachings but also by the strangeness of his appearance, marked by burning eyes and an excessively large, sharp nose. Two European Lazarist missionaries who visited Tibet in the first half of the nineteenth century stopped at Kumbum, site of Tsong Khapa's childhood and often heard their appearance referred to as being similar to that of Tsong Khapa's teacher; it was even concluded by some that they came from the same remote land in the west. We Tibetans ourselves often refer to Tsong Khapa by his nickname 'Amdo Nawochi' which means 'Big Nose from Amdo'. But we know his teachers to have included the great Karmapa teacher and Dongrub Rinchen, both from the west.

It is not until the seventeenth century that there is any definite record of the arrival of Christian missionaries in Tibet, though they themselves were lured on by stories of missionaries who had preceded them. At first the missions were established on the outskirts, around Leh and Ladakh, where for a time they had a warm and friendly reception. So it was when they arrived in central Tibet, but it was inevitable that their presence should be considered a challenge to the authority of the Buddhist monks, and they received increasing opposition from some of the monasteries.

The Capuchins were the first to establish a mission in Lhasa. It was short lived and was followed by the arrival of the Jesuit Fr. Ippolito Desideri. Desideri was made particularly welcome because of his great scholarship and his willingness to study under Tibetan teachers. The regent who was ruling at that time gave Desideri every freedom, but said that if he was going to teach he would first have to prove the superiority of his teachings. This is always done in Tibet by public debate, so Desideri set about preparing himself by a remarkable study of the Tibetan language and scriptures. At Sera Monastery he was given his own private rooms and allowed to use one as a chapel for Christian worship. He was expected to conform to the rules of the monastery and to attend and take part in the daily debates. He prepared, in Tibetan, a lengthy exposition of Christianity, which he presented to the Court; he also made several important translations of Tibetan scriptures, which he passed on to the Capuchin monks who eventually moved back into Lhasa. His only real difficulty was with the pillar of Gelukpa doctrine, the Tangyur, which includes the doctrine of nonexistence and illusion. Desideri took this to be a denial of the existence of spiritual reality, which it is not. It is rather a denial of *non-spiritual* reality; we believe that all things exist only through the Buddha. The Buddha himself only took on the outward form of life as we know it in order to teach us. The Theg Man school believes differently – Buddha was born as a human and lived and suffered as a human.

We Tibetans do not think like this at all. The Buddha only

took on the appearance of a human body, the appearance of suffering – for the Buddha is real, and the body and suffering are unreal. Through the Buddha we can know what reality is, not through the body. All Buddhists want to reach this true reality, to know what it is, and we all believe that existence is not what it seems to be. There is no great difference there. But whereas other Buddhists like the Theg Man, in the south, believe that the sole concern of every individual should be for his own enlightenment, in Tibet we believe that we should try to help each other. If one of us feels strongly that he must shut himself up and devote himself to his own liberation, then of course that is good and we respect and honour him. By his own effort, which is good, he will benefit the rest of us. But this is only for a few; for most of us this would only be selfishness.

Also, in Tibet, we believe that we each have an individual soul (*Namshe*), and that we retain this until reaching Buddhahood. But what this state of enlightenment is, what the nature of reality is, cannot be taught or explained, it can only be experienced by each individual for himself. So for us religion is not a statement of truth but rather a way *towards* the truth that each of us must find for himself. None of this could have been easy for Desideri, who believed in a very specific stated truth and who believed that an act of faith was necessary to achieve liberation.

There were other things that worried him and other Christian missionaries who have visited us, but such issues are mostly due to misunderstanding. Frequently they mistake symbolic acts for real acts, or else they accept stories with symbolic significance at their face value and then attribute the miraculous powers of those concerned to the direct intervention of some evil force. They would have us believe that Tibet is full of miracles, populated by monks who live for hundreds of years, and by magicians who can change their form at will and transport their bodies instantly from one part of the country to the other. We believe that such things may be possible, though rare, and that when they do occur there is good reason for them to occur.

If Desideri had been able to stay longer and had been able to continue his debates with the monks of Lhasa, he himself would have understood our teachings better, and his own in turn would also have become better understood, and there might quite well have been a Christian church in Lhasa today, just as there is a Mosque. As it is, when the Capuchins returned there was some feeling of rivalry between the two orders, and despite his protests Desideri was recalled by the Vatican. The Capuchins, who did not have the other's deep scholarly interest and who were more easily disturbed by their living and working conditions left not long after.

The reports are not clear, but it seems that some early Christian missionaries became pawns in a struggle for power that was beginning to develop between the two high Rinpoche of the Gelukpa sect, the Gyalwa Rinpoche and the Panchen Rinpoche. This rivalry was quickly exploited by the Chinese and has been used by them to this day to try to split our country. Yet the office of Panchen Rinpoche was brought into being by one of the Gyalwa Rinpoche and owes everything, including its wealth, to him. But again foreigners have failed to understand what to us is so clear, and their attempts to create a political rivalry have failed because the Panchen Rinpoche was never accorded any political authority, and as a spiritual authority is one of many, all equally under the leadership of the Gyalwa Rinpoche.

The office came into being because the fifth Gyalwa Rinpoche wished to show his gratitude to his teacher, Losang Chögyan, a highly influential and venerated incarnation of Opagmé. It was claimed that the great teacher was in fact a reincarnation of Khadrub, Tsong Khapa's disciple, further enhancing his prestige; and the fifth Gyalwa Rinpoche gave him land and farms near Shigatse, where the monastery of Tashi Lunpo was founded. That is why the Panchen Rinpoche is sometimes known, mostly in the Western world, as the Tashi Lama. Losang Chögyan, with all these additional honours, survived Ngawong Gyatso and was tutor to his successor. It was he who was so hospitable to the Christians coming in from Bhutan hoping to establish a church at Shigatse. There was certainly no thought of power on his part, or he would have listened to those who argued that these foreigners had come to undermine the Buddhist religion. As it was, he gave them every help he could, even appointing a representative to look after all their needs.

It was the Chinese, fearful of the very real power of the Gyalwa Rinpoche, who tried to divide the power. They invited the sixth Panchen Rinpoche to Peking, according him the full honours they would normally have reserved for the Gyalwa Rinpoche. The Panchen Rinpoche delayed acceptance for a long time, giving as reason his fear of smallpox, associated throughout Tibet with China. Eventually he accepted and proceeded to Peking with a vast retinue, being received at every stage by representatives of the Imperial Court. In Peking riches as well as honours were showered upon the Panchen, but it was all to no end for before he could return to Tibet he was struck down by the disease he dreaded and died.

Unexpectedly this led to an invasion of Tibet from a totally different quarter, Nepal. The Panchen Rinpoche's brother, Dza Marpa, had hoped to inherit some of the immense riches lavished on the incarnation at Peking. Disappointed, he intrigued with the Nepalese who sent a Gurkha army into Tibet in 1768 to take control of Shigatse. Dza Marpa, however, failed to keep his side of the bargain and three years later the Gurkha army returned to claim what they considered their due. They met with little resistance until the Chinese, hearing of the invasion, sent troops of their own and finally helped the Tibetans drive out the Nepalese. The Chinese were now in a position to exert more direct political control over Tibet. They had already established two representatives at Lhasa, and these *Ambams*, as they were called, were now given political authority, backed by the force of the Chinese army, and were charged with the supervision of the selection of each succeeding incarnation of the Gyalwa Rinpoche. The Chinese suggested that the final choice should be made by drawing lots from a golden urn which they presented to Tibet. This gave them a chance to select an incarnation of their own choice, yet the system may not have worked as well as they had hoped for every Gyalwa Rinpoche following the seventh, until the one before the present, the thirteenth, died (many say of poisoning) before achieving full manhood, leaving the power continuously in the hands of the Chinese-appointed regents. It was also at this time that the Chinese Ambams in Lhasa closed Tibet to the outer world, refusing to allow Tibetans to have any communication with foreigners except through their office. The influence of the Chinese was finally broken by the thirteenth Gyalwa Rinpoche, though during his reign and more recently during the present Rinpoche's reign the Chinese have done what they could to subvert the Gyalwa Rinpoche's authority by supporting the Panchen Rinpoche, trying to make him into a Chinese puppet. The Tibetan people, however, all know an ancient story that tells how they may expect a certain snake to come between the two incarnations.

Somewhere to the south there was a king with two wives, each with a royal son. The brothers were very fond of each other, always playing happily together, but between the wives there was much jealousy. The people all wanted the son of the first wife to be king. The second wife went up on to the roof of the palace, and she asked to the south, to the east, to the north and to the west, but everywhere the answer was the same – that the oldest son would become king over all.

The second wife then pretended to fall ill. Her physician could not cure her, and finally she said she could only be cured if she was given the heart of her stepson to eat. The king, to save his wife, sent his oldest son to the butcher, but the butcher told the boy to hide, killing a dog and sending the dog's heart to the palace. The young queen ate it and seemed to get better. But the two brothers were so drawn together that the older boy came back to play, and was seen. Once again the second wife fell ill and demanded the death of the oldest boy. The people then told the two children to escape and helped them run away into the mountains. Up in the mountains there was no food, and the younger boy finally collapsed with exhaustion. Dondrup, the older, told him to rest while he went in search of food and water. He searched for a long time but found none, and when he got back his young brother was dead.

Dondrup buried his brother under a pile of stones under the

shade of a fruit tree, and from higher up he dug a little channel leading down to the stones above his brother's head so that when it rained his brother would be able to drink and eat of the fruit of the tree and come back to life.

The oldest son of the king continued on his way until, nearly dying himself, he heard the sounds of people talking and chanting. It was a monk instructing his followers. The monk asked Dondrup whether he was a devil or a human and where he was from. But the boy just said he was a beggar who had lost his way and was hungry. He said nothing about being from a kingdom on the other side of the mountains. The monk gave him shelter and fed him and began to instruct him, but when he discovered that the boy was born in the Dragon Year he warned Dondrup never to mention this to anyone else. Dondrup began to wander down to villages near by, however, finding food for his teacher. Sometimes he played with the village boys, and once after a successful bout of wrestling he shouted boastfully, 'You can never beat me, I am a Dragon Year boy and am as invincible as the Dragon'. He proudly told the monk of his success, but the old man was dismayed. He said that Dondrup would have to leave and go into hiding because every year there was a custom in which a Dragon Year boy had to be thrown into a local lake to propitiate the demons and ensure a fruitful harvest. If the sacrifice was not made, there were always disasters, sickness would strike the people and hailstorms destroy the fields.

It was too late, however. The children Dondrup had defeated told their parents, and the king sent out to seize the Dragon Year boy and prepare him for the sacrifice. The monk and the boy had already run into hiding and were living in a cave, so when the people came to take the boy the monk hid him in the straw they used for bedding, covering it up with pots. He refused to say where the boy was, and the people began to beat him. Hearing the old man's cries the young boy came out from the straw and begged them to stop beating the monk, his teacher, saying that he was willing to be sacrificed.

Dondrup was then prepared for the sacrifice, treated like royalty, living in the royal household. During this time he met the king's daughter, and they grew so fond of each other that the king relented and told his ministers to find another boy. But they refused and said that once the choice is made it cannot be changed. When the day came, the boy was taken to the lake and thrown in. He sank down and down and eventually arrived at the palace of the Nagas, the water spirits. When the Nagas saw the boy they were all very happy, for he reached them alive and well. They begged him to stay, promising to send good harvests, better than ever, because every year the boys usually arrived dead, even bleeding and making all the water dirty. Dondrup must be something very special, they said, to come to them alive.

Dondrup lived with the Nagas for some months in their underwater palace, but then he said he had to return to the surface to see his old teacher again. He explained how the monk had tried to protect him and had been beaten, so the Nagas gave him many presents and allowed him to leave. Dondrup went straight to his teacher, who at once recognized he must be a Changchub Sempa, come to help mankind. That year the harvest was better than ever, and there was no sickness or death in any village throughout the land. The king called the monk to come to a celebration, and sent a horse for him. The horse was too spirited, however, so the monk told the boy to put a mask on his face and to come with him and lead the horse. When they arrived he explained to the king that the boy's face had been badly burned and had to be kept covered to avoid infection. He went on to tell the king, and his daughter who sat beside him, of his meditations in the mountains and of all he had learned. While he talked, however, a great wind blew up and tore away the mask from the boy's face. At once the girl, then the king, then all the people recognized the Dragon Year boy, and realized that he must be a Changchub Sempa. The boy told them all about the Nagas in the lake, and said that from that year onward they must stop making human sacrifices to the lake if they were to expect the Nagas to continue giving them good harvests. So from that day on human sacrifice came to an end.

Dondrup then told the monk, his teacher, the story of his

young brother and together they went to search for the place where the boy lay buried under a pile of stones beneath a shady fruit tree. After much searching they found it, but under the pile of stones there was no sign of the boy, not a hair of his head nor a bone from his body.

Each year Dondrup came back to visit the spot, and one year, while calling his brother's name, he heard a sound, and there stood his younger brother, the boy whose mother had wanted him to be king, with his body covered by long hair like an animal, making sounds like an animal. Dondrup and the monk took the boy and began to lead him back to the palace, but on the way they came across nine deadly snakes coiled up in the middle of the path. The old priest insisted that he go first, to test the way, for if the boys went they would surely get bitten. He would go first, praying, so that either the snakes would leave or else they would bite him and then go away. He stepped carefully and then jumped, but he stumbled and, falling, bruised two of the snakes with his feet. Dondrup leaped in among the snakes to save his teacher from falling farther, and in so doing he saved the snakes from being crushed. Seven snakes fled into a cave; the two that were bruised praised the boy, but nonetheless made a curse that whenever the monk and his ward, the young Changchub Sempa should try to join each other, to work together, there would be trouble between them, separating them by quarrel.

We believe that the monk was the incarnation of Opagmé, who is also incarnated in the Panchen Rinpoche, and that the boy was the incarnation of Chenresig, who is also incarnated in the Gyalwa Rinpoche; that is why there is so much trouble between the two Rinpoche. When foreigners see any disagreement between the two high lamas they see it as a struggle for power, and they try to twist this for their own ends. We see it differently. We respect both the Panchen and the Gyalwa Rinpoche, and if there is any disagreement we think of the story, and remember that it arises from their care for each other.

It would have been good, perhaps, if there had been more foreigners in Tibet, instead of the few individuals who came to teach or to trade and the few powers who came to use us for their own ends. If there had been more they might have understood us better, and we might have understood ourselves better. Now it is too late. The very religion that gave us our strength sapped our military strength, and that is perhaps one reason why the Chinese paid so much homage to our priests. It was partly out of fear for their power, or rather for the power of religion over the people, and partly because they knew that Buddhism, teaching us not to kill, leaves no room for warfare. Yet we would not have it otherwise; we still believe that religion is a stronger power than any other power of man and that in the end it will win.

It is strange that some of the most bitter critics of Tibet have been Buddhists from other lands, from China, Japan, and from the south. Yet the Christian missionary Desideri, who believed so strongly that many of our religious achievements were due to the dark forces of evil, could nonetheless write: 'The Tibetans love the Dalai Lama because he has, an infinite number of times, become a man, and taken upon himself the hardships and misery which afflict fragile, decrepit, and mortal humanity.' The same man, writing in 1714, described the Tibetans as 'not at all arrogant, rather submissive, kindly, cheerful and courteous under religious rule'.

That, in itself, is perhaps a good argument for the Tibetan beliefs concerning the nature of reality, for how could this description apply to the same people described by Desideri's fellow Christians in the same country as 'uncivilized and rude', and with 'no shadow of religious sense'? Perhaps we learn, from the few foreigners who have visited Tibet, less about Tibet than about themselves.

CHAPTER FOURTEEN

A Riddle of Love

In my Palace, the place of Heaven on Earth,
They call me Ringdzen Tsanyang Gyatso,
Chenresig Reincarnate.
But, below my Palace,
In the little town of Sho,
They call me Chebo Tangsan Wongbo, the
    Profligate,
For my loves are many.

— TSHANGDBYANGS RGYAMTSO,
sixth Gyalwa Rinpoche

There are certain houses in Lhasa, as elsewhere in the world, frequented by ladies and their lovers. Among these you can see many that are washed with yellow. Inside, as in the others, Tibetan girls serve steaming chang to their visitors, and the men make love to the girls. But the yellow-washed houses are special because long ago they were the houses most favoured by the sixth Gyalwa Rinpoche, whom we call 'Merry One'. There is also, in Lhasa, the Khrungser Khang, or House of Birth. Here, it is said, there used to be great dances for the sixth Gyalwa Rinpoche. And just behind the Potala, on the other side from the little hamlet of Sho, set like a precious stone in the lake, is the Lu Khang, with its own beauty matching the beauty of the lake around it and the Potala towering above. This 'House of the Serpent' was a favourite retreat of the same Tsangyang Gyatso, where he could meet his loves without desecrating the holy precincts of the Potala.

This may seem strange behaviour for the highest of all incarnations, and many have described Tsangyang Gyatso as debauched and dissolute, utterly unfitted for his high office, and an example of laxity in performing all the necessary rituals and making all the necessary tests in the selection of the Gyalwa Rinpoche. The Chinese themselves tried to make this an excuse for replacing him with an 'incarnation' of their own choice. But the Tibetans would have none of it and despite all the stories about him, have continued to revere him to this day. If anything the stories only serve to make him all the more popular and beloved for it seems to us that to be born great and good makes great and good living and dying too easy. To be born otherwise, to grow as an ordinary man, with all the desires, the loves and the hates, of ordinary man, then to *become* great and good, that is

285

an achievement deserving of respect. It is also a lesson from which we can learn, for what can we learn from a man born otherwise than ourselves?

Some say that the sixth Gyalwa Rinpoche was dissolute because unlike most incarnations he was not discovered until he was already a well-grown boy. Even those of us who do not think of him as dissolute agree that the circumstances of his discovery were responsible for the strange shape his life took. Most of us who are chosen as incarnations are chosen when we are only a year or two old. Although we may not be taken away from our parents at that time, we are immediately put under the most careful supervision, and as soon as the monastery authorities think we are old enough to leave our homes we are taken to the monastery and enter into a life of seclusion. So we really never have time to develop a taste for the pleasures of the world, pleasures that would distract us from our duties and make it difficult for us to keep all the vows we must take.

It was different with the selection of the sixth Gyalwa Rinpoche because of the nature of the death of his predecessor, Ngawong Gyatso, the great fifth Gyalwa Rinpoche, rebuilder of the Potala. In fact the Potala was not yet finished when Ngawong Gyatso died. There are stories even about him, perhaps resulting largely from his unorthodox interest in the Nyingmapa sect. There is quite a famous song telling how his rosary was found at a house near Sera Monastery and that there was no reason for it being there, unless it had been left there by the Gyalwa Rinpoche himself. In that same house a boy was born who was to become the Rinpoche's most trusted minister, Sanggye Gyatso. Many say they were in fact father and son. Sanggye Gyatso took over more and more of the power as the Rinpoche increasingly withdrew from public life. He directed the rebuilding of the Potala, and it was out of devotion to Ngawong Gyatso that he concealed the Rinpoche's death. Had the death become known, it is almost certain that the work on the building would have been stopped, and Sanggye was determined to see it finished. From an inscription carved into one of the stones in the Potala walls however, we can see just when the death actually took place, in the early 1680's.

Sanggye Gyatso continued to rule, allowing the people to believe that the Gyalwa Rinpoche was deep in meditation, in complete seclusion. It was some nine years before news of the death leaked out, and so it was nine years before the task of searching for the new reincarnation was even begun. By the time it was complete, the new Gyalwa Rinpoche was already twelve or more years old.

The minister, Sanggye Gyatso, was a good man, and he had performed all the necessary funeral services for the dead Gyalwa Rinpoche. He did this publicly, at the time of the death, but by using very poetic language he managed to conceal just whom the service was for. To further allay suspicion he also composed a prayer that outwardly praised the long life of the Gyalwa Rinpoche, but which had a double meaning and really begged for the speedy rebirth of Chenresig in the body of the next Gyalwa Rinpoche. At each of the great monasteries he held services, and all the time he was looking to see if anyone in the congregation might suspect who the dead person really was. At Drepung he saw that one of the monks had concealed his head in his robes and was crying. This monk was Kunkhyen Ngagwang Tsondru, builder of Labrang Monastery. He heard the prayers and understood their secret meaning, and he wept at the death of the Gyalwa Rinpoche while he prayed for his speedy rebirth and discovery. So the minister called him and told him the secret and why it had to remain a secret. But there was one other thing he had to do and that was to consult the oracle at Nechung to see about the rebirth. When he had done this he was filled with fear that his secret might leak out this way, so he disguised himself as a beggar and returned the next day to Nechung, to the house where the oracle's mother lived. As he was begging for food, the old lady came to him and told him to be quiet, that it was no time for begging, the Gyalwa Rinpoche was dead. Then Sanggye Gyatso knew that the oracle, when freed of possession, had remembered all that had passed. Sanggye Gyatso was so determined to keep his secret that he had the oracle and his mother put to death. When the Chinese finally came to learn of the death of the Rinpoche, several years later, they had Sanggye Gyatso himself put to death.

The new Rinpoche was put under the care of the Panchen Rinpoche, who acted as his tutor and did his best to teach the boy the discipline to be expected of any monk, let alone of the reincarnation of Chenresig. The boy was enthroned as the rightful Gyalwa Rinpoche, but a long period of training lay ahead before he would be fit and ready for ordination as a monk. This training must have seemed unnecessarily harsh to a boy unused to any such discipline and totally uninterested in an academic education. But we know that he worked hard and did in fact discipline himself to a very ascetic, simple life. In spite of his high position he refused to wear the rich clothes laid out for him for he was still unordained and so could not wear the robes of a monk. He wore simple clothes and went about on foot, spurning to use a horse and insisting that he should not be accompanied everywhere by a large number of officials headed by his chamberlain. As part of his training he had to give lectures, and when he went out to give these he gave them in the park, in public, arriving alone and on foot, dressed like the simplest of men in his audience. Even in the Potala, where he could have had all the luxuries of life, he chose simplicity. He lived without servants. If he wanted tea he made it himself, and whoever came by was welcome to share it with him. Yet to almost everyone except Tibetans this sixth Gyalwa Rinpoche is held up to be an example of depravity simply because of his high office. All the things he is said to have done are no more than any man might do and still not be considered a wrongdoer. But we have to consider just what he *did* do.

We know he used to leave the Potala at night-time and go to Sho, and there he visited the little houses, later painted yellow in his honour, where he drank chang and made love to the girls. But although he was Gyalwa Rinpoche, he never took the vows of a monk and so was not actually bound to a life of celibacy except through the wishes of the Gelukpa officials. He led an austere enough life within the Potala, but even so there are those who say that his excesses outside the Potala are sure indication that a mistake had been made in his selection and that he was not the true reincarnation. Others see no inconsistency, for regardless of what actually happened between Tsangyang Gyatso and his lovers, we are very aware of his attitude towards them as expressed in his poetry which, apart from that of Milarepa, is perhaps the most lyrical we have in Tibet. It shows a profound religious emotion, by no means merely sensual. It also shows an awareness of something taught by all Buddhists – that if we look for goodness, we can find it anywhere and everywhere, that there is nothing in this world that cannot be turned to our advantage and made to help keep us to the Middle Path.

For none of us, except the most brutal, is man's relationship with woman only one involving physical contact and pleasure. But few can have raised the relationship to such heights as Tsangyang Gyatso, the man of many loves as he was known in Sho. His poetry tells more than anything how different was his feeling for women. It also tells of the struggle between Tsangyang the youth and Tsangyang the reincarnation of Chenresig, as monastic discipline slowly attempts to obliterate the pleasures of the outside world.

> *I went to my teacher, with devotion filled,*
> *To learn of the Lord Buddha.*
> *My teacher taught, but what he said escaped;*
> *For my mind was full of compassion,*
> *Full of that Compassionate One who loves me.*
> *She has stolen my mind.*

Compassion is the quality above all others that the Buddhist must cultivate, and Tsangyang, unable to concentrate on his studies, turns a phrase so that his wandering mind is not led altogether astray, as it was evidently inclined:

> *In meditation I think of my teacher,*
> *I see his face come before me;*
> *But the face is that of my lover.*

For Tsangyang Gyatso, his love and his lovers more and more appear as his teachers.

> *My Compassionate One, be like the holy mountain,*
> *Rirab Lhunpo.*
> *Stay still, and let the sun and moon encircle you,*
> *Day and night.*
> *Faithful, like the sun and moon,*
> *Shall I be to you.*
>
> *The cuckoo bird from the land of Mön*
> *Brings rain.*
> *It descends from the sky,*
> *It brings blessings to the earth;*
> *Life grows and blossoms.*
> *When the cuckoo bird comes from Mön,*
> *My lover and I join as One,*
> *In body, heart, and mind.*

Even further removed from the libertine that has often been painted are two more of his poems:

> *To say farewell*
> *Is to be sad.*
> *Be not sad, my love,*
> *For after every parting*
> *Comes another meeting.*
>
> *What you write with ink, in small black letters,*
> *Can all be lost*
> *Through the work of a single drop of water.*
> *But what is written in your mind,*
> *Is there for eternity.*

To anyone who knows Tibet, there is something at work here that is a great deal more than the mere love of a man for a woman, something that is much more consistent with the simplicity of life led by the Gyalwa Rinpoche at the Potala. It seems most possible that the young Tsangyang was initiated into tantric practices which involve physical, rather than mental, sexual intercourse with women. There are various degrees of this, all of which rest in the belief that semen is possessed of a vital force that is both physical and spiritual. By correct expenditure of the physical, the spiritual force can be released for the further elevation of the adept. The correct practice may involve the withholding of the semen just as it is about to be ejected, or else it may be ejected and then drawn back again, a practice that can only be achieved after many years of physical training. In the latter case, according to some teachings, the male sperm may draw back with it the female ova, further enriching the practitioner, though at the expense of the female who is carefully chosen and who, in turn, may draw into herself something of the male element and transform it likewise into spiritual, rather than physical, energy.

This energy is drawn upward, as if along the spinal column, until it reaches a point at the base of the neck; when it reaches this point the practitioner enters a state of higher awareness. The sexual act performed normally may give a slight notion of the nature of this higher consciousness, but more than that it cannot do since the energy, instead of being trapped and put to use, is expended and lost to physical ends – creating a physical body instead of spiritual consciousness.

Those who object that this is a mere rationalization designed to excuse the grossest misbehaviour ignore two facts. First, ritual sexual intercourse is performed considerably fewer times than marital intercourse might, without being considered excessive, be practised by any layman. Not only is there long and special training before the rite can take place, but even then it can only be performed after the severest and most arduous preparations, the discomfort of which could hardly be justified by a few moments of purely physical gratification.

More important still is the fact that anyone, even before entering on such a course of instruction, must already have achieved a high level of discipline and must be prepared for a great deal more. There is no doubt that the young Tsangyang had all the physical urges of any youth when he entered monastic life. We can also be sure that his instructors, headed by his tutor, the Panchen Rinpoche, will have done everything in their power to lead him away from purely physical pleasures, and for this reason it is even more likely that he may have been initiated into tantric practices that would divert his physical desires into spiritual channels.

I can remember very well what it was like for me, as a boy of nine, when I was accepted as a junior monk and allowed to put on, for the first time, the simple red robes of the order. I was so full of happiness at my good fortune that I did not think for a while of what lay ahead of me. The next step lay several years ahead, when I would take my first examinations and so become qualified to enter the main assembly hall at Kumbum. To begin with, life seemed not too different except that I had to get up even earlier in the mornings. Before four o'clock I was awakened and my previous day's lessons, which I had had to memorize, were heard. I would then be taught another before being allowed any breakfast. The actual lessons did not occupy much more time than before, but they were much harder and I found myself working for longer and longer hours, having less time to play with my friends. Often I would work on through the evening until midnight. Only in the afternoons, for two or three hours, could I sometimes get away to play. Once, for two months, I was taken away to a remote little hermitage so that I could get better training in a special form of dialectics studied and taught there. The trip was made in winter so that I should feel less inclined to run away from my lessons, which seemed far above my head.

In the end, although I was not a model student, I found life more agreeable if I worked hard. When I did not work my lessons seemed twice as hard, and the public sermons and debates that I had to attend daily bored me to the point where I could hardly stay awake. I wanted to graduate so that I could become a full member of the assembly, and, rather than protract my training I worked all the harder so that I could take my examinations the sooner. When I took the entrance examinations I was fourteen years old. I had studied many branches of Buddhist doctrine and had memorized some two thousand pages of the scriptures. The examination was conducted in the abbot's private quarters. He had a number of texts spread around him, and from these he selected passages quite at random, reading part of the text then asking me to finish it. But my teachers had prepared me more than adequately, and not once did I even falter. Now, thirty years later, I marvel that as a young boy I could ever have had the patience or the ability to learn so much, but I had been brought up to it since I was a few years old.

After my admission to the assembly there were several days of celebrations, then my new life began. The main difference was that my lessons were no longer held in my own monastery, with my own tutor. I was now a member of a class in higher studies, entered in the College of Logic. The work was harder, but it was also more interesting as we could attend any of the debates and discuss the subject with any of the other monks. And when we had to debate in the assembly it was in front of four thousand others, all more advanced than ourselves and ready to shout us down with their laughter if we did not do well. At the end of such a debate we would be told, in front of all the others, how well we had done, or how badly, and given advice for our further studies.

Up to the fifth class, debates are only held between individuals of the same class. They are chosen in pairs and given a subject to study on which they will be expected to debate. But for the fifth class examinations each individual has to come out by himself and face all the others, from the fifth class down to the first, any of whom can ask him any question on any subject that pleases him. Each person can take twenty or thirty minutes to question him, and the examination for each person may last five or six days. I was about eighteen years old when I took my fifth class examinations and moved from the *Tsoglang* grade into that of *Tamcha*. At this point, far from becoming any easier, life only became harder.

It is not difficult for me to imagine how hard it must have been for twelve-year-old Tsangyang to give up all the freedom he had known and enter such a disciplined life, for far more would have been expected of him than is expected of a lesser reincarnation. It would be surprising if he had not been hard to restrain, but it would be equally surprising if he were not profoundly affected by his new position and by the teaching he would have begun receiving from the moment of his installation.We feel that there is no point in our questioning the situation; it is better to take it however we find it and see what we can learn from it. If, as some claim, a mistake was made in the selection of Tsangyang, there is no less to learn from his life, which teaches us how to find much more in the relationship between a man and his wife, or lover, than mere sexual gratification. If, on the other hand, he really was the true reincarnation of Chenresig, then we can not only learn the same lessons, but we can renew our faith that all around us there are Changchub Sempa, apparently no different from ourselves, with all our weaknesses, come to test and teach us. We should be prepared to learn wherever we look; to criticize is idle and wasteful.

The death of Tsangyang Gyatso is the subject of almost as many stories as his life. Some say that apart from his many lovers he had a special lover who remained with him throughout and by whom he had a boy child. According to those who tell this story, the high monks were afraid that if the boy were allowed to live it would turn the office of Gyalwa Rinpoche into a hereditary office, and to this they were opposed. Accordingly they imprisoned the woman and her child and drove the still young Tsangyang Gyatso into exile, where, in inner Mongolia, he became a goatherder and quietly lived out the rest of his life in the mountain wilderness. Considering the trouble that the succession to the office has often caused, some claim that it would have been a good thing if a hereditary system had been established.

More frequent accounts say that the Chinese saw in Tsangyang's unorthodox activities an excuse for intervention. They stirred up rumours that his discovery had been either a mistake or a fraud and that the real reincarnation in succession to the fifth Gyalwa Rinpoche had not yet been found. A powerful Mongolian general, Lhazang, resident in Lhasa, saw that it was in his own interests to support the Chinese and persuaded them to invite Tsangyang to Peking so that he could be conveniently murdered while on the way. It seems that there really was a plot to murder him when his party arrived at a lake known as Gunga Nor.

Before leaving Lhasa, the Gyalwa Rinpoche made a strange pronouncement, which people later took to be a prediction of his rebirth. He saw a white crane flying eastward over the city. He sang:

> *White bird in the sky,*
> *Lend me but one great wing*
> *That I too may fly eastward;*
> *Soon I shall return, from Litang,*
> *And give you back your wing.*

When he left Lhasa, it was with a large retinue of Tibetans and an escort of Mongolians. When he arrived at Gunga Nor, on the northern plateau, the Tibetans came to him and told him that they knew him to be the true reincarnation of Chenresig, but if he insisted on going on to Peking it could only bring death to them and disaster to Tibet. They begged him either to die there at Gunga Nor or to save them by some other feat.

That evening, when Tsangyang was in his tent, an old man appeared at the opening and came in. Tsangyang Gyatso asked him who he was, and the old man replied, 'Sengge', meaning 'lion'. The Gyalwa Rinpoche then asked the name of the lake near by, and was told, 'Gunga Nor'. Tsangyang Rinpoche thought for a moment, then said: ' "Sengge" means lion, a beast that stands for power; "Gunga" means happiness. It is a sign that it is right for me to depart from here so that my people can be happy.' Saying this he left, and though there are stories that he reappeared from time to time, he never reclaimed his throne as Gyalwa Rinpoche.

At the following New Year's festival in Lhasa the regent saw a beggar in the streets and suddenly bowed to him as he should bow only to the Gyalwa Rinpoche. Everyone noticed and cried out that the beggar must be that person and tried to hold him back; but he disappeared. Then a beggar appeared among others before the state oracle at Nechung, and the oracle turned and bowed to him, and once again the beggar disappeared. This time he reappeared again in eastern Tibet, in the land of Kham. There he met a Kham beggar, and together they travelled to India and made pilgrimage to all the holy shrines. When they returned to Kham the beggar from Lhasa demanded of the other a keepsake and was given a knife. With this he travelled far to the north, to Alekcha, in Mongolia. There he was given work by a wealthy lady, looking after her sheep. Once she complained that he was not doing his work properly and that a wolf had been killing her sheep. The next day the beggar, armed only with his small knife, went out into the hills and brought back the wolf alive, saying to the lady, 'Here is the wolf you say killed your sheep; now, if you wish, you can punish him yourself.' The lady then recognized that this beggar must be someone special, but she said nothing and allowed him to continue tending her sheep until he died.

When the Gyalwa Rinpoche disappeared from Gunga Nor, word was given out that he was dead, and immediately the Chinese, together with Lhazang, brought in a new Rinpoche, of their choice, who they said was a true reincarnation of the fifth, that the sixth had proven himself false by his dissolute life. The Tibetans believed otherwise, for they had seen Tsangyang's life differently and believed him to be true. Moreover, they began to hear tales of a young boy born in eastern Tibet, at Litang, who showed every sign of being a reincarnation.

Unwillingly Lhazang sent monks to look into the history of the boy, and on finding that he did indeed bear all the signs expected of a new Gyalwa Rinpoche, Lhazang had him confined to Kumbum Monastery and ordered everyone to accept the person whom he claimed to be the true sixth Gyalwa Rinpoche. The people would not accept the trick and appealed to a relative of Lobsang, another powerful Mongolian chief, to come to their aid. Much fighting ensued, and finally Lhazang was defeated and killed. The Chinese, seeing the way things were going, promptly seized the boy incarnation at Kumbum and with a large army escorted him to Lhasa, telling the people that they could have the Rinpoche of their choice, as the new seventh, provided only that the Tibetan people contribute to the maintenance and manning of the army, deemed necessary at this point to 'liberate' Tibet from the Mongolians, who by then had made a bad name for themselves by continuous looting and vandalism.

These troublesome times are all described by Fr. Desideri, who was in Lhasa at the time. He escaped detection by remaining in his chambers at Sera Monastery, then a little later he fled to a monastery in the south but was commanded by the Chinese to join the Tibetan army, bringing with him a horse, baggage mule, and two armed servants, under pain of death for disobedience. It was only through intercession by the local officials on Desideri's behalf that the order was rescinded. It was shortly after this that the Vatican recalled him to Rome. It is evident from his account, written at the time, that he believed the stories of the dissolute Gyalwa Rinpoche, and he could not understand how the Tibetan people, whom he respected as a religious people, could continue to respect such a leader. It may well be that the Chinese were equally sincere in their wish to see a fit person in office, but it is also quite plain how quick they were to turn the situation to their advantage. Their mistake, however, arose perhaps out of their basic disbelief in the whole system. In allowing the Tibetan claim for the installation of the young seventh Gyalwa Rinpoche, the Chinese may have felt that really it did not matter much who was put in office, so long as the Chinese Ambams retained political control. In this they were wrong, for we believe the seventh Gyalwa Rinpoche to have been a true reincarnation of Chenresig, just as we believe the sixth to have been. And if the sixth had caused any Tibetans to lose faith in their leader, the seventh brought them back to belief, uniting them even more firmly than before against foreign interference. One of the holiest of all our Gyalwa Rinpoche, he took pains to honour the memory of his predecessor. If non-Tibetans choose to criticize the sixth Gyalwa Rinpoche, then they not only fail to understand us and our religious belief, but they fail to understand Tsangyang Gyatso's most fundamental teaching, namely that life itself, in whatever form it appears to us, is one of our greatest teachers.

CHAPTER FIFTEEN

The Discipline of Religion

*May all beings be strengthened with Happiness,
   And the Source of Happiness;
May all beings be delivered from Suffering,
   And the Source of Suffering;
May all sentient beings be free from lust and
      hatred,
   And be united with the thought of equality.*

– from TSHADMED BSHI

No two people could seem less alike than the sixth and the seventh Gyalwa Rinpoche (1683–1706 and 1708–58), but to us they are in essence the same, for both are the embodiment of Chenresig. The sixth came in the guise of a lover of life; the seventh came, and lived, as a saint.

Kalsang Gyatso was born in Litang, not far from my own home, in eastern Tibet. He was born in 1708, at exactly the right time and in the place prophesied by Tsangyang Gyatso before he left Lhasa. His birth was accompanied by all the right omens, and very quickly he began to draw attention to himself by his actions and his words. He claimed to remember his previous incarnations and his fame spread to the authorities at Lhasa, who were looking for the successor to Tsangyang Gyatso. The military commander, Lhazang, supported by the Chinese, was busy furthering the choice of another candidate, and did not welcome the news from Litang. A number of influential people in Amdo saw that the safety of young Kalsang was threatened so he was sent to Kumbum Monastery for safety. There his religious education began in earnest, and by the time he was eventually recognized and brought for his enthronement to Lhasa, when he was nine years old, he was well within the discipline.

From the outset Kalsang showed a disinclination to make use of any of the power that had come to him so easily and surely. Despite the fact that he even had the Chinese behind him, as well as the Tibetans, his interests were religious rather than secular. Even when he was old enough for the regency to come to an end, he left most secular matters to others, particularly to the Panchen Rinpoche. The more Kalsang Gyatso retreated into religious life, the more the work of secular government and political control was taken over by the Panchen Rinpoche and the two Chinese Ambams stationed in Lhasa. The pattern was

Tibet

set for the Chinese to try to follow down to the present day. But they, and other non-Tibetans, have always made the mistake of assuming that the two great religious leaders of our country must necessarily rival each other for political power. On the contrary, none of the Panchen Rinpoche, not even those brought to China and held there under Chinese influence, have ever sought to take away from the power and reverence accorded by the Tibetans to the Gyalwa Rinpoche above all. Nor is it as others say, that the Gyalwa Rinpoche is the secular head of the country while the Panchen Rinpoche is the spiritual head. Some say this is because Opagmé, the Buddha of Infinite Light, is the traditional teacher of Chenresig, thus subordinating the Gyalwa to the Panchen as disciple to master. We see it rather as a reciprocal relationship between the two. If the Panchen Rinpoche has more often been tutor to the Gyalwa Rinpoche, in Lhasa, it is because of the chance that has more often determined their relative ages that way. The thirteenth Gyalwa Rinpoche, however, acted as tutor to the young Panchen Rinpoche, for their relative age was then reversed. For the Tibetan there has never been any doubt that the Gyalwa Rinpoche is our leader, secular and spiritual. Even a king must have a tutor, but that does not raise the tutor above the king. Both Gyalwa and Panchen Rinpoche are reincarnated for our benefit, as are all our reincarnations. Each has his own role, his own task.

Kalsang Gyatso, however, relinquished political control because he saw that at that time Tibet stood in particular need of spiritual help. The accusations levelled at the sixth Gyalwa Rinpoche and the subseqent dissension over succession, while causing no serious breach among the Tibetan people, nonetheless came as a threat to the authority of the Buddhist Church. This was the real threat, not so much the presence of foreign troops, Mongolian or Chinese. Kalsang Gyatso sought to restore that authority, not by physical force or political manoeuvre, but rather religious devotion. He led the most austere life and travelled widely, in simple clothes, on foot, teaching. He travelled without the attendants normally thought fitting to his station, and he stayed and taught wherever he felt moved to do so. Many people came to his religious lectures, especially those given from the mud throne in the park now known after him as Kalsang Park, in Lhasa. He also wrote many learned books, but more and more he retired to a life of solitary religious contemplation.

For all of us, good deeds done in this life will be of benefit to us in the next life. The more advanced we are along the path, the more our good deeds will benefit others. A Changchub Sempa's good deeds are entirely for the benefit of others since he himself has already achieved enlightenment. The life of renunciation led by the seventh Gyalwa Rinpoche was led directly for the benefit of his people and country, and all the hardships and sufferings he endured were for us, not for himself. Far from abandoning his country Kalsang Gyatso was working for it in the most direct and effective way possible. And like him we are all encouraged to enter a life of contemplation sooner or later.

Those who are not monks usually live out their ordinary active life first, raising their families and establishing them. They may then enter monasteries and retire from the world. Even those who enter monasteries as children may go through their entire lives without retiring into seclusion. There is no compulsion, for the life of a recluse is difficult and dangerous and must only be attempted by those who are prepared and who desire nothing else. After becoming a monk, because of my position as an incarnation, I was expected to go through the normal academic discipline, leading to a series of degrees. I was studying for my fifth-year (Namdrel) examination when my whole family moved to Lhasa, in accordance with custom, to be close to the Gyalwa Rinpoche, my younger brother. This distracted me very much from my studies, for my family were close to my heart, and although I saw little of them at Kumbum, at least they were not far away and there was always the chance of a surprise visit. Far from being a mere day or two away, Lhasa was many months distant, and I felt a great longing to join my family. I suppose I should have felt an even greater longing to continue my life as a monk and to fulfil my duties to Tagster Labrang, my monastery, but I did not. This too worried me, because I had no recollection of my previous incarnation and resented the fact that I had been given this doubt to live with.

I managed to pass my examination and requested permission from the abbot of Kumbum to allow me to join my family in Lhasa and to continue my education there. He refused and did his best to show me where my duty lay. I was obstinate, however, and even threatened to go through China and by sea to India and back into Tibet from that direction if I were not allowed to join a Lhasa-bound caravan heading westward. I had not only the abbot to contend with, but also my father, who as much as he wanted to have his whole family around him in Lhasa, also saw where my duty lay. Eventually I was given permission, and arrangements were made for assembling a caravan for myself and some twenty others. By the time we were on the road there were altogether some three hundred of us, our pack animals number-ing between fifteen and twenty thousand. We remained together for safety for the four months it took us to reach Nagchukha, a few days' ride from Lhasa. From that moment onward, until my return to Kumbum five years later, I was no longer the same person but the brother of the Gyalwa Rinpoche, and many things were made easy for me that would otherwise have been difficult or impossible. There were also many new opportunities open to me in the way of appointments in court or government circles, had I chosen to abandon the life of a monk. Had I wished to trade on my brother's position I could even have retired in material comfort; although I would have lost all respect, people would have tolerated my behaviour out of respect for the Gyalwa Rinpoche.

Not once did it cross my mind. My weakness brought me to Lhasa, to be near a family that perhaps I loved too much, but beyond that I was not even tempted. In fact, in Lhasa I saw little to tempt me at all. My training over the past twelve years, since I was a mere seven years old, had not only given me the strength, determination and will to resist temptation, it had given me such a very real joy in the life I was chosen to follow that the tempta-tion to go against it in any way barely existed for me. The life of a monk is not one long struggle against oneself, a life of regret and wishful thinking, a partial or stunted life. It is full and rich and brings an inner comfort that far exceeds any other kind of comfort I have known before or since. If temptation exists, it exists there, within the monastery walls and within the religious discipline – the temptation to be satisfied with the religious life as you find it, without striving all the time to get more from it. Our life, in a way, should be like that of the rich man who is never satisfied but always struggles for greater riches. The difference is that his struggles are rewarded by an ever higher degree of material comfort and security and often by an ever higher degree of mental discomfort and worry. As monks, our efforts are accompanied by steadily increasing material hardships and physical discomfort, but by a steady and sure increase in the well-being of our mind and spirit that renders our physical being insignificant to the point where physical discomfort no longer exists, where we are within reach of our goal: Sanggye Sa. Yet it is a goal that we cannot desire in itself, for in itself it is the annihilation of desire, the cessation of suffering, which comes through desire. Our minds then, are not so much set upon the goal as upon the path.

Upon my arrival in Lhasa I spent my time with my family, though naturally the amount of time the Gyalwa Rinpoche could spend with us was limited. I was taken around Lhasa just as any pilgrim would be, to pay my respects to the sacred places, and simply as a curious tourist. I moved in higher circles than I would ever have dreamed possible back in Amdo, but I actually saw little there that could claim much respect, still less envy. No man needs special respect for doing his duty, and nobles, who cannot help the accident of their birth that makes them noble, have duties like the rest of us. For the noble, however, it is easier to avoid duty, slipping into a life of wastefulness. Politics in Lhasa involve as much intrigue and subterfuge as elsewhere, for contrary to general belief our government is not made up entirely of monks, but is half monk and half layman. For the layman to hold government office is to be noble, and among the sons of such

305

nobles there is constant rivalry for the limited number of junior offices. For them it is harder to fulfil their obligations than for the simple monk.

It was not many days before I began making arrangements, with the help of my father, for my continued higher education. It was decided I should begin by applying for admission to Drepung, one of the 'great three' monasteries of Lhasa, about five miles from the city itself. The congregation of Drepung numbers about ten thousand monks, and it is divided, much like any university, into a series of residences and colleges and faculties. There were six abbots in Drepung, and when I arrived with my parents, others of my family and friends, they were assembled in a great tent to receive me and conduct me to my quarters. Many monks were there too, in welcome, but there was none of the music that there would have been at Kumbum, for the strict rules of Drepung forbid it.

My quarters consisted of a small apartment on the top floor of one of the many residences, overlooking the rest of the monastic city. I was allocated a monk to be my guide, and another, a great scholar, to be my teacher. My first duty was to take the entrance examination into the sixth level, and although nervous about my ability I found much pleasure in once more being back in familiar surroundings, leading a familiar life. The study was much more rigorous than at Kumbum. The day started, as always, with morning prayers at four o'clock, but then the classes, with a little interruption for exercise, lasted well into the evening, often to three hours before midnight, leaving little time for the private study that had somehow to be done. It seems strange to me now that four hours' sleep could have sufficed during those years, yet it did. The mental and physical exertion were well balanced with spiritual repose, beginning with the early morning prayers in the great assembly hall. It seemed that one's strength came from these periods of prayer rather than from the brief period of sleep that preceded it.

There was much less learning of scriptures by heart from the sixth level onward; more time was devoted to analysis of the scriptures and to developing skill in argument, particularly in debate. One is expected to pass from one class up into the next each year. On reaching the twelfth level the student who wishes to go further and take the highest degrees, equivalent to the doctorate of a Western university, must review all that he has done and further develop his skill in debate for another seven years. A boy who enters monastic life before he is ten, and is successful in his studies, may be about thirty years old by the time he completes his twelfth level, and so will be approaching forty by the time he is permitted to take his doctorate.

The doctoral examination, the highest of all, can only be taken in Lhasa. There are two types of doctorate, Lharampa and Tsogrampa, taken in the first and second months of the year respectively. The doctoral degrees are equivalent in that they cover exactly the same subjects, but those taking the Lharampa, in the first month, face a much more difficult audience during the debate because of the thousands who flock to Lhasa during this month for the New Year festivities. Among those present will be the greatest scholars in Tibet, yet sometimes it is an unexpected question from someone relatively untrained that will confuse the applicant most. The judges evaluate the applicant's success by the way in which he handles questions; the extent of his knowledge, at this point, is not really in question so much as his ability to make use of it. Some questions contain hidden traps; some are designed to lead the applicant away from the main issue under consideration; others may contain only part of a remote quotation that means one thing by itself, another in context.

I sometimes attended these examinations and myself asked questions; many of us did so just for the sport but sometimes also to help solve knotty problems that were bothering us. Each applicant (and there might be a dozen or more) is examined for a whole day, from the morning right through to nearly midnight. Then in the fourth week the results are given, and the Gyalwa Rinpoche comes to the great central temple to congratulate those who have passed.

Beyond this there are other colleges in Lhasa and elsewhere where more specialized teachings are given, teachings in special schools of philosophy, teachings of the various tantras and other esoteric doctrines to which only those with the highest qualifications are admitted. Not all of these are Gelukpa by any means, but once a Gelukpa monk has finished his formal eduction he is free to attend the specialized colleges as he wishes, even if they are under the Nyingmapa sect. All that is asked of him is that he does not introduce any Nyingmapa rites into a Gelukpa monastery; what he practises on his own is his own concern. Many are tempted towards the Nyingmapa teachings because whereas the Gelukpa teachings are designed to lead the monk slowly but surely towards enlightenment, there are shorter and more direct routes such as those taught by the Nyingmapa. Not everyone is fitted for the direct path, but many may benefit by the preliminary teachings and exercises, and I myself had many tantric teachers for some time. But by the time I had passed my seventh-level examinations I was already beginning to tire of academic learning and life in Lhasa, with all the attention paid to me as a member of the Gyalwa Rinpoche's family, left me little peace.

I was doing well enough in my studies, and I enjoyed them, but I felt I had gone far enough, that I needed something else. Some people are inclined to a purely academic life; they like to think and reason and argue, to arrive at truths by means of the intellect. To others this seems too cold and remote, and even within the limits of the Middle Path there is latitude for those who feel the need for a more direct, personal approach. After some five years in Lhasa I felt such a need, and I was also increasingly concerned about being away for so long from my own monastery. Many monks like to set aside one month of each year during which they retreat into a hermitage, or merely shut themselves up within their monastery, and spend their time in complete solitude, in religious meditation. Others spend longer, some devote their whole lives to solitude. Many private families are only too happy to invite in a monk who is searching for a retreat. They will look after him for three months or three years, for as long as he wants to stay, providing him with his food, looking after his needs, washing his clothes, and of course providing him with a small room of his own. Sometimes the monk will say prayers for the family at the family shrine, and perform services for them when there is need, but even if he remains for the whole time in complete seclusion, seeing no one and talking to no one, the family will feel well rewarded. The presence of such a person, engaged in meditation, will alone bring good.

In a monastery you must study; it is in seclusion that you can practise exercises such as those taught by the tantras. I had always found such exercises helpful, though being a member of the Gelukpa sect I did not believe in looking for the 'direct path'. Increasingly I longed for seclusion, for freedom from academic discipline. On the one hand I wanted freedom to attend at last to all the duties I had so long left to others, but which still remained my responsibility; on the other, I wanted to leave this world and renew contact with the world of the spirit. I decided to leave Lhasa and return to Kumbum.

I had not been back for long before I was once again drawn into the academic path. The abbot's term of office came to an end, and various names, mine among them, were submitted for election. The abbot himself indicated that he wanted me as his successor, and I could not refuse. Many things are considered in making a choice: academic ability, administrative ability, and financial support. An abbot has not only to administer his monastery, he has to see that all its members are properly taken care of, well fed and housed, and to this end he either has to raise contributions from others or he has to contribute heavily from his own sources if, as in my case, he has a wealthy endowment behind him.

His academic ability has to be at least adequate, since as abbot he is expected to take all twelve levels. I found myself once again back in my books, studying and debating, for being abbot in no way excuses you from your duties and your obligations as a student. I had two stewards to help me with the administration, but I still had to spend far more time in the official quarters of the abbot of Kumbum than back in my own more private quarters at Tagster Labrang. Once again I found myself being more and more involved with the world around me, and the hope of a prolonged period of seclusion faded.

The scriptures that have to be mastered in the full course of education are both canonical and non-canonical. The canonical scriptures include the Kagyur, which are primarily the direct teachings of the Buddha, embodied in some eighty-four thousand discourses on ethics, discipline, administration and philosophy, so that not only the Buddhist Church may take its law from this scripture, but it may also be used for the instruction of laymen according to their various characters and potentials. The Kagyur contains some expositions given by a few of Buddha's most chosen disciples, with his approval; it also includes the Four Great Tantras: the Tantra of Activity, the Tantra of Application, the Tantra of Perfection, and the Tantra of Perfection Supreme.

Following the Kagyur in importance is the Tangyur, a commentary written over many years by both Indian and Tibetan scholars, in two hundred and twenty-five volumes. There is also the *Tsanuyi Yikcha*, a university course in itself that must be completed by any monk before he embarks upon a study of the tantras. The canonical scriptures also contain numerous other volumes, including those of the Nyingmapa sect, precepts to aid in religious study and practice, hymns, invocations, and classical narratives concerning previous births of the Buddha.

The non-canonical texts deal with Sanskrit and Tibetan grammar, political science, medical science, astrology and astronomy, rhetoric, and general literature and arts.

These scriptures have been carefully preserved and are considered in many ways the most important means of instruction towards enlightenment that we have. However much we may revere and respect holy men and workers of miracles, we believe that the scriptures form a safer refuge. We symbolize this by placing them, in our monasteries and temples, in special places of honour, exalted above the mere images, which are considered as lesser aids to right thought and right action. This is best understood by remembering that the core of Tibetan Buddhism is represented by the Three Precious Ones: Sanggye, Chö, Gedun (the Buddha, the Dharma and the Sangha); the Buddha who is ever here to lead us to enlightenment, his Word (as given to us in the scriptures), and the brotherhood of his monks. This is our threefold refuge, symbolized in all our public and private worship by the images, the scriptures always housed around and above the images, and the congregation. This is where we all, monk or layman, find the inner security that has for so long been a part of normal Tibetan life.

There is a fourth refuge, the lama. The lama is simply a teacher, yet to every disciple his lama is the most important living being, for his mind, speech and body correspond to the Sanggye, Chö and Gedun. It is under a lama that one learns the process of concentration and then meditation, leading to Sanggye Sa. Concentration, by the application of proper techniques, is simply a means of getting rid of physical and emotional imbalance, arriving at physical and mental tranquillity. All wrong actions and wrong thoughts have to be utterly eradicated, and this can only be achieved after intensive training and rigid discipline and moral control. Meditation can then take over and allow the being to be pervaded by the truth that is ever with us but is obscured by precisely those personal emotions and thoughts and actions to which we cling so ardently, in the belief that without them we would be nothing. Without them, *only* without them, we are everything. Meditation demands absolute purity of mind and body, purity of purpose. It also demands watchfulness, patience and considerable exertion. The first three tantras demand religious devotion, concentration and meditation upon the aspirant's own tutelary deity (including his ngag and symbols), and breathing exercises; all based upon intellectual and moral training of the highest order. The fourth tantra also utilizes concentration and meditation, but focuses on the process of life and death, Bardo and rebirth, leading to the manifestation, out of the unreal, the real, the subtle body, and the transformation of this into a still higher state. Then, under the fourth tantra, follow six steps leading to the Great Bliss, utilizing the channel of spiritual energy, Tummo-me, which lies awaiting to be awakened and properly used for spiritual rather than physical creation. This step involves intricate breathing exercises and body postures. It is the most esoteric of all, given only to a few.

Together with these practices come the much talked of psychic powers. We believe that high spiritual attainment may free the body from natural laws. The body can then be legitimately used for the attainment of a still higher stage, but the goal is always one of enlightenment, to be achieved for the sake of all sentient beings. It is our duty to strive after enlightenment, for until we reach that state we are incapable of helping one another, we are still living in ignorance and illusion. Far from being an easy life, a way of escape, the way becomes harder the more directly it leads to the goal; the monk, whether of the lowest order or the highest, is making the supreme sacrifice when he undertakes a solitary life of concentration and meditation. He not only condemns himself to a harsh existence in his present incarnation, he also binds himself to return, again and again, to endure similar sufferings, so that he may help his fellows.

The renunciate is not a selfish man, cold and devoid of feeling for others. On the contrary, he is possessed of limitless love, limitless compassion, limitless joy, and limitless equanimity.

CHAPTER SIXTEEN

A Foreign World

Rest, my faithful ones;
Stay in peace, my beloved Khabachen.
In future times I shall come again,
Under a thousand different forms,
Bringing help and comfort.

— from MANI BKAHBUM

Of all the Gyalwa Rinpoche, we Tibetans probably respect the seventh, Kalsang Gyatso, most of all because of his saintliness, because he devoted his whole life to the Three Precious Ones, seeking refuge not for himself but for all his people. But we also honour most highly the fifth and the thirteenth, because they not only gave Tibet spiritual strength, they also gave her political strength, and during their reigns Tibet enjoyed long periods of peace and prosperity.

During the reign of the seventh, the Chinese tried to bribe the Panchen Rinpoche to come over to their side, so as to increase their influence in our country. But by the very honour they showered on the Panchen Rinpoche when he visited Peking, and by the respect they showed him, they only strengthened the Tibetan people's respect for their religion and their religious leaders. This respect is just what the Chinese wanted to break, for this far more than military strength has always stood in the way of Chinese control over Tibet.

This move having failed, and the Tibetan people still remaining obstinately devoted to the Gyalwa Rinpoche as their leader, the Chinese attempted to control the selection of the Gyalwa Rinpoche. It is perhaps more than a coincidence that between the seventh and the thirteenth holders of that office, only one reached his majority. The eighth, Gyampal Gyatso, died when he was in his thirties, Lungtog Gyatso when he was eleven, Tsultrim Gyatso at eighteen, Khadrup Gyatso when he was eighteen also, and Krinla Gyatso at about the same age. The circumstances are such that it is very likely some, if not all, were poisoned, either by loyal Tibetans for being Chinese-appointed impostors, or by the Chinese for not being properly manageable.

Many Tibetans think that this was done at the time when,

according to traditional custom, the young Gyalwa Rinpoche made his ritual visit to the sacred lake Lamtso. In this lake the Rinpoche was able to see the manner in which he was to lead his life and the nature of his death. The journey of some one hundred miles was always made with full pomp, a large retinue accompanying the Gyalwa Rinpoche. At the lake there is a special shrine sacred to Mogsorma, protectress of the lake, and protectress of all incarnations of Chenresig. She is considered to be particularly fierce in aspect, and none may enter the shrine other than the Gyalwa Rinpoche, and even he should only do so after long and proper preparation. Each of the four Rinpoche to die young expired shortly after his visit to the lake. Many said it was because they were not the true reincarnations, but impostors imposed by the Chinese. Others tell stories of how the cooks of the retinue, which in those days included many Chinese, were bribed to put poison in the Rinpoche's food. The thirteenth Gyalwa Rinpoche did not visit Lamtso until he was twenty-five years old. He was adequately prepared by spiritual exercise, and he also had faithful cooks. The Chinese were disappointed when he did not die like his predecessors, and he was to live long enough to give them much more cause for regret.

Life during the interval between the seventh and the thirteenth incarnations was almost equally hazardous for the regents, who were beset by powerful influences on both sides, and during this whole period of instability the Chinese resident Ambams, in Lhasa, exerted their strength to bring Tibet further under China's political control. When the twelfth Gyalwa Rinpoche died, however, the circumstances for the selection of his successor were different and left no room for intrigue. A highly revered monk had a revelation, there was an unmistakably clear vision in lake Lamtso, and the boy indicated (Takpo, in southern Tibet), showed all the expected characteristics, physical and spiritual. The oracles and omens were so unanimous that there was not the slightest question in the minds of any of the officials; the boy was brought almost directly to Lhasa, and installed as

Thubten Gyatso, thirteenth Gyalwa Rinpoche, about 1878. As he grew up he developed the qualities he was going to need the most. Although he was to become one of the greatest advocates of monks' leaving politics to laymen, as far as possible, he nonetheless became a shrewd and successful politician, while never neglecting his spiritual duties. Meanwhile Tibet was being drawn helplessly into the irreconcilable crosscurrents of international politics.

The great powers that surrounded Tibet, Russia, China and Britain were becoming increasingly interested in the trade potential of Tibet. The British, playing politics with the Chinese at the time, at first chose to support China's claim to authority over Tibet and signed various treaties with China concerning Tibet. This made the Tibetans aware of the danger of their position, for up to that point they had only had China to contend with and had always managed to keep her at a comfortable arm's length; the existence of the two Chinese Ambams at Lhasa was an effective face-saver for China and the Tibetans saw no harm in allowing her to pretend to an authority that she could not enforce in fact. With northern India, Nepal, Sikkim, Bhutan and Burma all under British influence, and with the British evidently supporting the Chinese, the position was different. The thirteenth Gyalwa Rinpoche sent an envoy to the Tsar of Russia to open negotiations. The Tsar was much interested, not only with an eye to trade, but also with the thought of using Tibet as a convenient back door into China.

Geographical barriers and the difficulty of communication hampered any practical agreement, but not before the British had become thoroughly alarmed at the prospect of an alliance between the two nations. Realizing that in effect Tibet was not the vassal of China that she supposed, Britain promptly repudiated her previous recognition of Chinese 'authority' and sent an armed expedition, under Sir Francis Younghusband, into Tibet. In the face of this invasion the Gyalwa Rinpoche fled through eastern Tibet, by way of Kumbum Monastery, and eventually arrived in Peking to enter negotiations with the

317

empress. Meanwhile the British signed a treaty in Tibet with the Tibetan government and withdrew their forces, leaving behind only a small commission. The Gyalwa Rinpoche returned, but the struggle between the great powers was not over yet. Britain persuaded Russia to join her in recognizing that Tibet was independent of China and that Tibet should remain closed to all foreign penetration. China made one last attempt, this time by armed intervention, and once again the Gyalwa Rinpoche, leaving the government in the hands of his representatives, left to attempt direct negotiation with his foes. This time he came to India and met with the British, who procrastinated until they saw the way the winds were going to blow.

The issue was finally settled by the internal revolt within China. The Tibetan troops who had been keeping the Chinese at bay now had no difficulty in driving them out. The empress, in a pathetic gesture that only served to underline the myth of Chinese authority in Tibet, had issued a proclamation deposing the Gyalwa Rinpoche, now Thubten Gyatso was back in Lhasa, and Tibet was as strong as it had ever been since the time of 'The Great Fifth', Ngawong Gyatso.

The Gyalwa Rinpoche issued a Declaration of Independence, deported all Chinese residents in Tibet, including the Ambams, and settled down to do what he could to strengthen his own country. It was during this time that the Chinese once again attempted to establish some influence by intriguing with the Panchen Rinpoche, in the nineteen-twenties. While the Gyalwa Rinpoche had been in India the Chinese Ambams had invited the Panchen Rinpoche to Lhasa, and had installed him in the offices and apartments of Thubten Gyatso. This in itself had not caused too much bad feeling, for both Rinpoche were highly respected and when Thubten Gyatso returned to Lhasa the Panchen Rinpoche simply went back to his own monastery of Tashi Lhunpo. There was no bad feeling between the two, until the Chinese instigated disagreement among their followers. The followers of the Panchen Rinpoche were fed with the notion that it was really *their* leader who should be the head of Tibet, not the Gyalwa Rinpoche. The Panchen Rinpoche and his followers were also encouraged to avoid the increased taxes being demanded by the central government, claiming a privileged position amounting to independence. The Gyalwa Rinpoche's followers, on the other hand, resented the privileges already assumed by Tashi Lhunpo and resented still more the growing desire among the followers of the Panchen Rinpoche for political power. A division of Tibet was as unthinkable as it was impractical, and when the Panchen Rinpoche left Tibet, with many of his court, on a visit to Peking, it was known that he would not return. He stayed in China until his death, in 1937. The old story of the division between the two leaders had once again come true. Yet there was never any lack of mutual respect between the Rinpoche. And although the Panchen Rinpoche's successor was brought up entirely under Chinese control and subjected to rigid indoctrination, when he was brought to Tibet by the invading communists he was accorded all the respect due to his position by the Tibetan people and in fact quickly proved that he was not the puppet the Chinese had expected. The Chinese expectation that they could play these two Rinpoche against each other was based on the false assumption that our system was one of political significance and convenience. Not being a religious people themselves they could not understand that our government, which bore all the outward signs of being political, was in effect religious, and that the loyalty of the Tibetan people was not mere political allegiance, but an act of faith, fervent and unbreakable. They have always equally misunderstood, as have other non-Tibetans, the role of our Rinpoche, who have appeared to them merely as political leaders, relying on secular support, whereas to Tibetans the duty of the Rinpoche is above everything else the spiritual well-being of the Tibetan people.

It is our unshakable belief that there is no goal higher than the spiritual goal, and that nothing is worth more than that goal, for all else will be given to us on the way, and even then will appear as worthless compared with that which we all seek. This is no philosophy restricted to the wealthy Tibetans who have already achieved material well-being in this life; it is the belief of every farmer, of every nomad. In Tibet the wealthy and powerful have never had the monopoly of contentment. That has always belonged to all of us.

Chenresig is sent to protect Tibet, and the Gyalwa Rinpoche is the reincarnation of Chenresig, so it is natural for the Gyalwa Rinpoche to be accorded political power if he wishes it. Tibet has a complex governmental organization without any need for an active Rinpoche at its head, however. It can run just as effectively if the Incarnation of Chenresig prefers solitude, working for the spiritual rather than political protection of his people as in the case of the seventh. Nonetheless, the Gyalwa Rinpoche is always the nominal head of our government, just as he is by virtue of his office the head of our Buddhist Church. As such he commands respect, but during times of pilgrimage there are many who place greater importance on taking the blessings of other Rinpoche, of either the Gelukpa or the Nyingmapa sects, or of the Panchen Rinpoche himself. It is something quite apart from the authority they unanimously accord to the Gyalwa Rinpoche and the respect they feel for him. A pilgrim seeking a blessing is like a pupil seeking a teacher, a disciple seeking a master; it is an individual matter, and each must allow himself to be guided according to his own needs. To become a follower of the Panchen Rinpoche, then, is in no way an act of disloyalty, however it might appear to outsiders.

Thubten Gyatso, on his return to Lhasa in 1912, in no way concerned himself with the Panchen Rinpoche as a potential rival. He was much more concerned about the condition into which the internal administration of the country had fallen during this prolonged period of intrigue and foreign influence. He set about a series of reforms designed to remove a number of abuses that had grown up, even when such reforms constituted an attack on the behaviour of members of his own sect, the dominant Gelukpa.

There had been instances of corruption in some monasteries, and the giving of the highest degrees had also been open to criticism. Thubten Gyatso called the abbots of the large monasteries together and insisted on the restoration of the old discipline. A monastery was a place for work and study, and persistently idle monks were simply to be expelled from the order. Candidates for the highest degrees now had to appear at the Potala for examination there before the degree was conferred. Monks were discouraged from too much involvement in secular affairs, and to this end the thirteenth Gyalwa Rinpoche increased greatly the number of lay government officials, which in turn effectively reduced the political and economic power of the monasteries over the farmers. On one occasion monks from Sera themselves went to collect debts from an outlying village; when the peasants were unable to pay, the monks seized a great deal of property and carried it back to the monastery. The peasants organized a petition, and the Gyalwa Rinpoche called the Sera abbots to the Potala. He kept them waiting in his reception room for two days, to teach them humility, and then imposed a heavy penalty on them for having allowed their monks to behave in such a way.

With government officials he was equally severe. It was an accepted custom that any government official could demand horses or yaks for transportation from any local peasants when travelling on government duty. Properly used, the privilege was a sensible one and caused no hardship. Some officials, however, had in recent times been making quite unnecessary demands, and not always when on government business. Thubten Gyatso introduced a law whereby nobody could make such demands without written authority from the central government.

Nobles had grown into the habit not only of avoiding taxes by giving false information but of further abusing their position by demanding service without giving pay. This was now stopped, proper scales of pay and service were established and a national basis for taxation was organized and enforced.

With all these laws, made necessary by a growing laxity among both nobles and monks, there arose a need for police to supervise their enforcement. Up to that point there had been no police force in Tibet, the rule of the monasteries had been firm and just. At the same time, punishments had sometimes been excessive and often severe. Thubten Gyatso revised the penal system and again established a uniform system for the entire nation. Capital punishment was completely abolished, and corporal punishment was reduced. Living conditions in jails were also improved, and officials were designated to see that these conditions and rules were maintained.

The whole process of education had tended to be exclusive, only those dedicated to a full monastic life, taking all the vows, being able to receive the highest education. Even the children of nobility were restricted to some extent, but the children of peasants were customarily only given a rudimentary education together with a firm religious foundation. Now a secular educational system was to be introduced, though not divorced from the religious education, but rather superimposed, so that the religious foundation remained.

Thubten Gyatso was an enlightened ruler by any standards, and if Tibet had been as feudal and oppressive as many have held it to be, he could never have survived. As it was, there was little opposition, for the justness of his reforms was undeniable. What opposition there was came from monasteries which had, until then, wielded a large amount of political power and which had exercised almost complete economic authority over vast areas. Under the new reforms the whole system of government was revised, and an equable balance was struck between religious and secular power. Further, Thubten Gyatso, while intent upon keeping foreign troops out of Tibet, and resisting any attempt by foreign powers to exert even indirect control over Tibet's internal affairs, wanted to be well versed in what was going on in the world outside. He sent Tibetans out to study and learn, and he himself welcomed foreigners who visited him in Lhasa, among them being Japanese, British and Americans. Despite his mistrust of the intentions of the British government, he remained close friends with her representative, Sir Charles Bell, and frequently consulted him on matters of major importance.

Electricity was introduced to Lhasa for the first time in the nineteen twenties, and installed throughout the city, not merely for the benefit of the Potala. Some elementary work was done on road building, and the first motor car was laboriously carried over the icy mountain ranges and down into central Tibet. Telephone and telegraph systems were established, and Tibet, in a few short years, was ready to make its entry into the modern world. For reasons of its own, however, the modern world preferred to keep Tibet in isolation, and while world wars raged outside, and the great powers vied with each other for the territories of lesser powers, Tibet could do nothing but wait, halted on its first step into the international maelstrom. It was like a fruit, slowly ripening, waiting to be plucked.

The reforms instituted by Thubten Gyatso did not collapse after his death; they were furthered during the regency and the present Gyalwa Rinpoche began an even more vigorous series of reforms as soon as he took over control. We had all seen the practical benefits brought about by Thubten Gyatso's ideas, and even the rebellious monasteries felt the benefit of the new laws that reimposed the strictest discipline for anyone having taken holy orders. Above all, monasteries began to appreciate the wisdom of leaving the secular administration to lay officials as far as possible. There were two good reasons. In the first place, administrative work of any kind requires special training, and when untrained monks took the task upon themselves they inadvertently caused much hardship, even oppression; in the second place, the monks and even whole monasteries were becoming secularized, giving more and more time to the task of local government and less to spiritual development.

I myself saw something of this when I was appointed abbot of Kumbum. It was not a post I wanted, for my whole purpose in returning had been to live a quiet life, devoted to meditation. I could not refuse a direct request, however, and soon found out what is involved in being both a monk and an administrator. It was partly the matter of being compelled, by the rules of our sect, to continue my higher education to the doctoral level; as abbot one is in charge of what in effect is a university, and the abbot is himself expected to possess the highest qualifications. Rank matters so little that although abbot, and as such entitled to respect, I was also a student and had to join in the daily debates and contests. Such a situation can only drive one to redoubled efforts, yet this purely academic burden is only part of the burden of an administrator in a monastery.

As abbot I was in charge of all personnel and had to approve appointments to the various offices, from the treasurer down to the cooks. In the end I was responsible for anything that any of them did and felt obliged to learn at first hand the work that each officer had to do. Then there were disciplinary matters, which to me were a particular strain, and the overall responsibility for the administration of the monastery's large holdings of farmland, involving many complex loans of land, cash and grain to other monasteries as well as to individuals. One duty alone took much of each day, and that was the preparation of a lecture that, as abbot, I had to deliver each morning to the four thousand monks gathered together in the general assembly. With so much time devoted to administrative problems and to ordinary every-day routine work there was no time left at all for the quiet and peace I both wanted and needed. An abbot is expected to be more than an administrator; he is also expected to give spiritual leadership. Such leadership does not come easily, nor is it given easily. It is not enough simply to lead a good life; to be a truly spiritual leader the mind must be fixed on the spirit, not on matter. That is not to say that it is impossible for a spiritual person to be an administrator, nor is it impossible for an administrator to give spiritual leadership, but it requires the highest qualities and special training. In Lhasa such training is given; monks are taught how to combine their sacred and secular roles, but it is given to a relatively small number. If it was difficult for me, merely the abbot of a religious institution, then how much more difficult was it for a monk appointed to an office quite separate from his religious life. One side or other of one's life is bound to suffer, leading to either poor administration or spiritual impoverishment.

Not long before he died Thubten Gyatso made a prophecy. A high incarnation in a monastery in Outer Mongolia had been killed by communists. The monastery had been closed and people forbidden to pray; the priests had been forced to join the army. The thirteenth Gyalwa Rinpoche said that all this would come to pass in Tibet before long, and that we should prepare ourselves. He told us that there would be a time when there would be no Gyalwa Rinpoche and no Panchen Rinpoche and that all other reincarnations would die and nobody would be allowed to search for their successors. All memory of our ancient past would be wiped out; land and property would be taken away from those who held it; there would be a time of no food and a time when days and nights would be passed in fear. Against this time, so close upon us, we should prepare ourselves by building up our physical resistance, and by increasing our spiritual endeavour and purifying our spiritual lives.

This prophecy was given by Thubten Gyatso in the year of his death, 1933, when he was fifty-eight years old, and within two decades it was to come true.

CHAPTER SEVENTEEN

The New Order

To others give the victory and the spoils;
The loss and defeat, take upon oneself.

– Bsodnams Rgyamtso,
third Gyalwa Rinpoche

One of the most frequent accusations levelled against Tibet has been that the Buddhist Church is an autocracy, a despotism headed by the Gyalwa Rinpoche. Insofar as no human beings are perfect, no human system of government can reach perfection. There are many democratic forms of government that allow far less freedom to their people than does the Tibetan system, and although successive leaders have seen the need for reforms, and instituted them, the reforms have arisen out of human weaknesses, not out of any inherent weakness in the governmental system. While I personally, and I believe most Tibetans with me, would like to see still further reform, I cling to our traditional form of government. If we seek a good government, we must seek good men, and where better to look than among those who have taken monastic vows, devoting their lives to the religious ideal? I also believe that our system's greatest strength comes from the undisputed leadership of the Gyalwa Rinpoche; but this is an act of faith that must be difficult for others to understand. Others in our government can be weak, but never our highest authority, for he is the reincarnation of Chenresig, the embodiment of perfection and enlightenment. It is pointless to criticize the Tibetan system without considering and allowing this faith, for without it the whole system becomes a mockery. If it were a mockery, it could hardly have achieved the success it always has, for even in defeat we have never lost our ideals, our goal, our faith, and those things we cherish far above material well-being and possessions. If our faith were taken from us, then truly we would feel defeat.

The whole concept of status and hierarchy in Tibet also depends upon our religious attitude and can only be understood with that in mind. Social status is acquired according to various qualities such as moral character, intellectual capacity, religious

devotion, and age. Status thus acquired should then be respected
... that is another quality. There is no rigid division ordained
by birth; movement from one level to another depends entirely
upon individual attainment, and so although we can speak of
three classes in Tibet – the nobles, the middle (or trading) class,
and the peasant farmers and nomads (apart from the monks,
which in a way form a fourth class) – there is no class system,
and the mobility from class to class makes any class prejudice
virtually impossible. It seems strange to us that foreigners should
criticize us for respecting our superiors, as though that were a
degrading thing to do. To us one of the greatest virtues in an
individual is respect for those who are his superior in any of the
qualities that we admire. We see nothing but honour in giving
honour where it is due, and with us it is due by individual
attainment, not by inheritance. The only hereditary ranks –
those of our reincarnations – are hereditary in a spiritual sense.

Respect is part of our life, and our forms of salutation, our
manner of speech, the way in which we move and seat ourselves
in public, all vary according to relative status and age. This
respect for those who are pious and wise is at the root of our
system of government, and in the same way that there is a
social hierarchy, so is there a religious hierarchy, which finds
a place for all the various branches of Buddhism in Tibet, all
the established sects, each of which acknowledges the overall
authority of the Gyalwa Rinpoche who although usually of the
Gelukpa sect, need not necessarily be so. The head of the
Gelukpa sect is always another Rinpoche, highly revered as such.
The Gyalwa Rinpoche is above sectarianism, and in fact several
of them have leaned as much, if not more, to the teachings of the
Nyingmapa than the Gelukpa, though all have been brought up
in the Gelukpa tradition.

The Rinpoche, or reincarnations, are themselves graded in a
hierarchy, and their respective status can be determined in any
monastic assembly by the manner in which they greet each other
or in their order of seating. In a sense they are part of yet another
hierarchy, a spiritual hierarchy, descending from the Buddha
himself, through the countless thousands of Changchub Sempa.

Yet even this hierarchy is closed to no one. It has been our cherished belief, and our practice, that any individual desiring to enter a religious life should be encouraged and helped to do so and should be helped to the maximum of his capacity. In my own monastery at Kumbum I had among my monks a man well-liked and respected for he was deeply pious, yet he came to us as a murderer. The only qualification for entering the religious order is sincerity of purpose and a proper sense of responsibility. From then onward, it is a question of individual attainment and ability, and the ultimate goal for all is the same, enlightenment. With enlightenment comes the choice of whether to accept Sanggye Sa or to return as a Changchub Sempa to help those still in ignorance, and the Changchub Sempa ideal is the ideal of all Tibetan Buddhists. In this way, in our society, no doors are closed, and yet every man has respect for his fellows.

The head of every government is the Gyalwa Rinpoche, embodiment of Chenresig. His first and foremost duty is the protection of his country and his people, and to this end he must work in whatever manner he deems best; there is no fixed pattern to which he must conform. Primarily concerned with the spiritual welfare of the people, the Gyalwa Rinpoche is above all else a lama, or teacher. He instructs us in the Buddhist religion in general and in the teachings of the Gelukpa sect in particular. But he also governs the country through a series of councils. As the head of the government the Gyalwa Rinpoche gives it its essentially religious character, but the councils through which he works, and which are responsible for most effective legislation (the Central Government), together with the Assemblies that can be summoned whenever needed, are carefully divided so that secular as well as religious interests are equally served. Approximately half of the officials are monks, the other half laymen. Most of the monks, but not all, come from the three major Gelukpa monasteries, Drepung, Sera and Ganden. They may be recommended by officials about to retire, or they may themselves apply for government service. Service is open to any monk in any part of the country, but if accepted he must enter the special school at the Potala for the training of officials, and pass the necessary examinations, before assuming duty. The Yigtsang council makes all final decisions and the appointments come from it. This council is itself composed of four members of the government, elected by the other governmental members, and above them stands the high advisory council, the Kashak, usually four officers appointed by the Gyalwa Rinpoche from laymen and monks who are nominated by the National Assembly.

The lay officials mostly come from noble families, so in a sense it is a hereditary body; but the composition of the nobility is changing all the time, and in every government there are a substantial number of lay officials who are not from the nobility. Just as appointments to the ranks of monk officials are made by a council, the Yigtsang, so is appointment made for the lay officials by a similar elected council of four lay officers, the Tsikang. As with the monk officials, a layman can apply for government service, and his acceptance depends ultimately on his suitability and aptitude. As with the Yigtsang, the Tsikang falls under the authority of the Kashak. In this way, though the direction of government is clearly given by religious authority, the government itself is divided equally on an elective basis between monks and laymen.

The National Assembly meets only in times of the greatest crisis. It consists of the abbots of the three seats of learning, the Yigtsang and the Tsikang, further representatives of both monk officials and lay officials from the Central Government, and representatives from many different professions, blacksmiths, soldiers, carpenters, farmers, nomads, shopkeepers, and so forth. Most of them are Buddhist, but some are followers of the old Bön religion. This National Assembly acts as a check on the Kashak and can even prevent the Kashak from taking steps it considers unwise. It may also suggest a certain course of action and place it before the Kashak for action. Whereas the Central Government is concerned mainly with internal affairs, the National Assembly will be summoned to deal with any international question and with issues that affect the nation as a whole.

The work of government in this way is carried out primarily

by the Kashak, with the Gyalwa Rinpoche involving himself as much or as little as he sees fit. The assemblies are summoned whenever there is need for the Kashak to consult the people, or whenever the people wish to make representations to the Kashak. In order to implement the decisions of the government, and to enforce the laws and apply justice, Tibet is divided into a number of regional districts, each under the joint governorship of a monk and a lay official, nominated by the Yigtsang and the Tsikang. The appointments are generally held for only two or three years each time, and there are many checks that prevent governors from abusing their authority. Even in the remotest districts, several months' journey from Lhasa, where an appeal would take well over a year to reach Lhasa, be heard, and answered, the most effective check is the dual system of governorship itself. Every decision must be made by agreement between both the governors, monk and lay. Each is jealous of his own authority and reputation and would fear an unfavourable report either by the people or by the other governor. The people always have the right of direct appeal to Lhasa.

On the whole the system of dual governorships has worked well in all but a few instances. The Dzongpen, as the governors are called, act as representatives of the people, and if the people have any grievances about the rate of taxation or any other matter the Dzongpen's duty is to report such grievances to the Central Government. The Dzongpen also act as judges, sitting jointly in court and hearing all cases that are brought to them. Again, their judgement must be unanimous, and this effectively ensures a fair hearing.

Below the Dzongpen, between them and the people, are the Ganpo, or village headmen, and the Khanpo who act in the same way for each monastery. The Ganpo really has no authority, though he may have a great deal of influence. He is elected by the villagers, and is elected mainly because of his ability. He need not be wealthy, and he need not even be from a family that has lived for a long time in that particular village. If the villagers have several ideas as to who might be Ganpo, and cannot decide, they write the names on pieces of paper and draw one. They can

333

also ask a Ganpo to resign, but this happens very rarely, because we find that a man who is elected is anxious to do the best he can. If he does something that the villagers object to, they only need to tell him.

The Ganpo do not get paid, although they frequently have to do a great deal of work for their villages, and travel back and forth to the regional capital. The most that they can expect is the gratitude of their fellow villagers, who might sometimes give a party for them. The governors are paid fixed salaries, and apart from holding court they are expected to travel throughout their district so that everyone has a chance to speak his mind directly. The Dzongpen and the Ganpo meet regularly, and the only time there is trouble is when one or other Dzongpen tries to extract some benefit for himself, either by accepting bribes or by demanding service. Monasteries sometimes demand too much interest on loans that they make. When they lend out grain to the farmers they are entitled to be repaid, once the harvest is in, with a reasonable amount of additional grain as interest. This additional grain, in turn, is supposed to be handed over to the Central Government whose responsibility it is to hold a reserve for emergencies, and to subsidize the poorer districts. If the people suspect one Dzongpen of abusing his authority, they will complain to the other, and if they get no satisfaction that way there is nothing to stop them from sending their Ganpo to Lhasa. Dzongpen, monk or lay, found guilty of such actions are dealt with severely.

Each Dzongpen has a secretary and a treasurer to help him with his work. They see to all the needs of the district, such as construction of major dams and irrigation channels, relief from famine, medical treatment, and protection against bandits or others. There has never been a police force, as such, to enforce law, but since the time of the thirteenth Gyalwa Rinpoche, Tibet has maintained a standing army of some eight thousand men, and these have been drawn from all districts. Members of the army are increased in times of emergency by conscription between the ages of eighteen and forty. Even monasteries supply soldiers, recruited from the monks who have not entered academic careers, and from volunteers. Monks always form separate battalions and must be released from certain vows during their service. All the needs of the state are met, in this way, with the cooperation of the people and with a minimum of coercion. The Central Government maintains large reserves of grain and cash to alleviate hardship, either regional or individual, and Central Government taxes, payable in almost any useful commodity, are never excessive.

Perhaps the major fault of the old system was the lack of attention given to organized education. The whole concept of education was as an individual affair, except for reincarnations. It was open to anyone who wanted it and could be had simply by joining a monastery and proving one's readiness and sincerity and ability. Education was never thought of in terms other than religious, for it has always been and still is our belief that there is no higher goal than religious enlightenment. A secular education corresponds only to secular needs, and in Tibet these are minimal. The son of a nomad knows all there is to know about the life before him by the time he is nine or ten years old. So with the son or daughter of a farmer. Children learn by living close to their parents from the day of their birth, accompanying them in their work and daily rounds. Reading and writing are virtually unnecessary for there is no such thing as secular literature in Tibet, and one of the values of having such a large body of monks is that in every village in every part of the country there are monks readily available to read the scriptures, or recite them, to the villagers, often adding a sermon or moral instruction to the reading and performing a rite and offering prayers, benefits that no layman could get by a mere reading of the scriptures on his own. Nonetheless many laymen hear the scriptures so often that they come to know many of them by heart and are able to recite them themselves. Monks also are always available to perform death and commemorative rites and to fulfil any other ritual needs a family might have.

The lay public receives, in this way, a general religious and moral education, which includes much of the history of our country; our people grow up knowing enough to live their daily lives to the full, with a universal sense of direction that renders the comparative hardship of their daily life, in some areas, almost incidental. What intellectual development any layman wants he wants in terms of his knowledge and understanding of the scriptures, and this is always open to him. Further knowledge, to anyone with so clear a sense of direction, is meaningless.

In the monastic schools students are trained for their responsibilities as well as for their personal development, so that they can discharge their duties, as monks, to their fellows. Their studies include the sciences and the arts. Mathematics, astronomy and medicine rank alongside painting and sculpture, logic and philosophy.

As with writing, Tibetan art is all religious. With the coming of Buddhism it took on a distinctive style derived from the art schools of India and Nepal, though in eastern Tibet the style is markedly Chinese. Colours are prepared by pulverizing plants and even rocks, allowing for painting that is as exquisite as it is brilliant, in colour and detail. The most popular form of all is the painting of religious banners and wall frescoes. Even a poor family will try to have some of these in the family house, and the banners will decorate even a nomad's tent. The subject matter is the endless variety of different aspects of the Buddhist universe. The Buddhas and Changchub Sempa, the gods and spirits and demons, the heavens and hells, all these fill our banners and wall paintings. But every painting carries upon it an ngag, or prayer, consecrating it to the Lord Buddha, for each is painted with a specific purpose, to aid the viewer (and the painter) in his religious development, to instruct through the associated scriptural story, to direct the mind to the Buddha, to help in meditation. These paintings fill our monasteries just as they fill our homes, and just as painted rocks and boulders line our highways and mountain trails.

Certain skills, other than religious arts, are of course passed down in the villages themselves, outside the monasteries. The working of iron, weaving, pottery and woodwork are among these, and Tibetan peasant art, including these skills, is enjoyed and honoured throughout the country, adding a richness to our secular life. The real source of our richness, however, in both secular and monastic life, is that the one commodity we value more highly than any other, religious endeavour, is free, in any quantity, for us all to take as we feel fit and able.

However, for some unhappy reason, the very circumstance of our life in Tibet that made it possible for us to rank religious endeavour so highly, has changed. It has changed sadly and drastically, dragging us into a world where a little silver and gold count for more than a lifetime of religious thought, where political expediency counts for more than religious devotion, and where man's ideals and goals and whole life are centred on his present transitory existence on this singularly transitory planet, and where this is considered more 'sensible' than having his life directed towards the achievement of liberation through religious enlightenment. If this is because such people do not believe in the transitory nature of life, or do not believe in any life beyond what they can see and hear and touch with their feeble senses or comprehend with their earthly intellects, then by their own standards and beliefs they are right. But, also by their own standards, they do not live in such peace and contentment as we have lived in Tibet with our religious belief. And the tragedy is that we still believe, yet now we are irrevocably in a world of disbelief.

The people of Tibet heeded the warning of the thirteenth Gyalwa Rinpoche, and they brought the regency to an end in 1939 when my brother, Tandzing Gyatso, was only sixteen years old. The world had changed around us and we had not changed with it. Now that we were to be brought together there was no time to prepare. Tandzing Gyatso began a series of reforms. His predecessor had instituted a number of rural schools, and now the plan to broaden secular education for laymen was pushed further. If Tibetans were to be able to deal with the new world coming to them, they had to know about it. Tandzing Gyatso appointed a committee to study the whole question of reform. The taxation system consequently was revised, and it was made virtually impossible for regional governors or

337

officials to abuse their positions by extorting local taxes. All officials were paid directly by the Central Government and were compelled to account for all money or goods received and to turn them over to the authorities at Lhasa.

Many peasant families had, over several generations, accumulated large-sized debts to the Central Government as well as to others. These debts arose not so much because taxes or rates of interest were excessive, for on the whole they were remarkably low; it was rather that there was not enough consideration given to factors such as increased demands arising from increase in size of the standing army and rising prices. More was being demanded of the villagers by way of incidentals, and the burden had accumulated in this way to the point where many of them had no chance at all of ever paying it back. The Reforms Committee studied all outstanding loans and while it forced some to repay the capital with interest, they were only those who could afford to do so. Others were asked to repay the outstanding capital in instalments but were freed from the interest; the poorest were freed unconditionally of all debt.

Coupled with this, and so that the same situation would not arise again, the Committee prepared a plan for land reform. Virtually all land in Tibet belonged to the government. Farmers held land granted to them by the state, but to all effects it was as good as freehold, for they had the right to will it to their heirs, to divide it, even to mortgage or sell their right to its use. In return they paid a small annual land tax, usually in grain, which went to support the poorer monasteries. There was no grievance against this system, dispossession was only possible in the most flagrant cases of refusal to pay the modest taxes when able to do so. This rarely happened for every farmer was only too anxious to get what he could from his land, and by paying the taxes regularly he knew he could always count on assistance in times of need, or on loans if he wished to expand his farm or to make costly improvements. But some land had been granted by the governments, in the past, to families who had rendered special services to their country. The land grants were large, and the estates had grown wealthy in private hands. Each such estate was under an obligation, however, to pay for the training of one government official, to be supplied by the land-owning family. The estate further had to pay the official's salary. Most lay officials in the government were recruited in this way. This in itself was no particular hardship to anyone, though the fourteenth Gyalwa Rinpoche felt strongly that such inequality in wealth as existed between these private estates and the peasant holdings should be abolished, being contrary to Buddhist teachings. Apart from the inequality, moreover, there was room for injustice because these private estates included farmlands worked by villagers who in effect were vassals of the landowner, and the government had no control whatsoever over the conditions of this feudal relationship. This meant that the landlord not only had the absolute right to charge whatever rent he wished for the land he leased out, but he could also exercise justice in whatever manner he pleased. Technically his tenants, though they had no right of appeal, were free to leave and find land elsewhere, they frequently could not do so because they were so heavily in debt to their landowner. Not many landowners abused their privileged position, but there was far too much abuse even so, and its potential was unlimited. The situation was all the more dangerous because while the landowners themselves, constituting Tibetan nobility, were mostly upright and devout people, their duties kept them for much of their time at Lhasa, and they were forced to leave the control of their affairs to stewards who were frequently less scrupulous.

It was decided that all such lands should revert to the state. The peasants would be absolved of all debts; the landowners would be well compensated; the government officials drawn from those families would be paid their salary by the Central Government, like all other officials, and the peasants and landlords alike would be free to claim and work the same land, but each holding it directly from the government at the same rate of taxation and under the same conditions of tenure. Unfortunately, before this reform could really be effected the Chinese invasion took place, and effective government by the Gyalwa Rinpoche became impossible.

During his brief period of authority in Tibet, Tandzing Gyatso did his best to broaden his own knowledge of the outside world and to lay the foundations for future relations with other nations. Like his predecessor, he sent students out of Tibet, and he himself took every opportunity to meet with such foreigners as managed to reach Lhasa. He would have gladly welcomed more than the few who came, most of them by accident, but again we were shut off from the world by our neighbours. India not only sealed our borders against travel, she even effectively cut off our communications. Again, it was through no fault or desire on our part that we were isolated.

The government of Tibet, in exile, is still under the leadership of the Gyalwa Rinpoche, under whose guidance a new constitution has been drawn up for implementation whenever the country is freed of Chinese domination. In the foreword to the constitution the Gyalwa Rinpoche says:

Even prior to my departure from Tibet in March, 1959, I had come to the conclusion that in the changing circumstances of the modern world the system of governance in Tibet must be so modified and amended as to allow the elected representatives of the people to play a more effective role in guiding and shaping the social and economic policies of the State. I also firmly believed that this could only be done through democratic institutions based on social and economic justice. Unfortunately, for me and my people, all our efforts were frustrated by the Chinese authorities who had established in Tibet the worst form of colonial regime.

Soon after my arrival in India I decided that a Draft Constitution should be prepared so as to give the people of Tibet a new hope and a new conception of how Tibet should be governed when she regained her freedom and independence. . . . This [Constitution] takes into consideration the doctrines enunciated by Lord Buddha, the spiritual and temporal heritage of Tibet and the ideas and ideals of the modern world. It is thus intended to secure for the people of Tibet a system of democracy based on justice and equality and ensure their cultural, religious and economic advancement.

Although it is thus plain that there is no change in the nature of Tibet as a religious state, the new constitution guarantees freedom for any Tibetan to follow the religion of his choice by whatever worship or observance or practice may be required of him by his belief. Education is given special attention, and it is to provide seven years free primary education for all children above the age of six. Higher and technical education shall be encouraged beyond that point, and state scholarships shall be offered to those who are unable to pay but who deserve assistance through merit. The land reforms considered earlier are included in the new constitution, with safeguards to prevent the concentration of large tracts of land in single hands.

The national government is reorganized and membership reapportioned to give representation among lay officials, though the government as a whole still remains directly and unequivocally under the leadership of the Gyalwa Rinpoche as its supreme head. It is the Gyalwa Rinpoche who appoints the Kashak, or cabinet, which must consist of a prime minister and no less than five other ministers, none of whom may be members of the National Assembly though they may attend and take part in its meetings without having a voting right. Regular meetings of the National Assembly are ordained, and the former rather undetermined division of responsibilities between the two assemblies is ended. The one single Assembly consists of members both elected and appointed. Seventy-five per cent are elected from territorial constituencies by universal adult suffrage. Ten per cent are elected by monasteries; ten per cent are elected by regional councils, and the remaining five per cent are nominated by the Gyalwa Rinpoche, generally in return for special services or because of special abilities.

Regional governments maintain a slightly reorganized form of the old dual governorship. The Gyalwa Rinpoche is to appoint each Regional Governor, but a Regional Council is to appoint the Deputy Governor. Regional Councils in turn are chosen by the general electorate.

Justice is centralized in a way that was only informally achieved before. There is now to be a Supreme Court, appointed by the

Gyalwa Rinpoche, but also answerable to the National Assembly, a two-thirds majority of which can recommend to the Gyalwa Rinpoche the removal of any member. Under the Supreme Court are a number of regional courts. In this way there will be a national standard and code, and regional justice will be national rather than regional in character. The system of appeals is clearly set out, and any opportunity for corruption is removed.

One of the incidental benefits brought by the Chinese is an improvement in internal communications. There are now major motorable roads connecting Tibet with China, Mongolia and India, and a number of internal roads connecting administrative centres. Although these may well be destroyed, as may the present telegraph and telephone communications system, when the Chinese finally withdraw, they have brought the idea, and that will remain. Improved communications will be the key to improved government and to broader education. The Chinese have in fact established many schools, though with a very particular form of education in mind, aimed at the destruction of any sense of Tibetan individuality. Nonetheless, there are now said to be some 60,000 children at school in Tibet, and even to establish the habit of schooling is a positive contribution, though we may deplore the actual education given. In the schools that we were establishing ourselves, prior to the Chinese invasion, we taught subjects such as art, literature, and of course religion. These subjects are now all banned, and according to the Chinese, Tibetan children are now being given 'class education, socialist education, and education in patriotism, with class struggle as the central theme'. Special classes are devoted to attacks on Tibetan religion and tradition, the total eradication of which was and still is a major goal of the Chinese, for until they have succeeded in this they will not have conquered Tibet.

To this end there has been an unbelievably tragic attack not only on our ancient shrines and monasteries but also upon the monks whose homes they were. The toll is almost unbelievable, yet there is no room for doubt, for the Chinese themselves give the account as evidence of the progressive nature of their rule in

Tibet. To begin with a few monasteries were spared, to be kept
as museums and to show foreign visitors how liberal the Chinese
were. They even allowed a few old monks to stay in these
monasteries. But even this proved too dangerous, and these
also have now been destroyed and the monkhood entirely dis-
banded. The persecution of the monks, their murder, torture
and degradation, is a story that has already been told. Perhaps
it is precisely because the story is one of such horror that the
world at large seems to have chosen to ignore it. It is perhaps
only possible to believe when it touches you. Even I found it
difficult to believe until I was told that monasteries I had known
had been, not destroyed, but carefully dismantled, the materials
being used to build barracks for troops or residences for Chinese
officials. Kundeling Monastery, near Lhasa, is now the Chinese
Motor Transport Office. Moru Monastery is the Department of
Stores and Supplies. Tode Khangsar, Shete and Tsemonling
monasteries are now Chinese training schools for their dance
and drama troupes.

Monks and nuns have been forced to marry, and have otherwise been compelled to commit acts against all their religious
convictions and beliefs. Of the 20,000 monks at the three great
collegiate monasteries of Lhasa, only 300 remained in 1965. Now,
by action of the Red Guards, I believe that even these are gone.
All but 200 of Tashi Lhunpo's body of 4,000 monks were deported to concentration camps in 1962, for being pro-Tibetan
and for praying for the long life of the Gyalwa Rinpoche. Tashi
Lhunpo is the seat of the Panchen Rinpoche, whom the Chinese
had trained and mistakenly counted on as a puppet. I recently
heard that my own aged teacher, a highly revered monk of
Kumbum, died while still a member of a road labour gang.

There is no point in going over the disaster that has befallen
our country. What is known to have happened is bad enough,
and there is a great deal more that is unknown. There are likely
even to be marginal benefits, though even the most generous
mind would find it difficult to equate a few roads and schools
and hospitals (primarily intended and used for the welfare of

Chinese troops) with the destruction of all the material evidence of everything that has ever meant anything to us as a people. And in a way it does not matter all that much. It might have mattered if the outside world had been able to help. But it is done. All that matters now is that we preserve the one thing we have left, our faith.

The Legend of the End

Fearless, in the midst of your army of Gods,
Among your twelve divisions,
You ride on horseback.
You thrust your spear toward the chest of
*   Hanumanda,*
Minister of the evil forces drawn up
Against Shambhala.
So shall Evil be destroyed.

– from SHAMBHALA SMONLAM

If the world, or any part of it, were perfect it would be paradise, there would be no question as to right and wrong, good and bad. As that is plainly not so, nobody, least of all any Tibetan, would try to claim that his country was perfect. On the contrary, the very fact that we Tibetans are so bound up in our quest for enlightenment, and in our pursuit of the religious ideal, is evidence that we are very aware indeed of the lack of perfection. Nonetheless, looking back on the old Tibet, I cannot find that life there could be compared unfavourably with life anywhere else in terms of human rights and freedom. While there are certain aspects of that life that I, and probably many other Tibetans, disagree with, there is much I see that I believe good. Many non-Tibetans speak against the monasteries. I lived most of my life, from my early childhood, in monasteries, and in them I see our strength. Many are endowed with great riches, but there are few, even among the poor of the Western world, who live as simply and as frugally as do the monks and abbots of those wealthy monasteries. Nor are the monasteries exclusively for the benefit of the monks. Quite apart from their role as landowner helping the local farmers, they provide shelter at all times for visitors, strangers and pilgrims. No charge is made, any visitor is made welcome and treated as an honoured guest, provided with accommodations and food far above the standard maintained for the monks themselves. We enjoy having such visitors, and though we make no conditions, they are of course welcome to attend our services, regardless of their religion. Some monasteries make special arrangements for women guests because of the strict rules of their order. Many build special guest houses, or *chiso*.

It is certainly true, however, that any accumulation of wealth is in itself a temptation, and there are always accusations of abuse in one part of the country or another. In particular it seems wrong to me that so much land should be held by monasteries. This not only leads to the possibility of corruption, it also leads to the possibility of stagnation, for we become so tied up in the administration of our estates that we have little time left for religious life. Most monks probably welcome the reform that would return all land to the state, leaving it to the state to administer through its secular machinery. Then each monastery would hold land, just as the individuals would, granted them by the state according to their needs.

Although we have always held that monasteries should be places of learning, and we have always opened our doors to anyone wanting to learn, it is good that now there should be state schools to take care of secular education. But in every school I believe religion should be taught by a monk appointed for the task. The monastic schools would remain open for all those wanting a higher religious education. Ultimately it is for each person to make the choice for himself, how he wants to lead his religious life, or if he wants a religious life at all. But if we do not give him the opportunity for learning about religion we deny him the choice.

I am not happy about the ideas brought by the Chinese, however, which take away all individual rights. I believe in state ownership of land and state-controlled education because these are things all Tibetans should share in equally; without them we cannot live. But men are not equal and never can live equally. Some want to live one way, some another. Each should have the right to decide his own way of life, so long as it does not interfere with those of others. If someone wants to work hard for material gain, let him reap the reward. If another prefers to remain in poverty so that he can devote himself to religious contemplation, he should be free to do so. For this reason we have never had such things as mining rights in Tibet, though it is said that we have rich mineral deposits. Salt is a vital trade product, yet anyone who wants to is free to journey to the northern plateau and dig salt for trading. There are no rights or licences to purchase.

In the same way that salt can be had for the taking from the lakes and sands of the north, so can gold be had from the mountains and streams. Some people go every year. There is no need for them to make any claim, nor is there any need for much in the way of equipment, so even poor people can make a successful trip if they want to. Gold is panned from the mountain rivers in large sieves, and the nuggets are simply picked out and put into soft bags made from the bladders or kidneys of sheep. Few of those who search for gold become wealthy, though some make enough to employ several workers. The workers are all paid, and above their pay they are allowed whatever gold they can find by working at night.

Precious stones are said to be found in certain mountain ranges, and turquoise can be found in many places, but there is still a great lack of interest in mining, even with the prospect of large financial returns. It is partly because most Tibetans are not interested in wealth beyond what they need for their ordinary everyday use, but it is also partly because to many the act of mining seems almost sacrilegious, a desecration of nature. The very fact that so little advantage is taken of this opportunity, open to anyone, for obtaining wealth, shows how foreign are envy or jealousy to the Tibetan character. The Tibetan notion of equality does not centre around material property but rather on religious opportunity, and in these terms every Tibetan is as wealthy as his neighbour.

The new constitution, as set out and approved by the present Gyalwa Rinpoche, allows for the fact, however, that Tibet and Tibetans have irrevocably been drawn into a world where material considerations are dominant. It provides for greatly increased representation of and by laymen and reduces the political power of the monasteries. This is going to be all the more necessary when the Chinese finally leave Tibet and the task of government falls again upon the Tibetan people, for the Chinese have created, and will leave behind them, a legacy of desecration that cannot help having reached into the minds of many. Boys and girls are already growing into manhood and womanhood having lived their entire lives in a Communist-ruled Tibet in which religion is ridiculed and where the new schools set up

349

only serve to indoctrinate the young. Many Tibetan children have been sent to China and are scattered all over, in the cities and towns, learning the Chinese language, Chinese ways and Chinese thoughts. As long as they remember that they are Tibetan there will be hope, and as long as any are left alive who remember Tibet as it was and can pass this knowledge on to their children, religion will not die. I believe that this is a period of suffering that we have to go through, but that we shall eventually emerge from it, and perhaps be all the stronger.

The Chinese invited me to return, and although I very much wanted to, I could not trust them; I felt they only wanted to make use of me. For the moment we have to consider them as our enemies, but they too are caught up in this time of darkness. When we come out of it we shall both be the victors.

In our ancient scriptures we hear of a country to the north, the country of Shambhala, where there is to be a final battle between the forces of religion and those of atheism. Shambhala is described as a land ringed with snowcapped mountains, and at its centre is an enormous city in which the king has his palace. Some say that it was from here that the great Lamèd tantra originated, for King Suchandra, the first of Shambhala's priest-kings, took the teachings direct from Buddha. According to the scriptures the predicted conflict is due to reach its climax in three hundred or so years from now. The world will have grown colder everywhere, we are told, but men's passions will have become inflamed. We believe that this has already started. When the time comes, men will be fighting and killing each other even within the land of Shambhala. There will be no honesty, no love, no peace; only dishonesty, hate and war. Up to the very end the capital city of Shambhala will be the one place where the teachings of the Buddha are preserved. Peace will remain there until the corruption of the world around reaches the city walls. Then the God-King will muster his army of Gods and ride out of the city to engage the forces of evil and destroy them.

The city of Lhasa will be covered with water when all this happens: yak-skin boats will take pilgrims to see the pinnacles of the great Jo Krang Temple rising above the surface. And at this time, once evil is destroyed, the tomb of Tsong Khapa at Ganden Monastery will open, and Tsong Khapa will live again, joining the people of Shambhala once again teaching the religion of Buddha. For a thousand years religion will be taught, but then will come the end of the world. Fire will be followed by wind, destroying all we have built; then will come water to cover everything we know. Only a few will survive, in caves and in the tops of trees. The Gods will come from Ganden Paradise and take these people back with them. They will be taught so that religion will not die, and when once again the winds blow the milk-ocean and once again the world is formed, these same enlightened ones, saved from the world before, will be the stars in the sky.

Only one thing comes to a final end, and that is ignorance and evil, for they are one and the same thing. How many cycles of creation and destruction it will take we cannot say. In Tibet we believe that we should each help by trying to destroy the ignorance that is within ourself. It is this conscious recognition of his ignorance, and his longing for release, that makes the Tibetan what he is, and that makes life for me, in Tibet, so well worth living. Buddhism teaches us that our ignorance is suffering, and we know it, but even that little spark of knowledge brings beauty into our lives, helping us to see beauty everywhere, teaching us wisdom. I think of Tibet as a beautiful country, and so it is, but the greatest beauty to me is that the people live a life dedicated to religion. You know it when you meet them, without being told. There is a warmth that touches you, a power that fills you with new strength, a peace that is gentle. I remember such people, and I feel sad that now it is so seldom one meets their like.

I also miss the country. I miss the sound of the wind blowing softly, rustling the treetops; I miss Shardzong, perhaps the most beautiful place of all for me, my first monastery. I miss its red rocks, its trees filled with birds, the deer and other wild animals. I miss gazing down from that tiny, remote little monastery, across the trees, to the little stream rippling through the valley. I can still see that stream, with its blue, blue water. I miss the infinite peace I knew then, and the cleanness of the scents of pine and juniper and wild rose.

When I was in Tibet, I was conscious of being happy, and at peace, but I think I never really looked upon my country as particularly beautiful; it was all I knew, and I simply accepted it and loved it. I do not think I realized how beautiful it was until one evening, watching a television show in New York, I saw a film made in my country. I saw again those mountains, and I remembered how every spring I looked at them with longing, until I could bear it no longer and would set off to join them, as though they were a part of me. It was the same thing, once there, with the wild animals all around. Watching them you became a part of them, and somehow this always made me feel as though I were bigger, and closer to the truth I sought.

I remember little things, like the way we used to keep time in my parents' home. We did not need to measure time of day, but we needed to measure it for cooking. One method was to fill a special pot with water; the pot had a small hole in it, and it allowed the water to escape, drop by drop. My mother would know to put in so much water to measure the time needed to cook such and such a meal. If we needed to be wakened up at a certain hour, my mother would light a stick of incense, of the right length. When it burned down to the end it would burn through a thread that held a stone above an old metal pot, and we would be awakened by the clanging and clattering as the stone fell. Otherwise we simply awoke when the cocks began crowing. During the day we knew the hour by the sun, at night by the stars. Our lives in Tibet were spent without haste, and without the strange force that presses people down here, so that they always seem to be doing one thing and wishing they were doing something else, as though they were being driven like animals. In Tibet I felt more free, and more alive, and although life may have been harder, living it was easier.

One thing that made it much easier was the fact that nearly all Tibetans live by the same standards, with the same ideals, so that rich or poor, monk or layman, they all understood each other from this common ground. I cannot think of anyone whom I really disliked in Tibet, or who showed any dislike for me. This is not to say that everyone is perfect; that is certainly not so. But recognizing our own weaknesses we make allowances for them in others, and more important still, we place more significance on the fact that despite our weaknesses we are struggling towards the same goal. We judge each other more by the sincerity of our effort than by our momentary strength or weakness. I think the hardest feelings I ever had in Tibet were for people who borrowed things and then, having promised to give them back at a certain time not only did not give them back but pretended that they had actually bought them and owned them. After the Communist invasion I met people I did not like, but on political grounds, not personal ones. So all the time, in Tibet, you enjoy meeting people, and they give you a pleasant feeling and make the world seem good. Here it is not like that. For one thing people do not seem so happy and content, and they do not all seem to share the same standards and ideals. I have not met many that have made me feel bad, it is not that people have been unfriendly or unkind, or that they have taken advantage of me or stolen from me, for all those things could happen in Tibet just as well; it is rather that I miss the warmth that comes from recognizing someone who openly shares with me my most cherished dream.

Then there are others, here as in Tibet, who live lives of such goodness that to meet them is to feel refreshed and strengthened, clean and whole; but in Tibet such people are not all that rare. They are usually learned men, and are always ready to share their wisdom with others, offering help and advice. Even to be near them is enough. My teacher was such a person, at Tagtser Labrang. At first I was young, and I just liked him as I might have liked anyone. But by the time I was fifteen years old I wanted to spend more and more time with him, and I used to wait upon every word he spoke, as though waiting for jewels to fall into my hands. Every day that I spent with him I felt I had accomplished something, though I had done nothing; and every day that passed without my seeing him I felt as though something

353

terribly valuable had been taken away from me. Even now when I think of his long face and long nose, and his bright red cheeks, I feel good.

He was a quiet man, and though I loved him most of all, he kept very much to himself. Others become well-known, often without wishing it at all, for then pilgrims begin to visit them. I visited one such famous holy man in a small monastery near Lhasa. He was very old, and he lived there with five or six disciples and servants, and a whole pack of fierce Tibetan mastiffs. I arrived with a party of about fifteen pilgrims, and as we arrived the mastiffs all started barking and the disciples came out to restrain them. Then we were invited in to the lower level and given tea. After that we were taken up to his tiny room on the next floor. It was decorated with prayer banners, and the old man, Gonser Rinpoche, sat on a sheepskin rug in front of a low table that held his books, papers, and a pile of white scarves used in greetings. We all presented our scarves, and received the old man's blessings. We sat down with him, and he spoke with us for a little while. He spoke in a soft low voice, asking where we had come from and what we were doing. There was nothing very special about what he said, just as there was nothing very special about his appearance. He was about sixty years old, and had very white hair. He was rather short, with a not particularly striking face, and he had lost all his teeth. Yet when I was with him, and I went back many times, I knew I was with someone very special, and though we might not talk about anything seemingly worth-while, it was worth more than any number of sermons or readings. Anyone who went to see him expecting or hoping for a miracle would have been disappointed, he could not have been more ordinary, wrapped in a worn, maroon-coloured woollen cloth, sitting on an oily sheepskin in a bare room. Yet most who went to see him came away feeling as though they had been touched by a miracle.

Sometimes, because I am recognized as the reincarnation of Tagtser Rinpoche, people came to me and asked for my blessing. I used to tell them that I had no power to give them a blessing, that I was nothing special, and that perhaps I was much more in need of blessing than they were. I used to advise them to pray to their personal deities, or to the Lord Buddha. But they would reply that what I thought of myself did not matter, that *they* believed I must be a great person to have deserved such a high rebirth. Then I used to say a prayer with them, but it always worried me because they had so much faith in me, and I could not share it with them.

There are some places in Tibet that give one the same feeling of goodness. Sometimes it is the house of a private person; sometimes it is a monastery or a hermitage. It may be a mountain or a stream, and just as with good people, these places often acquire fame and become places of pilgrimage. I suppose the same thing applies; it does not much matter what the place is, but if the pilgrim invests it with goodness it will, for him, be good. The place I remember most strongly is the sacred lake Lhama Lamtso. This is two or three days' journey from Lhasa, southeast, and it is famous for the visions it gives of the future. This lake is consulted by the ministers seeking help in the search for each new Gyalwa Rinpoche. It is high up in the mountains, and we rested the day before we made the final climb. At the top, surrounded by the snow-covered peaks, was a tiny but deep valley, at the bottom of which lay the sacred lake. It was June or July, but it was snowing all the time we were climbing the mountainside, and we thought we were not even going to be able to see the lake when we did reach the top. We stopped on the way and burned incense, and when we reached the top we burned more incense and made offerings, for it was still snowing hard, and we prayed. The monastery of Chokorgyal lay some four hours behind us.

Quite suddenly it was as though it had not been snowing at all. The sky cleared and there was Lhama Lamtso, a brilliantly blue little droplet in the midst of the Himalayan peaks. There was nothing around but the barren, treeless mountains, boulders and stone shining through the snowy covering in a few steep places. As we were looking over to the east end of the lake we saw some kind of movement, a shimmering that was not on the surface, for that remained quite still, but somehow below it. It was like a band of sandy colour that slowly spread across the lake, from the east, moving hesitantly then disappearing altogether. Many of us saw this, but then we each only saw what was meant for us. I had not really been expecting to see anything, and when I saw the movement and shimmering I was happy and thought that would be all. But as I looked I saw other colours appear – a little bit of green, a fleck of blue, and some red – and all these colours moved slowly around below the surface of the lake. When they also disappeared the water was left as clear as could be, and I could then see the reflection of the mountain. But it was not any mountain that was near the lake, it was some mountain I had never seen before. The top of this huge mountain was covered with snow, but from the middle down, its rocky side was bare until, at the base of the mountain, I could see trees, dry and leafless as though it were in mid-winter. At first there were only a few trees, but they grew thicker and thicker as the ground fell away into the valley floor.

Among these trees was a fine three-storeyed house, and on the terrace on the roof of this house three people were standing. One wore the robes of a monk, the other two wore ordinary Tibetan dress. A courtyard surrounded the house, and at one end of the courtyard were a number of bushes that had been cut and were being dried to use as fuel for cooking. At the west end of the courtyard there was a gate, with a road passing in front of it, and near by a stream ran down from the mountainside and passed under a little bridge. Across the bridge there was a swamp, with mud, but also with a lot of lovely fresh green grass. There, too, was a small dog kennel with a mastiff tied to it by a rope. To the north the road wandered on, and coming down it was someone on horseback, riding towards the house, and behind him was a caravan.

This vision lasted for about half an hour, and I wondered to myself what it could possibly mean, whether it was something I was meant to see in this life, or a vision of some scene from a future life. I prayed to the Goddess Lhamo, that she should instruct me. Then the surface of the lake changed and became as though it were coated with ice. I saw one huge block of ice, about the height of a two-storeyed house, and drops of icy water dripped down from it and formed stalactites, thrusting thirty feet or more down into the waters of the lake.

As I was wondering what this new vision meant – for it lasted about fifteen minutes – it changed once again and I saw a little cluster of whitewashed houses, which I recognized as being at Kumbum. Then they too disappeared and for the last time I saw the great snow-topped mountain with the green, tree-filled valley below, the house with the courtyard and gate, the road, the stream flowing under the bridge, the doghouse and the mastiff. There was the horseman, and a caravan coming down the road; but on the roof, where the monk and the two men wearing black robes had stood, there was no one. I stood there for a long time, wondering if they would appear again, and thinking, but finally the vision became speckled, as though little clouds were passing between us, and when I looked again the surface of the lake was clear.

We all came down from the mountain then, and back in the monastery below we talked about what we had each seen. Some had seen nothing at all, others had seen things as clearly as I had, but all different. One friend, another monk, had seen a vision of fields with lots and lots of people working in them. Some had seen things and did not want to talk about them. None of us who had seen anything could say what the meaning of our vision could be. I still have not seen that house in the woods, nor have I again seen the monk and the two laymen who had stood on its roof.

There are many things in the future that are hidden from us, and the future is plainly not a happy one for the world, if we believe in the legend of Shambhala and the increasing destructiveness of man. Yet at least we believe that there *is* a future in Tibet, and whatever it may be like on this world, we know that the ultimate end – enlightenment, release from all ignorance and suffering – is bliss. We also know that this will come to all of us, sooner or later. This makes all suffering bearable. We do not believe that we can avoid the disasters predicted, but we do

357

believe that we can help ourselves, and others, to be better prepared for them, so that as few as possible shall have to linger
through another cycle of creation and destruction.

Educated Tibetans may think about this differently from the
uneducated, just as one sect may differ from another in its
interpretation of the scriptures. But there is no division of
opinion on the fact of suffering, and on our proper objective as
being the achievement of release from suffering. This is the teaching of the Buddha, and the Buddhist scriptures, the Buddhist
Church and the monkhood all exist to help us. We do not concern ourselves with questioning the nature of God, or the nature
of afterlife, and however much other religions may deny ours,
we are content in the knowledge that ours leads us into a way of
life where every human being we meet is as precious as any other,
to us. It is a way of life in which we do not expect to achieve
perfection overnight, but in which we all take delight in striving
for it. This striving is not a dull chore; it is a vital, exciting quest,
and we feel the rewards with every step we take.

As for me, I feel a great sadness and emptiness when I think of
the Tibet I once knew, for it can never be the same again, and I
can imagine nothing more perfect than that Tibet I knew not
many years ago. But it is a selfish sadness, for others will discover
the same truths, and maybe many more, from the new Tibet, or
wherever they are, just as long as they still know enough to seek
for truth.

The nature of truth, in the end, is the biggest question of all,
and we only blind ourselves and remove ourselves still further
from the answer if we deny the truth to others simply because the
form it seems to take for them differs from the form we think it
takes for us. I can see nothing good in Communism, or in all the
destruction it has brought to my country, yet perhaps in bringing
that destruction they have brought themselves, in their own way,
closer to the ultimate truth. That is for them to decide, if they
want to. Or if they prefer to remain in ignorance, then no matter
how close they are to the truth, it will remain hidden to them.

The only truth that is worth anything to anyone is the truth in
which he believes with his heart as well as with his mind, and

towards which he strives with his body. Let that truth be ever so different from the truth as seen by his fellows, it is still the only real truth for him, just as theirs is for them. Perhaps the greatest ignorance of all, and the greatest cruelty, is to try to force others to see the world as we see it. By all means let us look at the thoughts and beliefs of others, and they may help us to see more clearly, even if we do not accept them. It is for this reason I have told this story, not that others should believe it but that they may understand us the better, and perhaps also better understand themselves.

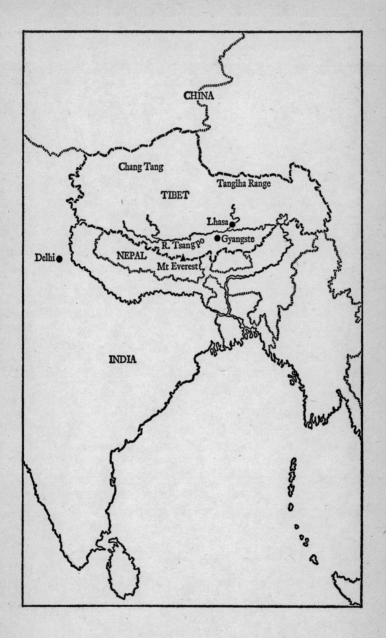

CHINA

Chang Tang

TIBET

Tanglha Range

Lhasa

Gyangste

R. Tsangpo

NEPAL

Delhi

Mt Everest

INDIA

More about Penguins and Pelicans

For further information about books available from
Penguins please write to Dept EP, Penguin Books Ltd,
Harmondsworth, Middlesex, UB7 0DA.

In the U.S.A.: For a complete list of books available
from Penguins in the United States write to Dept CS,
Penguin Books, 625 Madison Avenue, New York,
New York 10022.

In Canada: For a complete list of books available
from Penguins in Canada write to Penguin Books
Canada Ltd, 2801 John Street, Markham, Ontario,
L3R 1B4.

In Australia: For a complete list of books available
from Penguins in Australia write to the Marketing
Department, Penguin Books Australia Ltd, P.O. Box
257, Ringwood, Victoria 3134.

In New Zealand: For a complete list of books
available from Penguins in New Zealand write to the
Marketing Department, Penguin Books (N.Z.) Ltd,
P.O. Box 4019, Auckland 10.

A Choice of Penguins

WAYS OF ESCAPE
Graham Greene

The second part of Greene's acclaimed autobiography, which he began in *A Sort of Life*.

From Haiti under Papa Doc, Vietnam in the last days of the French, Kenya during the Mau Mau and Hollywood, to the making of *The Third Man* in Vienna and his time in the British Secret Service, Graham Greene writes exquisitely of people and places, of faith, doubt, fear and of the craft of writings, as he found himself repeatedly 'at the dangerous edge of things'.

'Marvellously rich' – William Trevor

THE BOOK OF EBENEZER LE PAGE
G. B. Edwards
Introduced by John Fowles

Stubborn, reactionary and oddly vulnerable, Ebenezer is a Guernseyman through and through. For him the smell of the sea, the tomatoes and his hatred of Jersey make up the stuff of existence. His long life, bounded by rocks and water and rooted in tradition, sees the destruction of the old ways . . .

'To read it is not like reading, but living' – *William Golding*

'Holds the reader in an Ancient Mariner grip' – *Daily Telegraph*

THE CHINESE
David Bonavia

'I can think of no other work which so urbanely and entertainingly succeeds in introducing the general Western reader to China' – *Sunday Telegraph*

'A timely book, informative, enlightening, intimate, based on personal experience, in which the reader quickly and easily gets to know the Chinese in their everyday life, at home, the city factory and country commune. Following, are insights into the fluctuating functions and fortunes of the inevitably strangling bureaucracy and the fields of education, medicine, commerce, the law, industry, consumerism, the arts – and politics' – Walter Tyson in the *Oxford Times*

'Excellent . . . He tackles the contradictions with an intelligent and well-informed approach: the violence and passivity, curiosity and apathy, collectivism and selfishness . . . avoiding the twin perils of inaccessibility and oversimplification' – Isabel Hilton in *The Times Educational Supplement*

THE HERMIT OF PEKING
THE HIDDEN LIFE OF SIR EDMUND BACKHOUSE
Hugh Trevor-Roper

It all began when Hugh Trevor-Roper acquired the voluminous memoirs of Sir Edmund Backhouse, up till then known only as a distinguished Chinese scholar who had lived quietly in Peking until his death in 1944.

The memories depicted a very different person – a man who said that he had been 'intimate' with many notables, from Lord Rosebery to Verlaine, and whose lovers had included the Dowager Empress of China.

In fact, they were so fantastic that the author felt obliged to discover all he could about the man who had written them: and what he reveals here is the story of one of the most outrageous forgers, confidence tricksters and eccentrics of the century.

'The reader is throughout amused, amazed and enthralled' – *The Times* (London)

'A fascinating book' – *New York Review of Books*

'An absolute corker' – *Paul Theroux*

A Choice of Penguins by V. S. Naipau

AMONG THE BELIEVERS
AN ISLAMIC JOURNEY

Tremendous acclaim for V. S. Naipaul's record of his travels in Iran, Pakistan, Malaysia and Indonesia –

'Naipaul's gaze, calmly intrusive, misses nothing . . . This book investigates the starry-eyed barbarism of the Islamic revolution and tries to understand the fundamentalist zeal that has gripped the young in Iran and other Moslem states . . . He is a modern master' – John Carey in the *Sunday Times*

'One of the greatest living writers in the English language . . . His themes, his vision of human destiny in our time, are composed with a perfection of language . . . a flawless structure – and above all a profound knowledge of the world' – Elizabeth Hardwick

'Pleasures, surprises and adventures . . . Naipaul is a superlative traveller who misses nothing worth the record' – Michael Ratcliffe in *The Times*

INDIA: A WOUNDED CIVILIZATION

In this sharp and reflective book V. S. Naipaul explores the feel of the fragile societies.

Beginning on a human – rather than a national – scale with a study of the racial clichés and fantasies which formed Michael X, and a detailed investigation of the events and psychology behind the killings at the Trinidad commune, Naipaul goes on to examine the uneasy society of Argentina during the years of Peronism and urban violence. He continues with an examination of the paradoxes inherent in the cult of Africanization in Mobutu's Zaire.

The last piece, an account of the author's own discovery of Conrad, forms a retrospective look at the preceding themes.

'The sharpness of V. S. Naipaul's words is that of a razor, dangerous and everyday . . . He takes his antiseptic intelligence, his steeled heart and his measured anger to the half-made societies . . . and what he has amazingly done is bend the level tones, the wisely withering wit, of Jane Austen upon societies utterly different from hers' – *Sunday Times*

THE ZOO QUEST EXPEDITIONS
David Attenborough

'When we get to Mars Mr Attenborough ought to be the first to land'
– *The Times* (London)

Sloths and snakes, butterflies and birds, Lord Lucifer and the Great
Smasher – strange people and bizarre animals abound in David
Attenborough's exciting narration of three zoo-collecting expeditions.
From the broad savannahs of the Rapununi, the remote forest reserve
of the Amerindians, to Indonesia and Paraguay – no one writes as
amusingly or as irresistably.

'Will fascinate armchair travellers and amateur naturalists' – *Sunday
Express*

THE WHISPERING LAND
Gerald Durrell

Gerald Durrell is among the best-selling authors in English. His
adventurous spirit and his spontaneous gift for narrative and anecdote
stand out in his accounts of expeditions to Africa and South America
in search of rare animals. He divines the characters of these creatures
with the same clear, humorous, and unsentimental eyes with which
he regards those chance human acquaintances whose conversion in
remote places he often reproduces in all its devastating and garbled
originality. To have maintained, for over fifteen years, such unfailing
standards of entertainment can only be described as a triumph.

In *The Whispering Land* he searches windswept Patagonian shores
and tropical forests in the Argentine for additions to his private zoo.
Penguins and elephant seals make way for an absurd family of foxes
who dance gracefully with a roll of lavatory paper, and we see the
author baiting a trap for a recalcitrant vampire bat with one of his own
toes.